HAMBURG

INSIGHT *City* GUIDES

Edited by Hans-Joachim Györffy
Principal Photography: G.P. Reichelt and Gerald Sagorski
Managing Editor: Andrew Eames

A P A
PUBLICATIONS

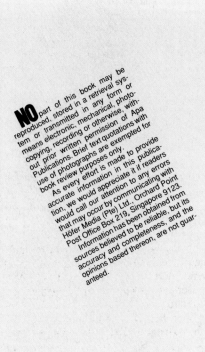

First Edition
© **1992 APA PUBLICATIONS (HK) LTD**
All Rights Reserved
Printed in Singapore by Höfer Press Pte. Ltd

ABOUT THIS BOOK

For many years Hamburg, the second largest city in Germany, was off the beaten track for tourists, with a reputation for seediness, dull tradesmen and rain. Indeed, as early as 1617, an English writer, Fynes Moryson, set the tone in *An Itinerary*: "Hamburg, where the people after dinner, warmed with drinke, are apt to wrong any stranger, and hardly indure an English-man in the morning when they are sober." In 1798 the poet William Wordsworth delivered his verdict: "It is a *sad* place."

Much has changed, thankfully, and the city has at last begun to fulfill its publicity slogan: "Hamburg – Top of the North". Visitors still may not encounter an excess of brilliant weather or breathtaking scenery, but they will discover distinctive qualities in Hamburg that are not found elsewhere.

Despite the enormous amount of damage caused by World War II bombing raids, the city still has numerous architecturally fascinating office blocks, aristocratic villas, well-to-do townhouses, traditional redbrick warehouses down in the port, and vast areas of parkland, lakes, rivers and canals at the heart of the city. All in all, it's a place well worth getting to know in some detail.

The writers

In *Insight Cityguide: Hamburg* a carefully chosen team of writers – some native Hamburgers and others relative newcomers – have depicted all aspects of the city in all lights and weathers. Editor **Hans-Joachim Györffy**, who assembled the team, was born and raised in Transylvania (Romania), moving to Germany with his parents when in his late teens. Although he initially had difficulty in coming to terms with these north German "lowlands", he now brings an outsider's sharp eye to the city in which he has lived and worked for nearly two decades, and, as a former editor of the German culture and travel magazine *Merian*, he has had wide experience in producing travel literature.

Also much involved in writing for travel guides, freelance journalist **Michael Auwers** studied German and worked as a copy editor before setting up his own business. He takes the reader through his own district, Altona, and neighbouring Ottensen.

Doris Cebulka works as a freelance journalist for various publications, including *Stern* and *Die Zeit*. In these pages she gets to grips with one of Hamburg's problem areas, St Georg, and presents a fascinating outline of life in a colourful quarter known for its intellectuals, prostitutes, foreigners and history.

There could have been no better candidate for the Bergedorf chapter than **Ulrike Esterer**, who used to work as a journalist on the local newspaper, *Bergedorfer Zeitung*.

Julica Jungehülsing also worked as a staff journalist before going freelance. Her chapter on Hamburg's red-light district, St Pauli, necessitated numerous research trips lasting well into the early hours. After all, when the sun shines on St Pauli, not much else is up.

Nina Köster, who has written for many other Insight Guides, moved to the city in the early 1970s, and felt instantly that this was where she belonged. In this book she describes the city centre, its shopping arcades, the districts of Eppendorf and Eimsbüttel, the outlying regions of Altes Land and Vierlande, and Hamburg as a media metropolis.

Historian by profession and politician by

Györffy

Auwers

Cebulka

Jungehülsing

persuasion, **Dr Franklin Kopitzsch** describes Hamburg's eventful history in these pages.

Christine Kruttschnitt, who works in the cultural department of *Stern* magazine, tackled a topic close to her heart for the book: Hamburg's theatre world – everything from Germany's largest theatre, Deutsches Schauspielhaus, to the Piccolo Theater, so small it qualifies for the *Guinness Book of Records*.

Klaus Martini teaches at a vocational training college and works as a freelance author. For *Insight Cityguide: Hamburg* he discovered all there is that's worth knowing about Hamburg's north-eastern suburbs, the Walddörfer.

Freelance journalist **Anke Möller** wrote the chapter on Ohlsdorf and Alstertal, in which she takes the reader round the world's second-largest cemetery, describes its origins and points out the graves of some of its famous "inmates".

Recently appointed official writer in the small town of Ottendorf on the Lower Elbe, **Norbert Ney** wrote the chapters on Uhlenhorst and Wandsbek for this book. As the author of a travel guide for children, he was also able to provide numerous useful tips for younger visitors.

Bettina Peulecke works in radio and writes film reviews for a Hamburg daily, *Morgenpost*. So it was only natural that she should be asked to write the article on Hans Albers, the cinema star who typified the rough but softhearted seaman on the big screen.

Andrzey Rybak was born in Warsaw but studied in Hamburg, where he now works as a journalist specialising in Eastern Europe for a Hamburg daily, *Hamburger Abendblatt*. In this book he contributes the chapter on the Elbe suburbs.

Jürgen Saupe, newspaper journalist and racegoer, is mad about horses – and he reveals all about horses and Hamburg.

Michael Studemund-Halévy lives and works as a freelance author and translator in Hamburg. He has published short travel guides on Israel, Portugal, Gomera and Sicily. His contributions to this book are the chapters on Jews, the city's characteristic redbrick architecture and the districts of Harvestehude and Winterhude.

Christian Venth studied literature and history and writes for the travel magazine *Saison*. His goal as a journalist is to travel in search of art – the subject of his contribution to this book.

Fritz Wiegand, artist and freelance journalist, is a football fan. But the team he supports is somewhat special: FC St Pauli. What's so unique about this club? Its supporters, naturally.

The photographers

G. P. Reichelt, an old Apa hand who provided the bulk of this book's images, set out on his motor bike innumerable times in search of unusual perspectives for *Insight Cityguide: Hamburg*. **Gerald Sagorski** put equal time and effort into looking for the best shots to capture the various moods of the city. The picture agency **Transglobe** supplied some vital shots.

Max Michael Hobst, a graphic design graduate, brought his artistic talent to bear in drawing the maps. The English version of the text was translated and adapted by **Andrew Craston**, an Oxford-educated Englishman who has lived in Hamburg since 1974, and was edited by **Andrew Eames** at Insight Guides' editorial office in London.

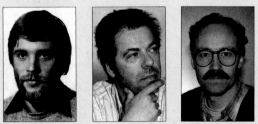

Ryback   *Ney*   *Martini*

History

Features

Places

Maps

TRAVEL TIPS

**For detailed information
see page 265**

It all began with the Hammaburg. The growth of this palisaded 9th-century settlement into Germany's second-largest city with 1.6 million inhabitants was mainly due to the power of the port, which celebrated its 800th anniversary in 1989. "Moneybags" the people of Hamburg were called – or at least the ones who had made it. And they were not too bothered about the means of making money, either. Hamburg kept out of as many wars as possible – if the matter could be settled by financial means.

But it would be wrong to assume that the city has numerous historic buildings. It never thought much of preservation, and considered demolition to be the only way to deal with anything that was no longer profitable. It even tried to make money in the face of certain death: when, a century ago, cholera broke out in the city and doctors warned of the dangers of an epidemic, the powers-that-be refused to impose quarantine to avoid any loss of business. The result was an epidemic.

Hamburg has always remained a proud, independent-minded trading city. As an indication of this republican spirit, when the German Kaiser, Wilhelm II, came to visit, the Mayor of Hamburg didn't think of addressing him as "Your Majesty". Moreover, Hamburg does not award any civic orders; the highest distinction it can bestow on anyone is of freeman of the city. After that, there is only the *Portugaleser* award, an imitation of a Portuguese coin which was once used in local trade.

Hamburg has always been a hub of traffic and trade between East, West, North and South as well as an emporium for merchandise, people, ideas, information and, unfortunately, disease and drugs. The cityscape has gone through radical redevelopment but, thankfully, some plans were never put into practice – including Hitler's idea of turning Hamburg into a model Nazi city.

Instead, the bombing raids of World War II killed 40,000 Hamburgers and totally destroyed large areas. The results of this wartime devastation are clearly visible today; the rush to reconstruct has produced many a housing monstrosity and wide roads dissect the heart of the old city.

People of all races, nationalities and religions have long flocked to Hamburg, contributing to the flair that is one of its outstanding characteristics. A British journalist who openly confesses his love for the city recently described Hamburg as Europe's least appreciated metropolis. He's right.

Preceding pages: anniversary celebrations in the port; Neptune looks towards the Rathaus (City Hall) in the city centre; St Pauli Landungsbrücken in the snow; facade of the Sprinkenhof; clocktower on the Landungsbrücken which shows water depth. **Left**, Jungfernstieg and the Inner Alster.

FROM THE HAMMABURG TO GREATER HAMBURG

Archaeological excavations have always been a source of new insights into the past. In the 1980s a new chapter in Hamburg's history was uncovered through excavations at the city-centre Domplatz, which as the name suggests was the place where Hamburg's cathedral once stood. These excavations unearthed the remains of a much earlier, pre-Christian settlement. In the 7th, and at the latest by the 8th century, Saxons had built a fortified camp on tongue-shaped higher ground rising up to 15 metres (50 ft) above the level of the river Alster.

The height of this land offered the first settlers protection from the waters of the Alster, Bille and Elbe. Soon agriculture, fishing and trade were established here. In the early 9th century a tribe of Slavs known as the Abotrites captured the settlement but soon afterwards the Franks under Charlemagne pushed north and took possession. These were the people who built the fortification known as the Hammaburg, located above Reichenstrassenfleet (both have since disappeared). The name came from the Old Saxon word "Ham" which was used to describe the bank or shore of a river or marsh.

A community of craftsmen and merchants grew up next to the Hammaburg and the first harbour was built at Reichenstrassenfleet. In 831–32 Emperor Louis the Pious established the bishopric of Hamburg. Ansgar, a monk from Corvey monastery on the River Weser, had been sent as a missionary to northern Germany and he became the first bishop of the new diocese.

Right at the heart of the fortified settlement around the Hammaburg a cathedral was built. In 845 Vikings attacked the Hammaburg and the surrounding settlement, plundering both and burning down the Hammaburg and the cathedral. As a result, the bishopric of Hamburg was merged with that of Bremen and the whole diocese declared an archbishopric in 864. Bishop

Ansgar moved across to Bremen as well.

The archbishops of Bremen remained lords of Hamburg while the settlement continued to develop as a market and harbour. In the 11th century the Abotrites destroyed the settlement several times. In 1030 the fortifications were strengthened and extended. In the basement of St Peter's church hall (Petrikirche, at the corner of Speersort and Kreuslerstrasse) you can see the foundations of the bishop's tower built under the supervision of Archbishop Bezelin Alebrand (1035–43).

Soon afterwards, the Billunger counts, commissioned to secure the eastern borders against the Slavs, built a fortress where Hamburg's City Hall (Rathaus) now stands. In 1061 a second fortress was built, an event commemorated in the present-day street named "Neue Burg". The Billungers were then replaced by the counts of Schauenburg who came from the mid-Weser region.

Stronger and stronger: In the 12th century Hamburg began to take on a more urban character. The cathedral chapter was re-established as a spiritual college and Hamburg was reinstated as a centre of church life. The population grew and trade increased. Under the archbishop's rule in 1188, Count Adolf III of Schauenburg established the new town (Neustadt) on the opposite bank of the Alster to the old town (Altstadt). A year later, he persuaded Emperor Friedrich I Barbarossa to grant Hamburg its first independent charter. Interestingly enough, however, only a forged copy of this charter exists today – a copy which was made by Hamburgers themselves in 1265.

What the Emperor granted the citizens of Hamburg-Neustadt in this charter was, however, most significant: unrestricted use of the Elbe for their ships from the mouth of the river as far as Hamburg and exemption from customs dues on the river. To the Church of St Peter in the Altstadt was added the Church of St Nicholas (Nikolaikirche) in the Neustadt.

The years before and after 1200 were politically volatile times. For a while Hamburg came under the influence of the Saxon King, Heinrich the Lion and then the Danish King. It was during these years that the Altstadt and Neustadt were combined to form a single town which was governed by a self-perpetuating council.

As a result, the first municipal laws were enacted in Hamburg. No knight was allowed to live in the town and no official or any count or earl permitted to become a member of the governing council; clearly, the newly-formed town was the work of self-assured citizens. In 1228 the Archbishop of Bremen assigned his rights as lord of Hamburg to the

wards the status of a free city-state, a mercantile republic. Hamburg then began to acquire lands around the city to ensure its safety and adequate supplies of food. The inhabitants of these lands became subjects of Hamburg.

In 1420 Hamburg and Lübeck captured Bergedorf and Vierlande from the duchy of Saxony-Lauenburg. Until 1867 this area was under their joint rule but from 1868 onwards Hamburg assumed sole government. In 1459 the Schauenburg dynasty died out and a year later King Christian of Denmark took over.

The Hamburgers were able to avoid the oath of allegiance demanded of them by their

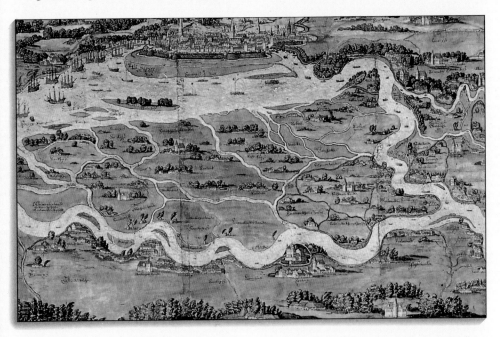

Schauenburgs. Hamburg joined the Hanseatic League and another two parishes were established, St Catherine's (Katharinenkirche) and St James (Jacobikirche). The Alster was dammed so that its water power could be used to drive mills.

At this time some 1,000 to 1,500 people probably lived in the Altstadt and Neustadt. By 1300 that figure had risen to around 4,000 to 5,000 for the whole of Hamburg. The rising population and economic growth were accompanied by an increasing degree of emancipation from the city's feudal lords. The first steps had already been taken to-

new king but had to accept his jurisdiction. Then, from the late 15th century onwards, the Holy Roman Emperor began to make claims on the city. In 1510 the Imperial Diet of Augsburg decided that Hamburg was still to be regarded a Free Imperial City, but Hamburg's legal status remained unclear for a long time. The smart citizens of Hamburg did not seem worried. Emperor Maximilian I was amazed by these "strange Hamburgers" who would show respect to their feudal lord in his presence but when negotiating with him, they would cite the Emperor.

From 1375 onwards there were several

incidences of civil disorder which forced the city council to make certain concessions to the people. In 1410, for example, it had to guarantee its citizens protection from arbitrary arrest. The latter also earned themselves a say in issues to do with war, peace and taxes.

Reformation: By the beginning of the 16th century Hamburg had some 14,000 inhabitants, a medium-sized town for those days. In the 1520s the Reformation reached Hamburg, which soon became a resoundingly Lutheran city. This was mainly due to the efforts of one of Martin Luther's closest colleagues, Johannes Bugenhagen.

when they assumed responsibility for the treasury.

Of no less significance for Hamburg's development was the arrival in the city of Lutheran and other Protestant immigrants. A tolerant attitude to strangers and the neutrality that guaranteed the undisturbed development of trade became Hamburg's policy. By 1600 Hamburg was the largest city in north Germany, and one of the most important in the Holy Roman Empire, with around 40,000 inhabitants.

Well-fortified city: Hamburg stayed in close contact with Bremen and Lübeck, its fellow cities in the Hanseatic League, but now had

Hamburg was one of the few cities in which the new ecclesiastical order was accompanied by political reforms. Periodically, landowners made up the "propertied citizenry" who exercised spiritual and temporal power in the city. But the formation of new "colleges" based upon the various parishes brought political change. In 1563 the "propertied citizenry" took a major step forward on the path to political independence

Left, Melchior Lorich's 16th-century map of the Elbe was the basis of Hamburg's claims to the river. **Above,** Hamburg circa 1730.

its own foreign policy. The city's new fortifications, designed by the Dutchman Johan van Valckenburgh in the early 17th century, proved the guarantee of its independence during the Thirty Years' War. In order to safeguard the city approaches, Neue Werk was built to the east in 1679–80 and Sternschanze to the northwest in 1681. During the 17th century the population grew to around 75,000. The new fortifications meant there was room for a new parish in the west, St Michael's (Michaeliskirche).

In the 17th and early 18th centuries, bitter struggles between the council and the "propertied citizenry" (Bürgerschaft) characterised political life in Hamburg. The issues were political authority and rights, with social and religious struggles mixed up with these political conflicts. Cord Jastram and Hieronymus Snitger became spokesmen of the Bürgerschaft. The Holy Roman Emperor, Brandenburg-Prussia and the Duke of Celle were all drawn into the conflict. In order to ward off attacks by the Duke of Celle, Jastram and Snitger made approaches to Denmark. But when Danish troops turned up in 1686 to make good their claim to sovereignty of the city, the tables were turned. The Danes were forced back at Stern-

legislative and executive power" was in the hands of the council and Bürgerschaft.

Powerful men: Only prosperous landowners were to be admitted to the Bürgerschaft. Around 1800 no more than 3,000 Hamburgers probably belonged to this elite group. When it met, there were rarely more than 230 landowners present and between 1709 and 1756, 193 sittings were called off because of lack of the necessary quorum. Only 204 actually took place.

Although Hamburg grew to a city of some 100,000 inhabitants during the 18th century, it managed to get by with a very small number of civil servants. In the age of abso-

schanze while Jastram and Snitger were accused of treason and executed.

A few years later, a new conflict arose. In 1699 the Bürgerschaft, to which every Lutheran citizen was now admitted irrespective of their property ownership, took over government and the Council was made subject to what was now more or less the City Parliament. In 1708 the Emperor intervened, sent in troops and gave an imperial commission the job of sorting out the conflict. Finally, in 1712, the Parliament and Council agreed on a political system which virtually re-established the old order of 1529. The "highest

lutism and the associated increase in bureaucracy, this self-government was a major achievement even though changes of personnel, confusion in the decision-making process, departmentalism and muddling along did lead to problems. The legal and administrative systems were organised in an extremely complicated way but legal and penal reforms could make no progress in the face of prevailing opinion. As late as 1806 a simple thief was condemned to death.

Centuries of conflict about Hamburg's exact legal status were finally terminated by the Treaty of Gottorp in 1768. Denmark recognised Hamburg as a Free Imperial City and the city's representative was finally able to take his seat in the Reichstagssaal (Diet Hall) of Regensburg City Hall. Of the 51 remaining Imperial cities Hamburg was by far the biggest.

The Hamburg Society: In the final decades of the 18th century, the Enlightenment became the engine of political reform in Hamburg – as a kind of practically-oriented movement for the welfare of the public. The driving force behind these reformist efforts was an association set up in 1765. Originally known as the Hamburg Society for the Furtherance of the Arts and Useful Crafts, it soon ac-

The Society members were a mixed bunch in denominational terms too: Lutherans, members of the Reformed Church, Mennonites and Catholics. After 1800 there were even some Jews. In terms of democratisation and tolerance, the Society was well advanced. Members of the Reformed and Catholic Churches were granted freedom of religion in 1785–86. From then on they were allowed to worship and build churches; up to then they had been forced to hold their religious services at foreign embassies. However, Lutheran orthodoxy had lost a lot of its vitality and support over the years. It wasn't always thus: as late as 1719 a church service

quired the more practical title of Patriotic Society. Patriotism in those days meant unselfish commitment to the community's interests and by no means excluded cosmopolitanism. The members of this new organisation included citizens who were already involved in the political machinery of the city and others who were still excluded, primarily academics and merchants. By the end of the century, there were even a few craftsmen and schoolteachers.

Left, access was only possible through the city gates. **Above,** Spitaler Tor (Gate) in 1600.

at St Michael's had been followed by the destruction of the Catholic chapel of the emperor's ambassador.

Social work: The reforms initiated and to a large degree carried out by the Patriotic Society included the beginnings of a vocational training system in 1767; a lifeboat organisation in 1768; a pensions fund with a variety of insurance schemes and the world's first savings bank in 1778; and a poor-relief fund in 1788 which set itself the task of providing for the non-employable poor, organising jobs for those who could work and giving schooling and job-related education to the children of both groups. Helping people to help themselves, work instead of charity and citizens' self-government – these were the guiding principles behind the Society's efforts. Some 200 citizens were involved in an honorary capacity.

Financial accountability and publicity were a matter of course for the new facilities. During the first decade of their work, the poor-relief fund proved extremely successful, a factor undoubtedly assisted by the economic prosperity of the period. The Society's work also attracted a good deal of attention at home and abroad. However, in the political and economic crises of the years

Klopstock, who was made an honorary citizen of France in 1792, and Adolf Freiherr Knigge, a supporter of the Enlightenment from Bremen. Hamburg and Altona became centres of a political press in which liberal and revolutionary-democratic voices prevailed over conservative.

French occupation: During the bitter years of the Revolutionary and Napoleonic Wars it became more and more difficult for Hamburg to maintain its neutrality. In 1801, with Napoleon trying to break up the empire, the concluding assembly of deputies led to a division of nearly all ecclesiastical territories in the old empire and gains for Hamburg

to come, the original concept was increasingly abandoned and the social reforms of the Enlightenment became a mere episode. Social work was given a new stimulus in the 19th century by committed Christians in Hamburg.

The French Revolution met with an enthusiastic response in Hamburg. On 14 July, 1790, a leading merchant and supporter of the Enlightenment, Georg Heinrich Sieveking, organised a freedom festival in idyllic Harvestehude – to celebrate the anniversary of the storming of the Bastille. Those attending included the writer Friedrich Gottlieb

in the form of its cathedral (Dom).

In 1806 the French occupied Hamburg, and in 1810 the city was assimilated into their empire. The French forced through the separation of judiciary and administration and equal rights for all citizens irrespective of their faith – including Jews. In March 1813 Russian troops liberated the city but in the following May the French returned with a vengeance.

The following 12 months of hardship and deprivation have influenced the picture most people have of the French occupation to such an extent that the 1806–13 period is simply forgotten. The latter years might have been years of foreign rule but they also brought with them cooperation and modernisation. From May 1813 onwards, however, Hamburg was turned into a fortress by the French and made ready for a possible siege. Anyone unable to obtain six months of provisions had to leave the city at the turn of the year. As a result some 20,000 people were thrown out and 1,100 of them died, evicted from their own homes. Fortunately, at the end of May 1814 the French returned the city to the control of its council and left.

The old order was largely re-established in 1814–15. Members of the Reformed, Men-

opposition. In 1848–49 there were bitter struggles for political reforms and the introduction of a representative constitution. However, the presence of first Prussian and then Austrian troops helped the council maintain the old order.

The worldwide economic crisis of 1857 had a particularly severe impact on Hamburg because of speculative commodity transactions and risky loans, but it did prove an impetus to change. The council wanted to assume responsibility for financial and economic policy but the Bürgerschaft opposed it. As a result, a new Bürgerschaft was appointed in 1859.

nonite and Catholic Churches were admitted to the Bürgerschaft and from 1819 onwards they were permitted to stand for election to the council. But Jews lost the equality of status they had been granted under French rule and did not regain it until 1849.

The Great Fire of 1842 uncovered the shortcomings in Hamburg's constitution and administration. The Patriotic Society became a forum of political discussion and

Left, St Georg when it was still a village outside the walls of Hamburg. **Above**, the old towers of Hamburg viewed from Stintfang.

This new grouping was now more like a real parliament since it was composed of equal numbers of representatives of the old "propertied citizenry" and deputies elected by the "ordinary" citizens of Hamburg. A new constitution was finally passed in September 1860. From then until 1918 the city parliament was composed of elected deputies mainly representing the notables of Hamburg, as well as office holders from the legal and administrative systems and property owners. An elitist group, maybe, but a start had been made on the road to true parliamentary democracy.

In the 50 years between 1860 and 1914 Hamburg developed into a cosmopolitan city of world standing. In 1860 some 250,000 people lived within its boundaries. By the start of World War I the population had risen to over a million. In 1861 the ban on settlement beyond the city gates was lifted and urbanisation began to spread into the surrounding region. Neighbouring towns or villages were officially incorporated into the city in 1894 and 1913.

seen, involving up to 16,000 workers. Although the action finally had to be called off, working conditions in the port did improve as a result. The strength of the labour movement was symbolised by the erection of the Trade Union House at Besenbinderhof in 1906. It was built, and then extended in 1913, as a counter-balance to the Rathaus.

Hamburg developed into a centre for co-operative societies, a pillar of the German labour movement. In 1901 the first Social

Industrialisation turned Hamburg into a centre of the labour movement. Hamburg, Harburg and Altona-Ottensen were early strongholds of the Social Democratic Party (SPD) and trade union movement. Up to 1890 all three Hamburg constituencies in the German Reichstag were in the hands of the SPD, and Hamburg was represented by the leader of that party, August Bebel.

From 1892 to 1902 Hamburg was the seat of the General Commission of German Trade Unions. The dockers' strike in the city in the winter of 1896-97 was the biggest industrial conflict the Second Reich had ever

Democrat Otto Stolten, was elected to the city parliament. By trade a locksmith, Stolten was editor of the *Hamburger Echo*. In 1904 a further 12 Social Democrats were elected to join him. The majority of Hamburg's bourgeoisie sought to stem the "red flood" by introducing a class-related electoral system. However, the SPD continued to flourish and many workers were willing to pay higher taxes for the privilege of voting.

Integration into the Reich: Hamburg had long kept aloof from the old Reich and the German Federation but now was pulled into Bismarck's Reich. Traditionally-minded

Hamburgers were extremely distrustful of what they termed "prussianisation". An archivist, Otto Beneke, wrote on 22 January 1871 as the new Reich was saluted in: "It's a funny business that *faute de mieux* Hamburg will be firing this 101-gun salute out of its backside (at Kehrwiederwall) – and the salute will be fired from old ship's cannons manned by night watchmen and policemen. Hamburg hasn't got any other guns or gunners to celebrate the inauguration of the new 'Reich' and the new 'Kaiser', this King of

ter. Comprehensive democratisation did not take place until the November revolution of 1918. Although independent social democrats and left-wing radicals headed the revolutionary movement in 1918, neither they nor the SPD had any realisable concepts or strategies for reform in Hamburg. The SPD went for a policy of cooperation with the bourgeois parties. After the March 1919 election, when women were finally allowed the vote, the SPD and DDP (German Democratic Party) formed a coalition gov-

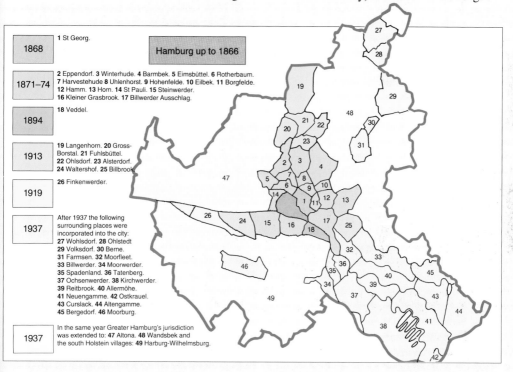

1868

1 St Georg.

Hamburg up to 1866

1871–74

2 Eppendorf. **3** Winterhude. **4** Barmbek. **5** Eimsbüttel. **6** Rotherbaum. **7** Harvestehude **8** Uhlenhorst. **9** Hohenfelde. **10** Eilbek. **11** Borgfelde. **12** Hamm. **13** Horn. **14** St Pauli. **15** Steinwerder. **16** Kleiner Grasbrook. **17** Billwerder Ausschlag.

1894

18 Veddel.

1913

19 Langenhorn. **20** Gross-Borstal. **21** Fuhlsbüttel. **22** Ohlsdorf. **23** Alsterdorf. **24** Waltershof. **25** Billbrook.

1919

26 Finkenwerder.

1937

After 1937 the following surrounding places were incorporated into the city: **27** Wohldorf. **28** Ohlstedt **29** Volksdorf. **30** Berne. **31** Farmsen. **32** Moorfleet. **33** Billwerder. **34** Moorwerder. **35** Spadenland. **36** Tatenberg. **37** Ochsenwerder. **38** Kirchwerder. **39** Reitbrook. **40** Allermöhe. **41** Neuengamme. **42** Ostkrauel. **43** Curslack. **44** Altengamme. **45** Bergedorf. **46** Moorburg.

1937

In the same year Greater Hamburg's jurisdiction was extended to: **47** Altona. **48** Wandsbek and the south Holstein villages: **49** Harburg-Wilhelmsburg.

the Slavs. Went home without any breakfast about 2. Sunday spoilt."

The truce concluded in 1914 between German working-class and bourgeois political forces was linked to hopes of domestic reforms. But these hopes were not fulfilled in Hamburg – nor anywhere else for that mat-

ernment. The mayor was from the DDP, his deputy from the SPD. In 1924 the right-wing "liberal" DVP (German Popular Party) joined the coalition, a constellation which remained in power until 1933.

In Hamburg and Altona the political parties supporting the Weimar Republic did their best to promote local government policies of a modern and socially just character. The architects Fritz Schumacher in Hamburg and Gustav Oelsner in Altona shaped

Left, Steinstrasse in the 19th century. Above, map illustrating the growth of Hamburg between 1868 and 1937.

the city. Their buildings were a significant contribution to the development of a republican architectural culture.

The effects of the Great Depression and the increasingly radical nature of German politics put an end to many promising beginnings. Democratic forces did nothing to oppose the seizure of power by the Nazis in 1933. Only Communists and active young Social Democrats began building up cores of resistance in their local strongholds.

Nazi terror regime: Contrary to numerous legends the oppressive rule of the Nazis in Hamburg was by no means milder than elsewhere. Actually Hamburg was supposed to

the working class population was forced into a programme of sterilisation which was designed to create Hitler's beloved masterrace. Ever since then, Germany has refused to participate in any form of genetic experimentation that might have implications for human beings.

Greater Hamburg – a 1937 Nazi creation, the result of the forced integration of Hamburg, Altona, Harburg-Wilhelmsburg, Wandsbek and several rural communities in Holstein – was badly damaged in World War II. On 3 May 1945 the city capitulated to British troops who took over as the army of occupation.

become a "model Nazi district". As early as 1933 Communists and Social Democrats were brutally tortured to death in Fuhlsbüttel concentration camp; 55,000 died in Neuengamme concentration camp between 1938 and 1945.

Hamburg was no exception in the Nazi's persecution of Jews either. They were boycotted, hunted and deported, their synagogues desecrated and destroyed. Mentally handicapped patients from the Alsterdorfer Anstalten, an institution set up by Pastor Sengelmann, became victims of the Nazi murderers' euthanasia programme. Much of

The first postwar election of Hamburg's city Parliament in 1946 again produced a Social Democratic-Liberal coalition though it also contained several Communist ministers until 1948. Hamburg's mayor was Max Brauer, who had been mayor of Altona during the Weimar Republic and who had returned from exile in the US. Brauer and building minister Paul Nevermann (himself mayor 1961 to 1965) were the driving forces behind the reconstruction of the city.

The SPD's dominance of local government was interrupted from 1953 to 1957 by a bourgeois government under Kurt

Sieveking. The reconstruction of the city was itself interrupted by catastrophic floods in 1962 but by the end of the 1960s it had been completed.

New constitution: In 1962 the city parliament passed a new constitution. Whereas previously, legislative and executive power had been in the hands of the council and city parliament, the new constitution decreed that all power emanated from the people. The senate, which is voted into office by the city parliament, became a collective body in which the mayor (*Erster Bürgermeister*) was only *primus inter pares* and did not enjoy any policy-making powers (such as

tal departments. The administrative system is headed by the senate, all administrative tasks which are not undertaken by senate commissions or senate offices are carried out by state departments, which are equivalent to ministries in other German states.

Hamburg today is divided up into seven administrative districts: Altona, Mitte, Eimsbüttel, Nord, Wandsbek, Bergedorf and Harburg. When elections to the city parliament take place, the electors also vote for their local district assemblies. Each of these assemblies is involved in the government of that district and also elects a district executive officer who has to be confirmed in

the federal chancellor now has). Senators (i.e. ministers) could only be removed from office by means of a vote of no confidence.

Elections to the city parliament, which has 120 members, take place every four years and are conducted on the basis of proportional representation. One peculiar feature of Hamburg's system of government is that citizens are elected by the city parliament to serve on deputations which control and administer the various individual governmen-

Left, Nazis at the war memorial at Dammtor Station. **Above**, the war-damaged city.

office by the senate. The districts are themselves divided up into smaller units where local offices take on some of the administrative work.

In general, local politics were always apathethic. In 1961 the author Siegfried Lenz, who lives in Hamburg, appealed to the city's patron saint, Hammonia: "give us a bit of passion, a bit of anger and enthusiasm, give us a bit of temperament – something you have carefully kept from us for such a long time. Oh, Hammonia, let us get a bit excited, let us be frightened, let us protest! We don't want to rave just for the sake of raving. We want, for your sake, to remain citizens. But give us a bit of passion."

Synthesis of Atlantic and Alster: Just over six months later, an anonymous article, signed with three asterisks, was published in *Die Welt* and became the talking-point of Hamburg. The author, who had hidden his identity very skilfully, proved to be none other than Hamburg's interior minister (subsequent Federal Chancellor) Helmut Schmidt.

Schmidt was always full of praise for the metropolis of Hamburg, "this magnificent city, a synthesis of Atlantic and Alster, Buddenbrooks and Babel, life and *laissez-faire*. I love this city with its scarcely disguised anglicisms, ceremonial pride in traditions, commercial pragmatism and loveable provincialism. But it is also a love tingled with melancholy because my beauty is sleeping, dreaming; she is vain about her virtues without really making use of them; she enjoys today and seems to think tomorrow is a matter of course; she suns herself a little too complacently and takes things that much too easy."

In 1965, however, narrow-mindedness and provincialism once again dominated. The popular and successful mayor Paul Nevermann was forced to resign from office because he and his wife had separated and she refused to undertake any more representative duties. His successor was the 69-year-old finance minister Herbert Weichmann, a temporary solution as many thought. But they were proved wrong. Weichmann, who had been a close colleague of the Prussian minister-president Otto Braun in the Weimar Republic and been called back to Hamburg from exile in the US by Max Brauer, became a great head of government – right up to the last. Under his leadership the SPD won the 1966 election to the city parliament with a healthy 59 percent of the votes.

Weichmann – a Jewish Social Democrat with a Prussian, Hanseatic background – was mayor until 1971. He gave Hamburg's administrative and planning departments important new stimuli. His wife Elsbeth served Hamburg magnificently in the fields of consumer advice and arts policy, and she wrote about the family's time spent in France and America (*Refuge – The Years of Exile*).

New ideas: Some of the mistakes made in the late 1960s and early 1970s – such as housing estates full of multi-storey blocks of flats or the hopes of industrialising the Lower Elbe – have since been recognised for what they were and stopped. Nowadays, Hamburg has some exemplary housing projects such as the Wolfgang Borchert estate in Alsterdorf or the whole new district of Neu-Allermöhe in Bergedorf.

Trade and the port continue to dominate Hamburg's economy, which produces the second highest earnings per head of population in the country (Frankfurt is the highest). In recent decades the city's manufacturing industry has gone through radical structural changes and electrical engineering, mechanical engineering and chemicals are now more important than the traditional shipbuilding industry. The petroleum and aerospace industries have increased in significance, and media has also become an important sector.

Since the late 1970s the ecological sins of earlier generations have been uncovered. Hamburg's economy has had to go through structural change. But now there are new perspectives, new opportunities in Germany and Europe, which can be exploited if Hamburg's political parties are able to free themselves from their self-absorption and provincial modesty. Hamburg's traditions of republican self-administration, commitment for the public good, tolerance and openness will continue to stand her in good stead.

Vital statistics: These days Greater Hamburg has a total population of around 1.75 million inhabitants, of whom around 10 percent are foreign nationals. As any visitor soon realises, the city-state is spread wide, covering 755 sq km (294 sq miles) and its area includes many islands which today are almost totally submerged beneath the city's infrastructure. Sixty square kilometres of the surface area is actually water, while Hamburg has the most bridges of any city in Europe. Roughly two million tourists a year visit this Venice of the North.

Right, the Heinrich Hertz Tower (TV Tower), Hamburg's highest building.

Hamburg has a long and unfortunate chronology of disasters – which have themselves perhaps helped cultivate the will to thrive. One of the city's first major blows was the Black Death. In the mid-14th century virtually the whole of Europe was hit by the plague, an infectious disease transmitted by rats' fleas. It reached Hamburg in 1350 and carried off a third of the population, and then kept on returning until the 18th century.

The last visit was one of the worst. In September 1712, the first cases were recorded in the rural areas around Hamburg and in the narrow lanes of the densely populated *Gängeviertel* at the heart of the city. In spring 1713 it disappeared, only to reappear in August 1713 in the slums of St Michael's and St James' parishes. With the whole of Hamburg in quarantine, trade and the port were brought to a standstill. There was mass unemployment, which of course increased the destitution of those most vulnerable. The epidemic did not subside until February 1714. Some 10,000 Hamburgers had died, out of a total population of 70,000–75,000.

Cholera: Untreated water was taken straight from the Elbe. Tap water was dirty and verminous. It wasn't just a case of small foreign bodies in the drinking water; turn on a tap and an eel might come swimming out. In 1832 no fewer than 482 Hamburgers died of cholera; in 1859 the figure was 1,300. Medical warnings about the state of the drinking water were ignored. Hamburg's government simply refused to listen, only deciding to build a central filter plant in 1891. That was too late. In August 1892 an appalling cholera epidemic broke out.

Robert Koch, who had discovered the cause of cholera, came from Berlin to see for himself what life was like in the slums. The leading bacteriologist of the time, he said: "I've forgotten I'm in Europe". In all, 16,596 people caught cholera and 8,605 died of the disease. The whole of Europe was horror-struck by what was hidden behind the splendid facade of Germany's rich and prosperous trading metropolis. The Senate was forced to admit its failure. It realised that something had to be done about the slums. Public utilities, which had become a matter of course elsewhere, had to be provided for the inhabitants of the city's poor quarters. Sadly, these measures were not solely taken on humanitarian grounds: the cholera epidemic had had a severe effect on business.

Fire: In the towns and cities of medieval and early modern times fires were a constant danger. Many of the buildings were constructed almost entirely of wood and there were numerous spectacular fires.

Religious leaders declared these fires divine punishment, although they had to think hard when the tower of St Michael's – affectionately known as "Michel" by Hamburgers – was struck by lightning. St Michael's, the church built between 1751 and 1786 under the supervision of Johann Leonhard Prey and Ernst Sonnin, had become Hamburg's most famous landmark. The burning tower collapsed, destroying the church.

The loss of St Michael's, the militant pastors claimed, was God's retribution on the free-thinking godless in the city. They even compared it to Sodom and Gomorrah. And 156 years after the fire of 1750, St Michael's was again in flames. In June 1906 a watchman, Carl Beurle, noticed the burning, which had probably been started by soldering work on the copper roof. He raised the alarm but there was to be no escape for him; Beurle was burned to death in his tower room. Just as in 1750, the burning tower collapsed and the whole church fell victim to the flames. It was immediately rebuilt.

The Great Fire of Hamburg in 1842 has gone down in history as one of Europe's worst, comparable with the Great Fire of London in 1666 and that of Magdeburg in 1631. It broke out in the night of 4 May in Deichstrasse, a fact commemorated by a plaque in the entrance to No. 42. Fuelled by

Left, Hamburg's most famous landmark in flames: the tower of St. Michael's, affectionately known as "Michel", burning on 3 July 1906.

the goods stored in the neighbouring warehouses and attics, it spread quickly, crossing the nearby canal. The chief fireman, Adolph Repsold, suggested following the American example and blowing up houses to stop the flames spreading. The senate refused, fearing claims for compensation from the owners, and the fire was able to burn on unhindered. When the senate finally realised that Repsold's suggestion was right, it was too late. By the afternoon the tower and church of St Nicholas were burning. The inhabitants of St Catharine's parish worked together and managed to save their church, houses and well-filled warehouses.

Fifty-one people had died, 120 had been injured, 1,100 houses and 102 warehouses had been destroyed, 20,000 were homeless. During the fire Hamburg had received a lot of assistance from neighbouring towns and villages. Two technical innovations were proven in the conflagration: one was the system of optical telegraphy, which had been used to pass on messages since 1833; the other was the railway which had just been opened from Hamburg to Bergedorf, the first stage of the route to Berlin.

Salomon Heine, a great self-made man and successful banker, ensured that the Stock Exchange continued to function. It was his

In the evening the flames spread across the Alster. Early next morning the Rathaus had to be blown up once all the documents and files had been removed to the cellar of St Michael's. The Stock Exchange, opened only a year before, was saved by the efforts of a few courageous men. The banker Salomon Heine had his Jungfernstieg house blown up to prevent the flames reaching Gänsemarkt. Though the fire faltered here, it continued to spread on the other side of the Alster. On the morning of 8 May the flames were finally extinguished in Brandsende, a street named after this fortunate event.

efforts that prevented any exorbitant profits being made. He purposely did not claim the insurance on his Jungfernstieg house to spare the fire-insurance fund. Hamburg had to raise a loan of 32 million marks after the fire; Salomon Heine's contribution was eight million. In addition to all this, he provided the city treasury with half a million marks of his own money. Hamburg awarded honorary citizenship to the mayors of Bremen, Altona and Magdeburg for their help during and after the fire but its senate felt it could not honour Salomon Heine or his colleague Jacob Oppenheimer, because they were Jews.

The Great Fire had clearly shown where the shortcomings in Hamburg's constitution and administration lay. A debate began about lasting reforms. But the fact that a professional fire service was not set up until 30 years later, in 1872, shows that the idea of somehow muddling through took a long time to die. However, modern principles were applied in the reconstruction of the city centre, a third of which had been destroyed. Water pipes and sewers were laid, streets widened and given better lighting. What's more, reconstruction also included the creation of "the work of art that is Hamburg", as the famous architect Fritz Schumacher put it. The attrac-

on German cities. From 25 July to 3 August, 1943 more than 3,000 British and American planes bombed Hamburg day and night. The first areas to be destroyed were the city centre around St Nicholas, Hoheluft, Eimsbüttel, St Pauli, Altona and Wandsbek; they were followed by Eilbek, Hohenfelde, Borgfelde, Hamm, Horn and Rothenburgsort; then came Barmbek and parts of Harvestehude, Rotherbaum, Eppendorf, Winterhude, Uhlenhorst and St Georg.

At least 35,000 people died and over 100,000 were injured in the worst catastrophe ever to hit Hamburg. Tens of thousands fled the blazing city. A secret report prepared

tive heart of present-day Hamburg – the Inner Alster, Alsterarkaden, Rathausmarkt and Ballindamm – emerged like a phoenix from the flames.

The blitz: Much of what was reconstructed in Hamburg after the Great Fire of 1842 was to be destroyed only a century later. Germany opened a new chapter in aerial warfare with its blitz on Coventry in 1940. The seed sown then was soon reaped with a vengeance

Left, the Great Fire caused widespread damage in Hamburg in 1842. **Above**, grave-diggers at work during the cholera epidemic of 1892.

by the police concluded: "Words fail us in describing the magnitude of the horror that struck people for ten days and nights. The traces of this horror are imprinted for ever in the face of the city and those of its people." A businessman, Hans Erick Nossack, was banned from writing in 1933 and lost nearly all his manuscripts in the 1943 bombing raids. In November 1943 he wrote a book simply entitled *Destruction*. Eventually published in 1948, it tells of the destruction of the city, of death and horror and of what really happened in the ruined and supposedly unharmed districts of Hamburg. *Destruction* is a testimony to the dangers of suppressing or forgetting such events.

Floods: Hamburg is situated on a tidal river. This is a fact most people were no longer aware of by the early 1960s. Actually, only a few years before, in 1953, terrible floods had hit Holland but the last to affect Hamburg were in 1906 and 1916. Only dyke builders and historians remembered the floods of 1771 and 1825 which had caused a great deal of damage in the rural areas around Hamburg.

In February 1962, storm areas in the North Sea produced enormous waves. On the evening of 16 February, the water rose 3.77

metres (148 inches) above normal in Cuxhaven and did not drop for ten hours. Northwesterly winds drove it into the mouth of the Elbe where dykes prevented it escaping onto the old flood plains. On the morning of 17 February the waters of the Elbe were 4.08 metres (160 inches) above normal at St Pauli, 46 cm (18 inches) higher than in 1825, the previous worst storm tide.

Whereas the sea dykes held and the inhabitants of the Elbe marshes were evacuated in good time, the storm tide devastated the Elbe island of Wilhelmsburg. In Hamburg 315 people were drowned, thousands lost everything. The man who was later to become Chancellor, Helmut Schmidt, had only joined the Hamburg senate in December 1961. As an expert on transport and then defence, he had made a name (and a nickname "Schmidt the Snout") for himself in the German federal parliament. When the floods hit Hamburg, he took control of the rescue operation and relief measures. He called in the Federal armed forces, frontier guards and Allied troops to help Hamburg's police, fire brigade and auxiliaries.

Just as the railway passed its baptism of fire during the Great Fire of 1842, helicopters now proved their worth; 2,000 people were saved and 20,000 homeless provided for. In the city centre the flood waters reached the Rathausmarkt, flooding cellars in the Rathaus, Stock Exchange, banks and insurance companies. For weeks there were problems with electricity and gas supplies as their production plants in the port area had been flooded too. On 26 February there was a commemorative service for those who had died. As Mayor Paul Nevermann said on that occasion, "In our vulnerable existence there is apparently no absolute security against the raging of the elements – though we so oft wish there were. However, we will increase the level of safety without delay."

As the interior minister and head of the police department, Helmut Schmidt organised rapid modernisation. Dykes were raised and strengthened, floodgates and locks constructed, a flood-protection built around the port and the old southern arm of the Elbe (Süderelbe) dammed up to the west of Finkenwerder. These dykes and walls are now 7 metres (23 ft) higher than the normal water level – 130 cm (51 inches) above the flood level of 1962.

On 3 January 1976 a storm tide reached the record level of 6.45 metres (21 ft), without causing harm. On 24 November 1981 the water rose to a level of nearly 6 metres (19 ft). Gale-force winds were driving the water direct into the mouth of the Elbe, but fortunately the tide turned just in time.

Above, some districts of Hamburg only existed on paper in April 1945. **Right**, Cars piled high in Wilhelmsburg after the 1962 floods.

Arable farming, cattle husbandry and fishing were the means by which the early inhabitants of what we now call Hamburg earned their living. The first trading links were forged in the 9th century with the Frisian inhabitants of the North Sea coastlands. When the fortress known as the Hammaburg was built, a settlement of skilled craftsmen and merchants grew up around this fortification.

Hamburg's first harbour at Reichenstrassenfleet is impossible to find in today's city centre. The small canal in question was filled in back in 1877. Early Hamburg traders also had ties to the Rhineland and millstones were transported from the Eifel region by water. It is possible that even in those early days grain was exported westwards from Hamburg. The town of Stade, half-way up the Elbe between Hamburg and the coast, was more important than Hamburg at the end of the 12th century, but this picture was soon to change. The colonisation of territories to the east of Hamburg, an increase in population in the Middle Elbe region and the founding of Lübeck were all points in Hamburg's favour as the city developed into the North Sea port of this new Baltic metropolis and the port for this large hinterland.

When Hamburg's Neustadt was established in the late 12th century, a new harbour was built at Nikolaifleet. Still visible today, it gives visitors a good impression of the modest beginnings to a port that was subsequently to become one of the world's largest. Safeguarding the transport of goods by land and water became one of Hamburg's foremost tasks. To this end, close alliances were concluded with Lübeck in 1241 and 1255. Hamburg also signed treaties with Hadeln and Wursen, territories at the mouths of the Elbe and Weser respectively, to safeguard the river's shipping.

Brewery city: Principal exports in those days

were grain from Dithmarschen, Holstein and Mark Brandenburg; wood from Saxony, Brandenburg; pitch and ash from the Middle Elbe region; dye from Thuringia; metal products from the Harz Mountains; honey from the Lüneburg region; and butter and ham from the neighbouring villages. These exports mainly went to the Netherlands and Flanders from where textiles in particular but also cattle and wine were imported. Hamburg's merchants also traded in wines from the Rhine and France. Spices and fruits from southern climes were imported from Flanders and fish came from Schonen and Norway. All these goods were also marketed in regions inland from Hamburg.

In the 14th century a product made in Hamburg also became an important export commodity: beer. A contemporary wit characterised the leading Hanseatic League cities as follows: "Lübeck is a department store, Lüneburg a salt store, Cologne is a wine house and Hamburg a beer house."

Hamburg, one of the hubs of east-west trade, was very much involved in the transition from the mercantile to the municipal Hanse. Since the sea passage through the Kattegat had become dangerous, many traders chose the land route via Lübeck and Hamburg. At the end of the 14th century another link was created between the two cities: the Stecknitz canal from Lauenburg on the Upper Elbe to Lübeck. From the 16th century onwards its importance declined but in 1900 the Elbe-Lübeck canal was completed as a replacement.

The Elbe: In the 14th and 15th centuries Hamburg skilfully established its control over the river Elbe. The acquisition of the island of Neuwerk in 1299–1300 and Ritzebüttel in 1394 ensured control of the Lower Elbe. Hamburg had to hand over Ritzebüttel, now the town of Cuxhaven, to the Prussian province of Hannover in 1937 but Neuwerk was recovered from the Hannoverians, now known as Lower Saxony, in 1962 so that Hamburg could build a deepwater port, at the time considered to be a necessity. A peel tower has become the most famous landmark of this tiny island at the mouth of the Elbe. In the mid-15th century Hamburg positioned buoys and beacons to mark the navigable channel in the river.

When conflict broke out in 1568 with the duchy of Brunswick-Lauenburg about the northern and southern arms of the Elbe (known as Norderelbe and Süderelbe), the city council commissioned a 12-metre (39-ft) long and 1-metre (3-ft) wide chart of the river. Melchior Lorich's magnificent work is now one of the splendid exhibits in Hamburg's state archives. The chart illustrates Hamburg's claim to the Elbe, the course of

from the Baltic to the Mediterranean and the North Sea, Hamburg was in a particularly favourable position. Grain and wood were the main products exported westwards. Spices and colonial goods were the imports.

Following the Dutch example, Hamburg established a Stock Exchange in 1558, the first in Germany. The city not only profited from the economic changes going on in Europe but also from its wars of religion. Dutch Protestants fled in front of the invading Spaniards to Hamburg. Lutherans were also welcomed but members of the Reformed Church were eyed with suspicion by some pastors and propertied citizens. The city coun-

which is mapped from Geestacht to Neuwerk.

In the 15th century Hamburg's links with the Hanseatic League became looser. The city's own interests, especially in trading with Iceland, went against those of other Hanse cities and the Hanse office in Bergen. Hamburg began to look more to the West and it was there, in Holland and Friesland, that Hamburg's beer found its markets.

Age of Discovery: In the 16th century Hamburg increasingly profited from the fundamental changes in world trade brought about by the Age of Discovery. Since the focal points of European trade were shifting away

cil, in contrast, recognised the benefits for trade and ensured they were accepted into the city community. In 1567 the Merchant Adventurers, English merchants, were admitted but resistance from pastors and some citizens meant their contract of residence was not renewed. In 1611, however, they were allowed to return.

Hamburg also opened its gates to Sephardim, Portuguese Jews who had come from the Iberian Peninsular via Flanders and the Netherlands, and Ashkenazim, Jews from the Holy Roman Empire and from eastern Europe. The know-how, experience and contacts all these immigrants brought with them were of great benefit to Hamburg's trade and industry. Trade with Spain and Portugal increased and ships began to sail to Italian ports. In 1619, these new merchants played a decisive role in the establishment of the Hamburg Bank, the first such institution in Germany.

Specialisation and diversification shaped Hamburg's economic life. Commission business, forwarding and bill transactions were commonplace. Shipping companies, bankers and brokers established their businesses. A messenger and postal system ensured the necessary means of communica-

burg and sold throughout Germany. Skilled craftsmen met the population's basic needs and worked for the traders and shipping companies whose demand for crates, barrels, boats and ships grew enormously. Even books were shipped in barrels because it was easier to transport them in this way.

Whereas the Thirty Years' War hit many German towns and cities very hard, Hamburg was safe behind its mighty fortifications. All the major powers used Hamburg for trade and finance, supplying and equipping troops and collecting news and views. Even the King of Denmark, Christian IV, had to admit failure in his attempt to break Hamburg's

tion with towns on the coast and in the hinterland. The brewery business, however, declined steadily – though as late as the 18th century, newly-elected city councillors still swore an oath to its prosperity in the speeches they made on entering office. Textiles, in contrast, became more and more important. Hammer mills and grain mills were built outside the city walls. Sugar and salt, key import commodities, were refined in Ham-

Left, copper stills in the St Pauli brewery; beer was an early export from the city. **Above**, researchers at DAISY particle acceleration centre.

power by establishing the town of Glückstadt further down the Elbe.

New competitors: A more dangerous threat was presented by Frederick III of Denmark in 1664 when he granted Altona – which was still part of Denmark – its municipal charter. This town, where freedom of worship and trade flourished and Northern Europe's first free port was created following the example set by the Italian port of Livorno, presented an extremely important challenge to Hamburg. The latter was forced to adapt its policies to become more tolerant and ease some of its customs practices.

However, it was not long before the two neighbours were trading and cooperating with each other. Altona made use of Hamburg's Bank and Stock Exchange while Hamburg merchants made use of shippers and ships under the Danish flag. When the Swedes burned down Altona during the Nordic Wars in 1713 as an act of revenge for the destruction of Stade by the Danes, the Hannoverian representative in Hamburg commented that its merchants had suffered more than those of Altona itself.

Hamburg set up an Admiralty in 1623. Its purpose was to safeguard and further the city's economy. In 1668–69 the Admiralty

began equipping its own men-of-war as convoy ships to protect Hamburg's merchant vessels. In 1665 a Commerce Deputation was established. This forerunner of the present-day Chamber of Commerce was to have tremendous influence on Hamburg's foreign and economic policies. France and Russia became increasingly important trading partners for Hamburg.

New trade links: France provided materials, velvet, silk, cane sugar, spices and wine as well as those new sources of pleasure, coffee, tea, tobacco and cocoa. In 1677 the first German coffee house was opened in Hamburg. Business life, a postal service and the press developed in a process of mutual interdependence and Hamburg became one of the leading news centres in Europe. A new industry to emerge was whaling off Greenland. The sailors for these dangerous trips mainly came from the North Frisian Islands.

The 17th century also saw the beginnings of what were later to become very important manufacturing industries: sugar refining and calico printing. The sugar went mainly to markets in Germany but the cotton cloth was exported to other countries in Western Europe. Tobacco products were another internationally significant industry in the 18th century.

Increasing competition and the mercantilist tariff policies of the major powers hit Hamburg hard. The economic crisis that struck Europe in 1763 at the end of the Seven Years' War badly affected the city too. A total of 97 bankruptcies were recorded. But towards the end of the century Hamburg began to profit from Germany's growing economic power – despite the numerous German states with their own frontiers and customs dues, which hindered trade. Many new trading links were established, for example to the newly independent United States of America. Between 1789 and 1791 the most important trading partners for Hamburg were France, England, Holland and Spain. In 1791 Portugal was pushed into sixth place by the US with Denmark dropping to seventh.

Hamburg's companies became increasingly involved in world commerce. Via Portugal, England and the Netherlands, Hamburg's merchants obtained resins from India and pepper, tea, ginger, indigo and opium from Java. From Smyrna (now Izmir) they got cotton. Silk was brought from Venice and Livorno. Olive and laurel oil came from Florence and Northern Italy; snuff tobacco, timber and sugar from Spain and Portugal; and wax from the Russian and Baltic ports. In the second half of the 18th century some 2,000 ships a year called in at the Port of Hamburg. Lübeck, with 950 ships, and Bremen, with 480, were left well behind.

Hamburg's economic achievements were the result of the combined efforts of merchants, shippers, bankers, brokers, sailors, dockers, porters, packers, carriers and skilled craftsmen, locals and immigrants, members of the Lutheran majority and religious minorities. During the 18th century new immigrants came to the city from France, Switzerland, England and Hamburg's own hinterland. They brought fresh stimulation to the city's economic life.

Waterways: In the centuries before the construction of decent roads and railways, waterways and even small rivers were extremely important means of transport. This was particularly true of the river Elbe and its tributaries and canals. In 1793, for example, over 5.6 million pounds of coffee, 4 million

before through the Hamburg Bank and an extensive insurance business. As early as 1676 the first public fire-insurance scheme was set up. In 1765 the first maritime insurance was founded and in 1778 the first life insurance. Speculative commodity transactions led to an economic crisis in 1799 with 152 Hamburg trading houses collapsing. A couple of years later, Hamburg's economy was devastated by the Anglo-French wars and in particular by the blockades of the Elbe in 1801 and 1803 and the French continental blockade in 1806 to which England responded with a trading blockade in 1807. Smugglers and illicit traders had a heyday but shipping

pounds of refined sugar and over 3.5 million pounds of cane sugar, over 3 million pounds of syrup, nearly 12 million pounds of raisins, 5.6 million pounds of tobacco and 3.3 million pounds of rice were transported up the Elbe to Hamburg.

Finance: With Amsterdam weakened by the political upheavals resulting from the French Revolution, Hamburg was, for a short time, the leading continental financial centre. Sound foundations had been laid long

<u>Left</u>, warehouse working in the Speicherstadt. <u>Above</u>, cars await delivery in the Free Port.

and foreign trade came to a virtual standstill with heavy losses for Hamburg.

In the post-1815 era England dominated commerce and Hamburg became the most English city of continental Europe. They used to say that when it rained in London, people in Hamburg would put up their umbrellas. Hamburg also developed its own trading links to the newly independent countries of Latin America. Boliva Park at Klosterstern with its monument to Simon Bolivar is a reminder of these close ties. In the 1830s and 1840s Africa and Asia became favoured destinations for Hamburg.

Industry: The year 1838 saw an end to compulsory guild membership in shipbuilding but general freedom of trade was not introduced until 1865. Industrialisation came very late to Hamburg, with mercantile interests, too, dominant in political and economic life. Up to 1856, industrialists were not allowed to attend the Honourable Merchant meetings, a tradition going back to 1517 and still in existence today. Another anomaly of present-day Hamburg is the fact that the city has no Chamber of Industry and Commerce; there is only a Chamber of Commerce, even though it does look after both fields.

Not surprisingly, the industrialisation of the Hamburg region began in Harburg and Altona-Ottensen with Wandsbek and Bergedorf also developing into industrial locations. But Hamburg was well off for trade and shipping. The Elbe was deepened and work began with extensions to the port. In 1842 the first railway line was completed between Hamburg and Bergedorf and in 1846 it was extended to Berlin. The Altona-Celle railway was opened in 1844 and in 1860 the link between Hamburg and Altona was finally completed. In 1865 the railway line to Lübeck was built and in 1872 bridges were constructed over the northern and southern arms of the Elbe. This made direct rail links to Bremen and Hannover possible. In 1906 the main station was built to replace the various terminus stations which had existed up to then.

Parallel to the development of the railways, Hamburg built up a system of public transport, starting with horse-drawn omnibuses and then progressing to electric trams, electric suburban trains and finally to the underground railway system which was opened in 1912. One peculiarity of Hamburg's underground system is that a good deal of it runs overground – and it is actually known as the "Hochbahn" (overground). The public-transport system was rounded off by Alster steamers and port ferries. But despite this progress, many workers still had to walk or cycle to work.

The port: Traditionally oriented towards free trade, Hamburg was faced with a completely new situation from 1867 when it became a member of the North German Confederation and then from 1871 as part of the newly created German Reich. For years Hamburg and Berlin conducted negotiations on joining the German Customs union to which Hamburg and Altona did not belong. It was only in 1888 that Hamburg finally became a member. However, it managed to maintain a Free Port area in which goods could be stored, treated and processed without being subject to customs dues. In order to create this new Free Port, 24,000 people were thrown out of their homes to make way for the so-called Speicherstadt, still the world's largest homogeneous warehouse complex, close to the city centre.

Membership of the Customs union brought a decisive boost to the process of industrialisation. In 1880 Hamburg had a mere 685 manufacturing firms employing only about 18,000 people. By 1914 the figure had risen to 6,715 firms employing some 110,000 workers. The leading industries were mechanical engineering, precision engineering, instrument construction and shipbuilding followed, at a distance, by the food, beverages and tobacco industry, the clothing industry, the metal- and wood-working industries, the printing industry and the chemicals industry. Some 40,000–50,000 people were employed in 15,000 business in the skilled trades. In the port the major shipyards were now the dominant industries.

Before World War I huge ocean liners of over 50,000 GRT were launched at Hamburg's shipyards – ships such as the *Vaterland*, *Bismarck* and *Imperator* which deserved the superlatives rained upon them but also symbolised Germany's imperialistic ambitions. The *Hamburg-Amerikanische Packetfahrt-Aktiengesellschaft* (HAPAG) was set up in 1857 and became the world's biggest shipping line under the directorship of Albert Ballin. In the world ports' league Hamburg was now third behind New York and London. In the South Seas and West Africa Hamburg's merchants were paving the way for German colonies.

In 1900 nearly 15 million tonnes of goods were imported and over nine million tonnes exported. In 1870, 4,144 ships had sailed into the Port of Hamburg and 4,101 departed. By 1900 these respective figures had risen to

13,102 and 13,109. Steamers made up 47 percent of the vessels in 1870; by 1900 the figure was 68 percent. The age of sail was slowly drawing to an end.

The World Wars: World War I and Germany's defeat in 1918 were decisive in Hamburg's economic development. Companies were faced by keener competition worldwide. Old ties were broken, areas of influence lost. Imports and exports only reached their pre-war levels in 1928 and 1929. However, this upswing was brutally stopped by the Great Depression which began with the Wall Street crash in October 1929. Hamburg's dependence on trade, the port and on shipping meant

especially in the big shipyards. During World War II forced labour was introduced into many firms. "Extermination through work" became the ruthless aim of the Nazis' cynically brutal policy. The victims were the German and foreign inmates of Neuengamme concentration camp in Hamburg.

Reconstruction: After the war Hamburg was faced with utterly different economic conditions in which to rebuild its devastated city. A large part of its natural hinterland was virtually inaccessible as a result of the division of Germany and indeed Europe. Up to 1951 there were still restrictions on production in shipbuilding – only repairs could be

that the effects of this global crisis were particularly severe. The domestic market offered no alternative, especially since the economic and fiscal policies pursued by the Weimar government only served to weaken domestic demand even further.

During the first few years of Nazi rule, unemployment in Hamburg still remained at above-average levels, but it was not until armaments production was dramatically stepped up that jobs were created in industry,

Above, offloading of all types of merchandise continues round the clock in the port.

carried out at Hamburg's shipyards. But in the mid-1950s Germany's "economic miracle" enabled prewar figures to be equalled and then passed in terms of the volume of cargo handled and industrial production. The port and shipping shaped the city's economic fortunes, just as it had done in the decades before, and shipbuilding prospered.

In 1949–50 economics senator Karl Schiller propounded his ideas about attracting new industries to Hamburg but hardly anyone was willing to listen, not even at the Chamber of Commerce. Hamburg continued to bank on its traditional strengths. In the

1960s and 1970s the city's infrastructure was improved.

In 1967 Hamburg's various means of public transport were united to form a single Passenger Transport Authority (known as the HVV). It proved a model which several other German metropolitan regions later copied. In 1974 the Kohlbrandbrücke (bridge) was built to improve road connections to and from the port. In 1975 the new tunnel under the Elbe was opened to traffic, over half a century after the first Elbe tunnel had been opened to link St Pauli and Steinwerder in 1911. In 1976 the Elbe lateral canal was opened to link the Upper Elbe and Mittellandkanal.

From 1963 onwards, a new business park, City Nord, was constructed right next to the Stadtpark, mainly as a location for corporate headquarters. It has taken a lot of pressure off the city centre.

Structural change: International and national structural changes have brought about enormous economic upheavals in Hamburg since the 1960s. Whereas over 20,000 people were still employed in shipbuilding in 1966, that figure had fallen to 7,000 by 1989. Of the major shipyards that used to dominate life in the port, only Blohm & Voss remains – and its survival is due to a successful transference to other products. Now Hamburg's biggest shipyard is not even in the port: J.J. Sietas is located at the mouth of the river Este in the part of Altes Land belonging to Hamburg.

In employment terms, Hamburg's leading industry is now electrical engineering, followed by mechanical engineering and chemicals. In terms of turnover, the petroleum industry leads electrical engineering and chemicals. Shipbuilding has now been overtaken by the aerospace industry. MBB in Hamburg develops and manufactures parts for Airbus Industrie and the Lufthansa service yard is a major employer at the airport.

There has been a revolution in cargo handling in recent years with container traffic increasing dramatically from year to year. Mechanisation and rationalisation have radically transformed the nature of work in the port. In 1989 nearly 58 million tonnes of goods were handled from 12,500 ships. Over 14 million tonnes of these cargoes were containerised. In addition, inland waterway vessels carried more than 8 million tonnes of goods. Today Hamburg is the fifth most important port in Europe, after Rotterdam, Antwerp, Marseille and Le Havre.

The contribution to Hamburg's GNP by the various sectors of the economy is shown below (with the figures in brackets referring to the benchmark figures for pre-unification West Germany): public sector 9 percent (12 percent), services 34 percent (28 percent), sransport 13 percent (6 percent), trade 15 percent (10 percent), manufacturing industry 28 percent (42 percent) and agriculture 1 percent (2 percent). Hamburg has become a services city.

The traditionally strong sectors of banking and insurance have been joined by the media, a fast-growing industry with nearly 3,000 firms in the Hamburg region and a media workforce made up of some 45,000 permanent employees, 7,500 regular freelancers and around 20,000 casuals. Hamburg is the home of high-circulation dailies and weeklies, magazines, books, records, TV companies, radio stations and film production studios. Tourism is another growing industry in Hamburg. In recent years an annual figure of nearly 2 million guests came to the city with some 3.8 million overnight stays recorded. Thirty-four percent were foreigners.

German unification and the progress towards a single European market confront Hamburg with new challenges. The infrastructure needs further improvement. Measures required include the modernisation of Hamburg airport, the building of road and rail links to the airport, further extensions to the public transport system and improvements to the Elbe as an inland waterway. Hamburg can take on new functions as a bridge to northern and eastern Europe. The experience gained over the centuries will be of decisive economic benefit in future.

Its recently acquired significance as a centre of information and communication seems to be based on sure foundations – despite emerging competition from Berlin.

Right, the Speicherstadt, the world's largest homogeneous warehouse complex.

It is a strange and little-known fact that Czechoslovakia borders on Hamburg. It has done for years – and this has got nothing to do with German reunification. To be honest, it's not quite the whole of the country but only a 1.6-hectare (3.9 acres) enclave in the Free Port that was taken on a 99-year lease way back in 1929. This peculiar enclave, the so-called Moldauhafen, actually handles over a million tonnes of transit goods every year. It is not the only peculiarity you come across in the Port of Hamburg, a 6,250-hectare (24 sq. miles) area making up a twelfth of the entire city-state of Hamburg.

History: It took a thousand years for Hamburg to develop to one of the world's most important ports. It all began in the 10th century when a 120-metre (393 ft) wooden jetty was built at Reichenstrassenfleet (don't go looking for it now, it disappeared long ago). Today, the total length of the quays in the port is 70 km (43 miles).

In 1188, when Hamburg's Neustadt was founded, Graf Adolf III of Schauenburg had the first "real" harbour built at Nikolaifleet. A year later, Hamburg's merchants obtained from Emperor Friedrich Barbarossa the privilege of exemption from all custom dues on the Lower Elbe. Although the charter is now known to be a 13th-century forgery, Hamburg still celebrates 7 May 1189 as the anniversary of the founding of its port.

In the 14th century Hamburg joined the Hanseatic League in which Lübeck was then the leading light. But Hamburg became increasingly important as the hub of trade between eastern and western Europe, a role it maintained until Portugal and Spain established their overseas empires. The King of Denmark handed over some islands in the Elbe to Hamburg at the Treaty of Gottorp (1768). These islands were later used to expand the port.

The early 19th century was a time of renewed boom as the Spanish and Portuguese colonies in South America gained their independence and the colonial powers lost their trading monopoly. In 1862 work began on construction of the first artificial harbour basin, Sandtorhafen. It was the first step towards the present-day infrastructure with road and rail connections – an open tidal port with permanent berths for ships. This initiative was followed by buildings on the southern shore of the Elbe's northern arm (Norderelbe) and the construction of bridges to Harburg.

The Free Port: When Hamburg joined the German Customs union, it was the end of the city-state's privileges – apart from the vital fact that Hamburg's mercantile community struggled hard and long with Bismarck to obtain the right to establish a Free Port. The community was eventually successful but a solution had to be found to the problem that many of the warehouses were outside the newly-established Free Port enclave.

A whole residential area between Zollkanal and Sandtorhafen was subsequently demolished. Over 20,000 people lost their homes so that Hamburg's merchants could build their so-called Speicherstadt. The 17 seven- or eight-storey redbrick warehouses making up this "Warehouse City" are still the world's largest warehouse complex of its kind – covering nearly 500,000 sq. metres (123 acres) in all. Today, just over a century after they were built, there are plans to turn the Speicherstadt into apartments, offices and shops.

Customs frontier: Visitors to the Speicherstadt are on foreign, i.e. non-German, territory – at least in the customs sense. And you need to be careful. If you've just bought a new cassette recorder in some city-centre store or even are carrying a prayer rug under your arm, you can take them into the Speicherstadt (or anywhere else in the Free Port) but you could have difficulties getting them out again. Goods can be stored or treated in the Free Port but as soon as they cross the border into Germany, which circles the port,

Preceding pages: Hamburg to England ferry tied up at Landungsbrücken. Left, *Cap San Diego*, the port's museum ship.

customs duty has to be paid – even for that cassette recorder or prayer rug. The thing to do is register them with the customs officers before entering.

Quartermasters: Within the Free Port, all kinds of goods are stored: tobacco, machinery parts, carpets worth billions, tea and coffee. So-called quartermasters, specialists in their field, ensure they are stored correctly. They got their German name ("Quartierleute") from the fact that typical firms were made up of four such men. Company names such as Müller & Consorten are derived from the foreman's name and the collective term for his three colleagues.

Port of Hamburg.

Nearly 80,000 people work in and around the port, almost 10,000 of them in cargo handling. In 1990, for example 61.4 million tonnes of goods were handled by the port: 4.9 million tonnes of suction cargoes (e.g. grain), 12.6 million tonnes of grab cargoes, 15.3 million tonnes of liquid cargoes and 28.6 million tonnes of general and bagged cargoes. The total volume of cargo would weigh as much as 70 million VW Golfs.

Time is money: The port runs as a sophisticated system in which the individual operations fit together to work like clockwork. It all starts about 100 km (62 miles) down-

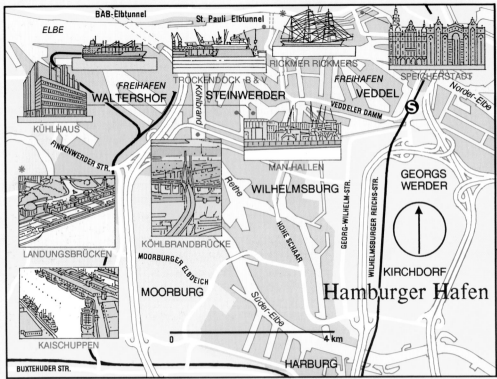

"Incomprehensible, unfathomable, indescribable: that's the Port of Hamburg, this huge world magnet… Its gigantic size and power, its gravity and work have stirred many minds…" This was how the poet Gorch Fock, born in Finkenwerder on the Elbe, described the port. Now he is better known for the fact that the German navy's sailing school ship was named after him. Fock was right. It is extremely difficult to grasp the magnitude of what goes on in the

stream where the Elbe flows into the North Sea. There a pilot goes on board one of the 70,000 ships which use the Elbe every year. The pilot's job is to guide the ship into the funnel-shaped mouth of the river. The Elbe pilot comes on board off Cuxhaven and is later replaced by a harbour pilot. Ships of more than a certain tonnage, and any carrying dangerous cargoes, have to take on a pilot, whose services are not cheap. A container ship of 51,000 GRT will have to pay upwards of DM 100,000 for pilots, tugs, port dues, berthing charges, quayage and brokerage. Not surprisingly, port life is dominated by the well-known phrase "time is money".

To ensure that everything runs smoothly, the whole port machinery is set in motion as soon as a ship reaches the mouth of the Elbe. It is allocated a terminal; brokers and carriers are informed about the kind of cargo and how much there is; a telephone line is installed; and as soon as the ship has been towed to its berth and made fast, the unloading operation begins.

Nowadays a shipping company's choice of port is dependent on the speed of cargo-service is also dependent on the highly specialised nature of the port operators' facilities. Any kind of cargo can be given the specialist treatment it requires. Besides the multi-purpose terminals where ships can be loaded and unloaded from all sides with the help of cranes and barges, there are also specialist terminals. For example, the cargoes unloaded from ships' holds at the fruit centre are immediately transferred to air-conditioned warehouses where a ripening specialist keeps a careful eye on storage conditions. The banana shed is so large that several lorries and railway waggons can be loaded inside without this sensitive fruit suf-

handling operations. So to stay competitive over the years, the port of Hamburg has had not only to extend its facilities but, above all, to modernise its cargo-handling gear. Back in 1969, 13,500 dockers were employed to handle 13 million tonnes of general cargo. Seven years later, 7,700 employees managed 21.5 million tonnes.

The fact that each of the more than 40 ships arriving daily can be given prompt and fast

Left, map of the Port of Hamburg. **Above**, Kohl-brandbrücke spans the waterway linking the Elbe's southern and northern arms.

fering any damaging change of temperature.

Port giants: The Port of Hamburg seems like a collection of superlatives. One floating crane, known as "Magnus X", can lift up to 1,000 tonnes of cargo. The heavy-duty pontoons can manage up to 25,000 tonnes. But the real revolution in recent years has been containerisation. Invented in the US during a transport workers' strike, these easy-to-handle boxes have triumphantly swept the field in the international freight business. Fifteen years ago, some 15,000 containers a year were handled by the Port of Hamburg. Now the figure is 10,000 – a week. The port now has 28 container bridges with 16 of them located at the Waltershof container centre. The container revolution has certainly done away with a great deal of back-breaking work but the fact is that even when container terminals are operating at full capacity, there is hardly a soul to be seen. Jobs have been done away with in the name of rationalisation and only a few new vacancies have been created in the container manufacturing, repair and leasing businesses.

Marshalling yards for Europe: Of course, the container's journey does not end in the port. To ensure it reaches its destination as quickly as possible, speedy trans-shipment is essen-

of their own, preferring instead to leave their goods in the port until required. The overseas centre, built as a collecting and distribution depot for general cargoes, now rents out two-thirds of its 60,000 sq. metres (14 acres) as storage space.

Liners and trampships: More than 300 liner services call in regularly at the port. The daily port report gives exact details of when each ship will arrive, where its berth will be and what cargo it is carrying. Shipping lines also make use of tramp steamers which can be chartered as needed.

Another feature of the port are the docks of the (erstwhile) great shipping companies.

tial. At the Port of Hamburg this is guaranteed: by road via the Waltershof motorway link-up or by rail at Maschen, Europe's largest marshalling yards where more than 10,000 waggons a day are made up into trains. Just as in the port, where nearly all the information is transferred between liner agents, forwarders and cargo-handling firms by computer, Maschen is a highly-computerised set-up where most data-transfer operations are done by computer. Close cooperation ensures that cargoes can be in Munich 24 hours after arriving in Hamburg. Lots of Hamburg firms have no warehouses

From the riverfront St Pauli Landungs-brücken you can see the huge Blohm & Voss dry dock. Blohm & Voss is just one of a long line of famous shipyards and shipping lines associated with Hamburg: others are Woermann, Vulcan, HAPAG, Laeisz, HDW, Sloman, O'Swald, Godeffroy and Hertz.

The port is full of history, stories and romantic tales – but for the people involved there is little that is romantic about the place. For centuries the living conditions of those who lived here (and those who went to sea) defied description. What's more the ship-owners and merchants were convinced these people ("a dissolute, drunken mob") had their rightful place at the bottom-most rung of the social ladder. It never occurred to them that this boozy, seedy lifestyle was the direct result of the infamous working-class slums.

"Pepper sacks" was the spiteful term used by the workers to describe Hamburg's rich merchants. After all, that spice was once worth its weight in gold. Since the motto of any commercial deal was profit maximisation, medical warnings about the health dangers lurking in the Gängeviertel, where 60,000 people lived in cramped slums, were simply ignored. Hardly surprisingly, cholera broke out here in 1892.

of Hamburg at the turn of the century. These served as hostels, eating houses, churches and synagogues. In the course of a single year 70,000 emigrants would pass through these halls.

But they were much better off than those who booked a steerage passage with Sloman. On the infamous "death ships" of this shipping line the sanitary conditions were so bad that one vessel docked in New York in 1868 with a hundred corpses on board of people who had died of typhoid. The port of Hamburg was the hub of traffic in merchandise and men – always in motion day and night.

Emigration: But misery was certainly not confined to Hamburg and the city became the transit port for those who couldn't make a living in their home countries of eastern Europe (and later Germany) and instead set off for the promised land of America. Some Hamburgers even made a mint out of these emigrants' distress. In order to control the crowds of potential passengers, but also for "hygienic reasons", HAPAG had so-called emigrants' halls built in the Veddel district

Left, before tobacco is processed, careful storage is essential. **Above**, warehouses in the port.

Transit traffic: For many eastern European countries (e.g. Czechoslovakia, Hungary, Poland and Rumania) but also for Austria, Sweden, Finland, Denmark and the Soviet Union, Hamburg is a vital transit port today. A whole host of inland waterway ships carry their cargoes from Hamburg up the Elbe and Moldau as far as Bohemia. Others turn off into the Elbe lateral canal where the "lifting lock" at Scharnebeck raises the ships a total of 61 metres (200 ft). The locals jokingly refer to it as "Suez in the Heath". Nearly half the Port of Hamburg's berths are reserved for inland waterway ships.

Quays and sheds: Building has been nearly continuous in the port, but in the past century or so the islands between the northern and southern arms of the Elbe have become almost permanent building sites. From Kleiner Grasbrook in the east to Waltershof in the west little can now be seen of the original islands. Kilometres of quays now wind their way between them. In some places there are still buildings of considerable historical interest – though World War II bombing raids on Hamburg did not leave much standing.

The most famous buildings are probably the riverside St Pauli Landungsbrücken with the pontoons and "clock" tower. What this "clock" actually tells is not the time but the depth of water in the Elbe. Between Landungsbrücken and Überseebrücke there is striking evidence of Hamburg's long-forgotten sailing past: *Rickmer Rickers*, a windjammer built in 1896, found its final berth in Hamburg after a lifetime of nearly 80 years under a variety of names. On the opposite bank of the Elbe, accessible on foot via the old tunnel under the river, are the Blohm & Voss shipyards and further south, at Vulkanhafen, HDW/Vulcan.

At Vulkankai several buildings have survived the wartime destruction: the shipyard's joinery workshops at Vulkankai (built in the reformist architectural style in 1906–07), the plate shop (built 30 years later) and the partly destroyed U-boat bunker. The latter serves not only as an "architectural monument" but also as a memorial to the U-boat war. Of the 39,000 U-boat mariners who fought in World War II, only 7,000 survived. To the east, at Hachmannkai in the Rosshafen, there are the six MAN halls where the engines for the U-boats were built. These steel constructions are actually rather impressive monuments to the industrial architecture of the Nazi period. Rosskai is also the site of the 10-storey refrigerated warehouse built in 1926. It is the only one of its kind still in use in the Port of Hamburg.

In the early 1970s a daring steel bridge was built across the waterway linking the northern and southern arms of the Elbe. Hung from pylons soaring 130 metres (426 ft) up into the sky, seemingly slender steel ropes carry the four-land roadway of the Köhlbrandbrücke at a maximum height of over 50 metres (164 ft) above the water. To bridge this waterway, a whole district, Neuhof, had to be flattened.

The quays at Kleiner Grasbrook have a variety of exotic names, relics of colonial times: Cameroon, Togo, Africa and Australia. At the last-mentioned quay (Shed 52) and at Bremerkai (Shed 50) you can still see two typical Hamburg quay sheds, built in the so-called reformist style with wooden rafters. And one basin further east is the Czechoslovakian enclave known as Moldauhafen, mentioned above. In this isolated outpost of Czechoslovakia the hotel ship *Praha* provides overnight accommodation and a bit of their homeland to the Czech crews of inland waterway vessels.

To the east, the port stretches beyond the Elbe to a small tributary known as the Bille. Billbrook, where in the 18th century rich Hamburgers had their summer residences well beyond the gates of the city, was turned into an industrial area at the turn of the century. It now has a waterworks, a power station, an incinerating plant and modern industry; there are also several old factories, relics of a bygone age, and numerous allotments, affectionately known as "Costa Billa" by their owners. Many of the colourful summer houses on the allotments even have their own landing stages.

Downstream there is a very special service for passing ships. At Schulauer Fährhaus near Wedel, the so-called *Willkommhöft* sounds out a unique greeting and farewell to every vessel over 500 gross tonnage. Since 1952, Hamburg's "national anthem" and the national anthem of the ship's home country have boomed out from the Fährhaus in personal tribute to each maritime visitor.

Another popular Hamburg institution is *He lücht* ("He lies"), the name given to the guides who accompany every boat trip round the port and provide their guests with solid facts and numerous yarns. And if you didn't know why a ship has two propellers, any *He lücht* will tell you: one for the journey there and one for the journey back.

Right, a port office entrance, showing something of the local traders' sense of self-importance.

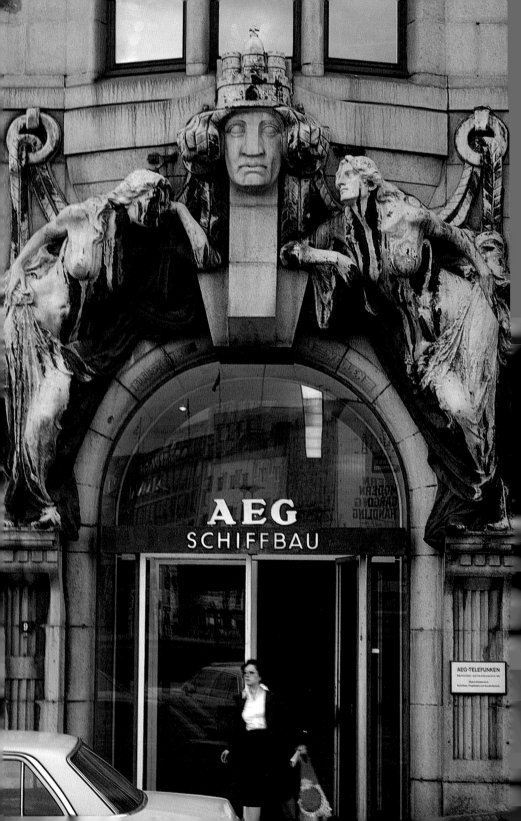

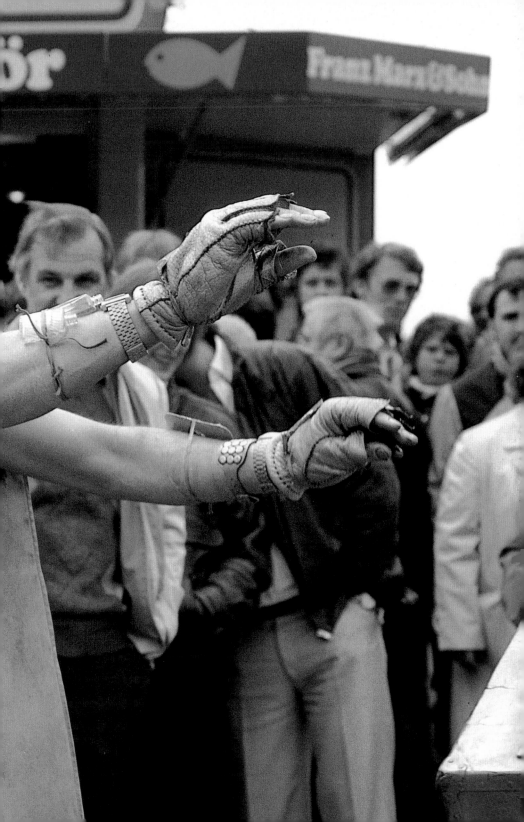

IN SEARCH OF THE REAL HAMBURGER

If you were to ask in New York, Moscow or Tokyo for a real Hamburger you'd be steered towards a fast-food joint, no questions asked. In most of the world the hamburger is the most consumed food of the 20th century. Ask the same question in Hamburg, however, and you'd not get such a easy reply.

Popular tradition maintains that citizens of Hamburg are cool-tempered and cautious people with blond hair and blue eyes, but this, like many a cliché, is only skin deep. The original Hamburger stock has long since been diluted by immigrant blood, which has given fresh life to the city.

If you investigated the background of the rich families in Hamburg you'd find that many are so-called *Quiddjes* or immigrants. Many *Quiddjes* have made their fortunes in the city, but nevertheless the man in the street still calls them *pfeffersäcke* (pepper-sacks). This is a term less indicative of low respect than of envious admiration of their wealth; after all, it wasn't so long ago that spices from the East Indies were worth their weight in gold. In those days anyone who owned a sack of pepper had a fortune and reason to be proud of it – and thus the name *pfeffersäcke*.

The pride felt by the rich merchants is intrinsic to the local character; typically this is a man's world, stern and unbending. During his time as Chancellor, Helmut Schmidt, who comes from Hamburg Blankenese, was often accused of being Hanseatically cold and aloof. The workers in the port used to say you'd stand more chance of getting a shilling from the man in the street than you would do from the rich merchants of Hamburg.

But under the surface most Hamburgers – even the *pfeffersäcke* – enjoy life. A typical Hamburger family will go on an outing to the port at least once a year, to breathe the fresh sea air and hear the sound of the sirens. And if you were to drag yourself out of bed at 6 o'clock on a Sunday morning you'd meet all varieties of Hamburgers in the St Pauli fishmarket, also a local tradition. Here

assemble farmers, fishermen, greengrocers and vociferous market traders such as slitty-eared Banana Harry, one of the local celebrities, who can make a normal bunch of bananas look so big with his words that his customers will pay far more than they would in a supermarket and still feel satisfied.

Some years ago the cheeky Hamburg Green Party re-wrote German history by being the first all-female party to enter the political arena. The whole nation turned on their televisions to watch these eight women enter parliament. They made an unforgettable sight, not least because they were dressed in black suits and ties – a reference to the traditional Hamburg world of men.

But not everyone is rich and self-important. In the St Pauli area of town anything goes, from the outrageous to the eccentric to the pitifully poor. In these areas the drug problem is considerable and prostitution is every-where, but it is not something that Hamburg tries to hide. The City Fathers are, however, doing their best to emphasise Hamburg's other cultural resources, such as the art galleries and theatres. Cynical observers say that this is for commercial reasons – the *pfeffersäcke* need more and wealthier tourism to keep the local economy growing.

You don't have to travel far to see the extremes of Hamburg: the rich merchants live in elaborate villas along the Elbchaussee, Germany's Beverly Hills; closer to the town centre in the now infamous area around Hafenstrasse a whole community of obstinate and persistent squatters has colonised streets of city housing, and there are occasional streetfights with the authorities.

The problems of Hafenstrasse, prostitution of St Pauli and *pfeffersäcke* of the port all suggest that the Hamburg character is not as straightforward as opinion would have us believe. Something has been mixed up in the protestant bourgeois Hamburg world of men; the key to it lies in the local dialect, which features the word *missingch* (mixed) a term which originated in the 15th or 16th century and described the mixture of Germans from the coastal plains with Germans from inland. Hamburg is *missingch* through and through.

Preceding pages: "Bobby", a familiar face in the city; punks in Altona; tending their Barmbek allotment. **Left**, ferry men at Landungsbrücken.

"Confidentially, a lot of things go on in our theatre that do not suit me. There is dissension among the entrepreneurs, and no one knows who the cook or the waiter is." This complaint is more than 200 years old. It was made by Gotthold Ephraim Lessing, writing to his brother when he was embittered and infuriated by the failure of the first German National Theatre. The latter was founded in 1767 by Hamburg merchants and famous actors who had become tired of small-time performances in various courts, and wanted to put an end to the pomp and affected mannerisms of courtly theatre.

In the beginning, the National Theatre looked promising. Lessing acted as advisor. His "contribution" to the Hamburg stage was his *Minna von Barnhelm*, which was first performed on 30 September 1767. However, within two years the various entrepreneurs had quarrelled terribly, and the liaison between art and commerce was broken. The Hamburg theatre encountered its first crisis.

Crisis appears to be an important word for managing culture in Hamburg. Yet it must be said that crisis in Hamburg has had little to do with weak performances, bad plays, or incompetent actors. Even at times of great crisis, renowned drama companies from all over the world come here to the Kampnagelfabrik (a converted factory) for experimental theatre workshops. Crisis simply means bickering. Crises arise whenever ministers for culture accuse creative artists of not being able to economise and the latter, in turn, feel insulted and grumble back that ministers do not know the first thing about culture anyway. At the height of such arguments, artists normally throw in the towel.

This makes a crisis. Two small private theatres had to close as a result of such crises in recent years, and the carousel of theatre directors has been revolving tirelessly for decades at the large, state-subsidised Deutsches Schauspielhaus. The questions

whether, when and why the trendy alternative venue, the Kampnagelfabrik, should actually close have been rumbling on for years.

In spite of the squabbling, Hamburg is a theatre city. One can see something unusual, exciting, or splendid every night of the week. The city offers the world's smallest theatre, the largest theatrical stage in Germany, as well as uproarious revues in the red-light district of St Pauli, and first-class ballet performances. "May Hamburg be fortunate in its prosperity and freedom," wrote Lessing in a more patient moment, "because it deserves to have fortune!"

Permanent crisis: The Deutsches Schauspielhaus is the ultimate in traditional theatres, with cherubs on the walls, Apollo on the ceiling, and shimmering gold balconies and plush velvet everywhere. As you emerge above ground from the main railway station, your heart beats a little faster as you are faced by the magnificent building. Pomp and elegance are joined together here in operetta fashion. The theatre was designed by a Viennese couple who had blessed Europe with such palaces in the second half of the previous century.

The stage, which originally had columns made from trees, was completed exactly at the turn of the 20th century. The 84 societies comprising the joint-stock company of the Deutsches Schauspielhaus paid merchants, solicitors, and artists 590,000 marks for it. Goethe's *Iphigenie auf Tarsis* was performed at its opening. The director, an aristocrat of course, was a short, portly man from Vienna with a pointed beard. One of his most important duties was to teach the enthusiastic public how to dress for such festive events; that is, elegantly. On one occasion the director paraded his actors dressed to the hilt through the vestibule. The public caught on and became stylish dressers themselves.

They truly loved their theatre. The Viennese director presented a selection of plays in the tradition of civic theatre with a smattering of realism. His successor, however, who turned up his nose at such "republican

Preceding pages: *Cats* in Hamburg's Operetten-haus. **Left,** *Black Rider* in the Thalia Theater.

courtly theatre," drove away audiences with modern ventures such as Hans Henny Jahn's *Medea*. Declining attendances forced the theatre to change its policy; it filled the house by presenting melodramas with final lines such as "Karl-Heinz, don't you ever come here again!" Clearly, the Schauspielhaus was in a critical state.

The most famous director after World War II was Gustaf Gründgens. Initially, the Hamburgers weren't quite sure what to make of him, but they were won over by his renowned production of *Faust*. From that moment on, all 1,400 seats in the theatre were often sold out for weeks in advance.

reputation. Concepts, ideas and schemes were never lacking. On the departure of the director Ivan Nagel in 1978, the newspaper *Die Zeit* asked anxiously, "How sick is the Hamburg theatre scene?" When Niels-Peter Rudolph left, *Die Zeit* predicted forebodingly that "the theatre crisis was approaching its 20th anniversary."

The next director, Peter Zadek, installed pinball machines in the magnificent 19th-century building, which had been renovated in 1982. These machines were used to produce a soundtrack by the rock band *Einstürzende Neubauten* ("collapsing modern buildings"). Finally, worn down by daily

The ensemble shone with names such as Elisabeth Flickenchildt, Werner Hinz, Antje Weisgerber, and Will Quadflieg. Gründgens had set standards, and many of his successors had problems living in the shadow he had cast. Again, there were crises. Hamburg was too gloomy for one director or too boring for the next. Brecht's student Egon Monk, for example, walked up to an actor on the stage in the middle of a monologue and said, "always remember what Biafra is thinking." Monk left after 75 days.

The Schauspielhaus has worked hard to acquire what usually comes easily: a bad

disputes with the ministry of culture about finances, Zadek left as well.

His successor was the Englishman Michael Bogdanov, a director who found the situation in Hamburg "okay" before he too departed after only two years. "Nowadays," said Bogdanov, "there is no city in Germany that has such credibility through theatre, including musicals like *Cats*, as Hamburg has." With a budget of 27 million marks a year, a good variety of shows can certainly be staged. But as far as the Schauspielhaus is concerned, there is always a crisis rustling behind the curtain.

Eternal second: When Boy Gobert gave his farewell performance of *Mephisto* in 1980, one critic actually suggested that the Thalia Theater was "Hamburg's number one theatrical stage." Gobert had rescued the venue from the imponderable morass of burlesque theatre and, with his gift for talent, had engaged great actors such as Ingrid Andree and Carl-Heinz Schroth for the company.

"Thalia" is the German muse of comedy, and so the theatre which bears her name began with robust slapstick. In 1843, amateurs eager to act banded together in the "Musentempel Thaljythalia" on Gerhart-Hauptmann-Platz to form a burlesque thea-

as sensational spectacles (a production of *Parsifal* by the mystic Robert Wilson) appear on the theatre's schedule. Like the Schauspielhaus, the Thalia Theater (the first "a" is stressed by most Hamburgers) has to calculate by how much taxpayers should subsidise each ticket. A recent article in *Manager* magazine suggested that this subsidy amounted to DM 230 a ticket.

There are also crises and financial woes at Thalia. The magazine *Theater Heute* coolly judged the theatrical craft of the house to be "partly superficial theatre," while the leftist paper the *Hamburger Rundschau* has been slow to make favourable criticisms. But

tre. They gave themselves complete freedom of expression in pieces about knights and knaves and every sort of riotous farce. At the time they had no competition; otherwise, as an angry critic wrote, "the management certainly would not dare to offer the public such impertinent rubbish."

Today, under the direction of Jürgen Flimm, good classics (for example Heinrich von Kleist's *Der zerbrochene Krug*) as well

Left, performance of Guiseppe Verdi's *Rigoletto* at the State Opera. <u>Above</u>, Hamburg State Opera on Dammtorstrasse.

Hamburg does still need the Thalia Theater.

Three burlesque theatres: You may come across it on television and think you have heard "Plattdeutsch" (low German), but you would be quite wrong: what the Ohnsorg-Theater presents to those at home by means of its television productions is actually "Missingsch" a dialect which turns the stomach of every true low German. On the stage in Grosse Bleichen, on the other hand, the language of "the man in the street" is always spoken. The farces are called *De Deern is richtig* (The woman is right) and *Een Mann is keen Mann* (A man is no man), and for want of current low German material *Arsenik un ole Spitzen* (Arsenic and Old Lace) and *De Biberpelz* (The Beaver's Fur) are sometimes produced. At least two of the eight productions each season, however, are more thought-provoking than farcical. The 348 seats in the house are sold out almost every evening, and the greatest hits are also available for sale on video. The star of the troupe, Heidi Kabel, has spent her entire professional life since 1932 on this stage and kept it in the family at the same time. Her husband was the director, her daughter an actress, and even her grandchildren occasionally appear.

The two other burlesque theatres are on the "sinful mile," nowadays the Eldorado of the alternative scene (and still sinful enough). One of these, the St Pauli Theater in the attractive building located near the police station on the corner of Davidstrasse and the Reeperbahn, is the oldest stage in Hamburg.

In May 1990, one year before its 150th anniversary, the actress Christa Siems died. As the original Hamburg "Zitronenjette" she had been playing from this stage to sold-out houses for decades. However, according to director Michael Collin, a theatre cannot earn its daily bread from burlesque pieces alone nowadays. Thus, he continues to offer

With 7,000 regular subscribers, the Ohnsorg-Theater is doing well. Yet, that is not the reason why it is called "ohn Sorg" (without cares). Rather, it was named after Richard Ohnsorg, who brought an amateur theatre into being in 1902 which became the predecessor of the present eight-member troupe. Since 1936, this private theatre has been located in Grosse Bleichen in the city's shopping area. When the doors close, the family experience begins: "Kommodig sitt'n an de Groten Bleeken, dor kann'n sik to Huus feuhlen" ("comedy situated in Grosse Bleichen, where you can feel at home").

his grass-roots audience guest performances by their favourites, stars such as Manfred Krug and Freddy Quinn. This private theatre has no ensemble of its own. Instead, guest artists perform modern classics like *The Little Shop of Horrors*.

Hamburg has had a third burlesque theatre since 1988, the cabaret theatre Schmidt. Corny Littmann and Ernie Reinhardt provide a variety show that is at the same time a parody of its motto, "honourable, German, and homosexual." Many sing at Schmidt without really knowing how to sing. Many show a lot of skin, but seldom with taste. It does not really matter. Cabaret artists from all over Germany and clowns from Moscow sometimes give guest performances.

Jugglers, strippers, antique bicyclists, and those, above all, who can do many such things at the same time appear at Schmidt. When Marlene Jaschke, the house's own "Heidi Kabel" of the red light district, performs, no one sitting on the pink bar stools can contain themselves. The shrill old maids in Schmidt's revue have become so popular that NDR (North German Broadcasting Corporation) shows them on their Channel 3. Even on screen the audience is the real public of crazies from the red light district.

ling productions and Bob Wilson worked?

At the Kampnagel, as the cosmopolitan Hamburger says, anything goes: modern dance, evenings of German lieder, large-scale productions, fireworks and evening serenades. You go in casual clothes, buy a *Schmalzstulle* (a lard roll), and take a seat in one of the halls.

It can be quite draughty in winter and oppressively warm in summer. Kampnagel was never intended to be more than a makeshift solution. While the Schauspiel-haus was being renovated, the ensemble from Kirchenallee performed at this old factory site in Barmbek. The public quickly

The dream factory: If all had gone according to plan, the city would have preferred to build blocks of houses on this 50,000-square-metre (12-acre) area on Jarrestrasse. However, year after year when such schemes were discussed, there was an uproar from theatre fans. Tear down the Kamp-nagelfabrik? Whose annual summer theatre programme has achieved worldwide recognition? Where Peter Brook staged his start-

<u>Left</u>, Piccolo Theater, so small it's in the *Guinness Book of Records*. <u>Above</u>, musician Tom Waits was involved in a performance of *Black Rider*.

came to like the interesting makeshift venue. The big, empty halls were so delightfully different. "Free-form theatre" – whatever that might be – should be staged here, they thought. However, the authorities were not aware of this feeling and threatened demolition. Cries for a reprieve went up; actors and spectators held sit-ins. Today, there is a private association of administrators which has wrested a six-year lease and an annual subsidy of DM 3 million from the senate. So the Kampnagelfabrik goes on.

The unique one: The Piccolo is the only theatre in Hamburg that is cited in *The*

Guinness Book of Records because it is the smallest in the world. It has 30 seats and its repertoire is devoted especially to pieces for up to four people – for example, those by Samuel Beckett. The theatre, with a separate pub in the foyer and a stage at the back, is located in Juliusstrasse in Altona directly opposite a cool, sparingly decorated café, whose stylish clientele would never enter the dark, plush pub in the Piccolo. The interior of the pub dates from the first decade of this century. Anyone who does not like the programme can have a beer instead. And which beer? Guinness, of course.

The versatile ones: In the postwar years, the aged by Ursula Lingen and is once more beginning to regain something like its former fame.

Since old favourites can often turn into financial flops these days, and since no-one attempts problem pieces any more, a sort of specialisation has emerged in the private theatres. The drama adviser at the Ernst-Deutsch-Theater near Mundsburg complains: "We cannot afford experiments." The Ernst-Deutsch-Theater, for example, has devoted itself to solid classics, especially during the 1980s when Peter Zadek (the director at the Schauspielhaus) was driving conservative spectators away from the state

Hamburger Kammerspiele was the most important stage apart from the Staatsoper (state opera). In 1947, the legendary premiere of Wolfgang Borchert's drama about homecoming, *Draußen vor der Tür*, was staged there. Works by Jean Paul Sartre, Jean Anouilh and Max Frisch had their premieres there as well.

The owner, Ida Ehre, honorary citizen of Hamburg and legend in her own lifetime, founded the theatre in order to show, as she said, "that tolerance is the most important thing in the world." Since her death in 1989, the house in Hartungsstrasse has been man-

theatres with his pinball machines. At the time the Ernst-Deutsch-Theater gained 20,000 new subscriptions, more than any other theatre in Hamburg.

Other venues: The sparklingly elegant Komödie im Winterhuder Fährhaus produces light material. The audience, seeking entertainment after hours, is welcomed by comedy stars such as Johanna von Koczian and Evelyn Hamann. Of course, for those who are particularly keen on variety shows, Hamburg offers the Hansa-Theater with its impressive claim, "never on television, only here with us." In this Hamburg institution (founded in 1894), acrobats, illusionists, and poodle trainers romp about. Asta Nielsen performed here, Josephine Baker shook her hips and Charly Rivel did acrobatics. The surrounding area is not elegant, with its peep shows in the neighbourhood, but you do not go to the Hansa to see *Hamlet*.

Musicals: On a typical premiere night at the Neues Flora near Holstenwall in 1990, the preparations were lavish. Awaiting the spectators, whose tickets to the premiere cost DM 1,000, were a 300-metre (426 ft) buffet, with 1,000 lobsters, 4,000 shrimps, and 30 kilos of caviar. Outside, however, were 1,000 demonstrators, twice as many police, and large quantities of tomatoes, bags of paint, and rotten eggs.

The protest against the gentrification of the Schanzenviertel quarter by the elegant theatre was one of the worst riots Hamburg has seen in recent years. With the spectacle outside the theatre, it was easy to forget what the work on stage was about: Andrew Lloyd Webber's musical horror trip through the Parisian underworld, *Phantom of the Opera*. The Wagner tenor Peter Hoffman occasionally sings here, and a gigantic, rotating chandelier hangs in the expensive entrance hall. The model for this mammoth show is, of course, *Cats*, the perpetually sold-out tourist attraction at the Operettenhaus on the Reeperbahn. Both musicals are managed by Friedrich Kurz from Württemburg, whose efforts brought a bit of Broadway to the Elbe, or what someone who has never left the provinces imagines Broadway might be.

Hamburg State Opera: On evenings when an opera is performed, there is no chance of getting a parking place on Stephansplatz. Women in long dresses and men with fat wallets emerge from the taxis. A little drink is necessary before the event and obligatory during the interval. Premieres at the Hamburg State Opera are always an event, though they are nothing in comparison to those of the past: the premieres were great events – for example, when "La Stupenda", Joan Sutherland, sang there in two new productions, when Mauricio Kagel enraged the au-

dience with his composition *Staatstheater*, and when director Rolf Liebermann transformed the State Opera into a first-rate international stage with a fantastic repertoire of contemporary music. At that time, even the girls from St Pauli are said to have had a subscription to the opera and their normal workplace in Herbertstrasse was closed on those evenings.

It was merchants and solicitors who founded the first permanent German opera on Gänsemarkt in 1678. Their creation was a prestige plaything that they could give up any time the troupe did not obey their wishes. The troupe did not toe the line three times, so there were frequent flashy re-openings of the opera. The fourth re-opening took place in 1827 in a building designed by Schinkel in Dammtorstrasse that was completely destroyed during the war. Another re-opening was celebrated in 1955 at the present building, whose facade unfortunately looks like that of a trade school.

Liebermann's successor following his first tenure of office (during a difficult period he stepped in again at the end of the 1980s), was the Munich director August Everding, who brought the dancer and choreographer John Neumeier to Hamburg in 1973. This German-American is the most successful ballet director in Europe, famous for his new interpretations of Gassenhauer's *Swan Lake* and *Sleeping Beauty* and his choreography of Mahler's music. He started a ballet school in Caspar-Voght-Strasse at the motorway junction in Horn. Students of the school often "take their first steps" by performing at the State Opera. In 1974 Neumeier initiated the Hamburg ballet days.

While the bickering at the theatres grew worse during the last decade, crisis was looming at the opera as well. The argument is over the payment of the equivalent of a top manager's annual salary to some singers for one evening's performance. Further criticism has been made of opera's non-political stance, and its old-fashioned approach. But the opera fraternity itself has been remarkably low-key about these issues. Instead, the two new directors, Gerd Albrecht and Peter Ruzicka, have reported "record financial results" for the beginning of the 1990s.

Left, Kampnagelfabrik, an arts complex in a disused factory.

In the summer of 1789 the young Danish author Jens Baggesen travelled through Germany on his way to Switzerland. "Hamburg", he noted "is not the temple of the muses but rather their lodging house. The Graces do not live there, they just stay the night." Nevertheless, Hamburg, he added, was "the meeting place for Europe's scholars and what you might call the general inn of the Muses".

Obviously the accommodation and standard of service in the inn was attractive enough, however, and several artists made Hamburg their home – most notably Meister Bertram and Meister Francke, two outstanding late medieval painters whose work can be seen in the Kunsthalle on Glockengiesserwall. This building contains a striking wealth of art history's treasures – yet, in typical Hamburg fashion, this is not visible at first glance.

The Kunsthalle, the flagship of Hamburg's aspirations for art seems to be physically a bit stranded. The raised piece of land on which it stands, sandwiched between buildings, is called the Kunstinsel (art island). The Alster does not flow around it as does the Spree around Berlin's famous Kunstinsel; this island is only encircled by the drone of traffic.

An outsider might consider this isolation symbolic of how the powers of commerce have restrained the unpredictability of art. At one time, though, this was indeed a desirable site, one of most beautiful in the city. Glockengiesserwall was a friendly avenue and the main railway station (finished in 1906) had not yet been built when the place of honour on the former rampart near Ferdinand's gate was chosen for the Kunsthalle in 1861.

On the island: Today, two buildings cover the encroached and disfigured area which has been virtually sacrificed to the traffic roaring around the outside. They are linked by a hall, yet their distinct styles suggest a basic dissension.

Hamburg actually has two art museums, although together they form one complex. Finding the entrance to the complex requires a bit of ingenuity. It is located on the front side of the modern building facing Glockengiesserwall. The entrance will certainly be changed and improved in the future, so that it leads visitors in more invitingly. Still more important is the fact that the designation "new" for the second, limestone-grey building dating from 1912–21 will clearly become meaningless when the initial construction work on a truly "new" building becomes visible. The new building has been long overdue: the award-winning design for a really new, third Hamburger Kunsthalle has existed since 1986.

The famous Cologne architect Oswald Mathias Ungers was both praised and chided for his design of the new Kunsthalle. Critics say that his severe cube at the end of the elevated area has nothing to do with the charm of the Alster landscape. However, the strength of the design lies in its response to and contrast with the two older buildings. The completion of the project will certainly improve the beauty of the art island and marks an epoch-making new arrangement in the Hamburg art landscape.

Planned relocation: The Kunstverein (Art Association), to whom the Kunsthalle owes its foundation, and the Professional Association of Fine Artists, regard or initially regarded themselves as the ones who will have to suffer for the redevelopment. Their buildings which are also located on the Kunstinsel will probably have to be given up to make way for the contemporary art which is intended for Ungers building (all this is said with reservation, as the situation at the time of this book going to press involved probabilities rather than facts).

There are new quarters for both the Kunstverein and the Professional Association of Fine Artists nearby in the Markthalle in Steintorwall. Both new homes are near the

Left, Meister Bertram's St Petri altar, now in the Kunsthalle, is a 14th-century masterpiece.

main railway station and the fantastic Museum für Kunst und Gewerbe (Museum of Arts and Crafts – the contents of which are described later in this chapter) is located on the other side of the tracks. The move could actually turn out to be an improvement for both institutions. They will have more room to spread out in the Markthalle and would perhaps get more attention from the public thanks to the planned installation there of a museum for games, a youth cinema, music rehearsal rooms and a youth theatre.

Deichtorhallen: They could especially profit from being in the same neighbourhood as the Deichtorhallen, a recent addition to the

But Hamburg is never slow to criticise, and the complaint made the rounds immediately that the whole thing had turned out a bit too flashy – in all senses. Körber, who is an immigrant from Saxony (perhaps itself a reason for the slightly less than enthusiastic welcome for his work), was criticised for not having kept his light under a bushel as the locals like to do. The fact is that the purists in the city, the hardened old traditionalists, find anything that is not understated extremely suspicious.

The opening exhibition in the Deichtorhallen was a great success. In autumn 1991 Zdenek Felix from Prague, previously head

Kunsthalle complex with 6,000 sq. metres (65,000 sq. ft) particularly for changing exhibitions. Architecturally interesting themselves, these impressive industrial buildings, erected in 1911–14, served the wholesale flower trade until 1983. In 1989 the halls were restored, thanks to the generous patronage of the industrialist Kurt A. Körber. Using the substantial sum of DM 25 million donated by this opera enthusiast and amateur painter, the Berlin architect Josef Paul Kleihues restored and transformed the halls into an exhibition centre whose light-grey rooms are illuminated with innumerable spotlights.

of the Munich Art Association, took on the directorship. His plans included an exposition of modern art, and promised to include "very important artists" as well as modern classicists.

Inside the Kunsthalle: Since January 1991, Uwe M. Schneede, the successor to previous director Werner Hofmann, has been managing the Kunsthalle (official address Glockengiesserwall 1, open Tuesday to Sunday 10 am to 6 pm). The latter was replaced after a tenure of 21 years. Werner Hofmann made the museum's strong point its inventory of first-rate 19th-century paintings, which he achieved through a series of very clever, analytical exhibitions.

His cycles of shows exposed misjudged aspects of the paintings and their interrelationships, even those between art and literature, as well as cross currents in European art. He gave the museum the image of an institution concerned with cultivating modern art, yet cultivating it with restraint. However, the stars of the present are also in evidence on these walls, with names like Anselm Kiefer, George Baselitz, A. R. Penck, Sigmar Polke, Gerhard Richter and several others.

The new director Schneede is working on a reconstruction of Beuys' projects and is planning a Beuys exhibition which will probably contribute towards clarifying new points of emphasis and describing the standing of contemporary artists, particularly Andy Warhol, Joseph Beuys, Iannis Kounellis, and Gerhard Richter.

Uwe M. Schneede is used to crossing Hamburg's thresholds. Before he became a professor of art history in Munich, he was director of the Kunstverein (Art Association) in Hamburg from 1973 to 1984, during which time his work aroused some conservative indignation.

Schneede is likely to revolutionise the interior of the Kunsthalle; fittings that convey the feeling of being in a labyrinth will vanish, as well as the careless impression made by cramming too much into a small space. With so many delectable tidbits, it sometimes seems a pity that they are swimming in an old gallery sauce. Of course, some visitors may have enjoyed the faded wall coverings and the occasional creaking floors as nostalgic remnants of the showcase atmosphere under the surface.

Whatever happens to the fabric of the building, the majority of the paintings in the historical rooms will remain connected with the memory of Alfred Lichtwark, who determined much of the collection's content as director of the Kunsthalle from 1886 to 1914. In order to appreciate his efforts, one

Left, Max Liebermann's 1902 painting of the patio of restaurant Jacob in Nienstedten, now in the Kunsthalle.

has to imagine him beginning like a gardener in withered fields which were then transformed into blossoming flower beds. As a gifted educator at all levels, he knew how to encourage others to weed and cultivate as well as when to offer them the handle of the watering can.

An example of his charisma is how, after one of his many lectures, his audience pooled their resources and acquired Max Liebermann's *Netzflickerinnen* (*The Net Menders*) for him. Lichtwark acquired the first work by Liebermann to be bought and placed in a museum, and followed this up with many more.

When assessing the content of the various art institutions, it is important to realise that the collecting, exhibiting, and handling of art in Hamburg has, until recently, been a concern of the city's citizens rather than its government. Moreover, no individual prince, archbishop, or noble could have enjoyed the limelight by putting himself on the city's art podium as patron or charitable distributor.

Art directors: Since ancient times, Hamburg has been a republic of self-governing citizens (and they have, oddly enough, long prized music and theatre more than fine art). Direction of the arts has been handled by citizen's initiatives. In 1765, the Hamburg Society for Promoting the Arts and Useful Crafts (Hamburgische Gesellschaft zur Förderung der Künste und nützlichen Gewerbe) was established. It has since operated under the designation "Patriotic Society" (Patriotische Gesellschaft) and still retains its headquarters in the House for Patriotic Societies at Trostbrücke, where the former Rathaus once stood.

The list of this Society's meritorious services is long, and not just confined to the arts. It cared for the poor, provided lightning rods for working class housing, helped to fund medical care, promoted business, and, especially, did much for the development of Hamburg's educational system. It was, as Lichtwark put it, "something like a volunteer ministry of education and cultural affairs" until 1870.

Even recently, when the senate established a new basis on which Hamburg's cultural life could be built, it still owed a debt of gratitude to the Patriotic Society for founding the Educational Association for Workers as well as for creating the botanical gardens, for constructing the public swimming pool at the Inner Alster, and, finally, for privately financing the public libraries.

In 1896, the Society founded the School of Arts and Crafts (Kunstgewerbeschule), which has since been succeeded by the College of Fine Art (Hochschule für Bildende Kunst).

Another great cultural dynamo of the same era, Justus Brinckmann, had a strong hand in the formation of the School of Arts and

to the Hamburg Art Association, with whom it shared personnel, the Kunstverein (Art Association) was established in 1817. One of the earliest associations of its kind in Germany, it is somewhat younger than the one in Altona (1812). It began exhibiting in 1826 and initiated a lottery in 1827. In 1836, it exhibited its own collection of copperplate engravings (the corresponding section in the Kunsthalle may be compared to that of the Albertina in Vienna). In 1850 in conjunction with the Patriotic Society, it opened the first public city gallery for paintings (Öffentlich Städtische Gemälde-Galerie) in the Stock Exchange arcades. Having raised DM

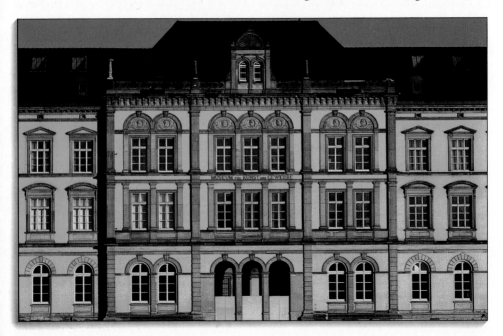

Crafts, where both Ernst Barlach and Lyonel Feininger studied. Brinckmann began collecting in 1869 and built up the Museum of Arts and Crafts (Museum für Kunst und Gewerbe), which the Patriotic Society had assisted in opening in 1877. Justus Brinckmann was, like the younger Alfred Lichtwark, a great personality and a boon to the city. Their friendship yielded much fruit in terms of the city's artistic heritage. Both men were more than just outstanding museum curators; in their work they were cultural revivalists.

Kunstverein: Thanks primarily, however,

300,000 itself, the association was soon able to build the Kunsthalle with other generous donations. This amount was two-thirds of the construction cost. The senate paid the remaining third and took over the institution's administration.

Lichtwark's work: Before Alfred Lichtwark became director in 1886, several paintings had been acquired by the Kunsthalle that indicated the taste of the times to an unfortunate extent. In 1881, a large sum was forked out for Hans Makart's *Einzug Kaiser Karls V. in Antwerpen* (Emperor Karl V's entry into Antwerp). The fashionable preference for ostentatious, large-scale paintings, of which this was one, completely pushed the modest, locally-orientated Hamburg painting tradition to one side.

As a result, this local tradition fell into oblivion, and Lichtwark's primary concern was to get it out again, to stimulate interest in it and to obtain models and patrons. At that time even the esteemed local artist, Thomas Herbst, could only survive in his city by giving painting and drawing lessons – in a city rich in capital that was truly the gateway to the world's trade.

Hamburg has honoured the memory of Alfred Lichtwark by naming its most important art award after him (an award first received by Oscar Kokoschka in 1952). A miller's son from Reitbrook near Hamburg, Lichtwark became a world figure and was the greatest art educator Germany has ever had. His collection of paintings by Hamburg artists alone proves this. It brought a forgotten past to life and aided a significant painter of the 17th century, Matthias Scheits, to take his place in art history.

The story of how Lichtwark tracked down the best works in the Kunsthalle was sensational at the time: he found the glittering, gold altar pieces by Meister Bertram and Meister Francke in the towns of Grabow and Schwerin respectively and brought them back to their home town, which had carelessly sold them off. Today, they are the most valuable objects in the collection of first-class masterpieces of the Middle Ages.

A great lover of Dutch painting of the 17th century, Lichtwark was the first to recognise the significance of the solitary figure Philipp Otto Runge, who died of consumption at an early age in Hamburg.

Lichtwark was busily procuring works by Caspar David Friedrich, at a time when it was not clear that they would later have such a magnetic effect on the public. And last but not least, this art-prophet with his collection of 19th-century German work – Moritz von Schwind, Hans von Marees, Arnold Böcklin, Adolph von Menzel, Ludwig Rich-

ter, Wilhelm Leibl, Hans Thoma, Max Slevogt, Lovis Corinth and the large block by Max Liebermann (who was too modern for many Hamburgers at that time) – preceded many art institutes by making his museum a school for cultivating a new, developing generation of young artists working in Hamburg.

Moreover, in the context of a series of commissions for views of Hamburg, he brought the French artists Pierre Bonnard and Edouard Vuillard to the Alster in the year before his death.

His successor, Gustav Pauli, made the art of Paul Cézanne, Henri Matisse and the Expressionists available. A reminder of this man's able continuation of Lichtwark's work is the impressive *Nana* by Manet, purchased from a private Hamburg collector in 1924. The Expressionists are present in a remarkable strength in the Kunsthalle, and they had another very committed defender in Max Sauerlandt, who was director of the Museum of Arts and Crafts (Museum für Kunst und Gewerbe) from 1919 to 1934.

Museum für Kunst und Gewerbe: This institution's development was even more influenced by Justus Brinckmann than the Kunsthalle. When he died in 1915, one year after the death of his friend Lichtwark, he had substantially improved the standards of the collection he carefully assembled in the course of 46 years. Because of Brinckmann's preference for ceramics and generous donations of porcelain, so many of these objects have piled up in the museum that it is scarcely possible to see them all without pausing for some sort of refreshment.

Fortunately help for the hungry or just tired is at hand in the extremely stylish Destille, which has a hearty buffet. (Actually, the restaurant in the Kunsthalle is better, although the Café Liebermann in the pillared hall there is also not too badly equipped).

One of the most inspiring sections in the Museum für Kunst und Gewerbe (Museum of Arts and Crafts, official address Steintorplatz 1, open daily except Mondays 10 am to 6 pm) is the Jugendstil (art nouveau) section, which is unsurpassed in Germany. In 1890, the Senate allocated a large supplementary budget of 100,000 gold marks, which

Left, the Museum für Kunst und Gewerbe (Arts and Crafts) near the main station has a unique Jugendstil (art nouveau) section.

Brinckmann was able to use for buying items at the World Fair in Paris. Since he was friendly with the art dealer Bing, who coined the French term "art nouveau", he acquired his pieces from their source. He reformed the museum's usual manner of presenting works by putting all his purchases together in the Paris Room.

Brinckmann stopped the custom of dividing objects according to style and material. Instead, he found a harmony in mixing elements. The visitor should approach this collection of combined art forms as if he were going through a collector's hall.

Brinckmann definitely had a hand in shaping Jugendstil or art nouveau. Seeking stimulus from Japanese art, he offered the richest diet of such work in a collection that was the largest in Europe at the time. In addition, the founding of the School of Weaving in Schleswig-Holstein was his work and his daughter became its director. The last carpet designed by the Hamburger Otto Eckmann, a showcase piece of Jugendstil art, came from this school. The museum also poked great fun at it by placing a contrasting work next to it, one of Eckmann's colleague's carpets depicting a pious, pastoral scene. When leaving, linger for a short while near the modern section, which offers all sorts of surprising utilitarian works of Expressionism, including an important photography collection.

Ernst Barlach: The Jugendstil section in the Museum für Kunst und Gewerbe provides a good initiation into the work of Ernst Barlach, the sculptor and dramatist. There is a wall fountain from the Altona pottery workshop of Barlach's friend Richard Mutz. During his early years, Barlach was also involved in designing the pediment for Altona's city hall.

These are, however, trivial efforts in comparison to the later works such as *Fries der Lauschenden* (frieze of the eavesdropper) in the Barlach Museum. It is thanks to the industrialist Hermann F. Reemtsma that Barlach was encouraged to complete this work and bring it to Hamburg. He showed a bit of character in doing this, as the Nazis had banned his work at that time; Slavic features in Barlach's work did not fit into the Aryan concept and his style was slandered for being decadent. The moving, unassuming memorial of a mother comforting her child on the square commemorating the dead of World War I was distasteful to the Nazis.

Fries der Lauschenden was first mounted at Schleusenbrücke in 1932, but this location was so controversial that it had to be taken down and replaced by an eagle. A copy of the original with a different, horrifying association was put back in the square in 1949.

It is also well worth visiting the functional, modern Ernst Barlach-Haus in beautiful Jenisch park (official address Baron Voght Strasse 50a, open Tuesday to Sunday 11 am to 5 pm) not far from the banks of the Elbe. Apart from the historical considerations and the surrounding landscape, the works themselves make the visit worthwhile.

When in Jenisch park, you shouldn't miss the museum in Jenisch-Haus, a collection of *haute bourgeois* interior design originated by Jenisch himself, a senator and member of the aristocracy (official address Baron Voght Strasse 50, opening times vary according to season).

Altona Museum: Since 1927 Jenisch-Haus has been part of Altona Museum, which also has a fine collection of paintings. Generally speaking, its enthusiasts usually recommend the museum's collection of picturesque figureheads, examples of rural life and models illustrating the history of shipping and fishing. But the two collections of paintings of everyday life and north German landscapes are more long-term attractions. Many of the painters of everyday scenes were those who Lichtwark brought out of obscurity, in particular Hermann Kauffmann.

The landscape gallery has paintings of contemporary scenes. There are works by Max Pechstein and Franz Radziwill as well as contemporary Hamburg artists. Here, they seem to be gathered in the silent expectation that the final word has not yet been said about their position in art history.

Have a look yourself and decide to whom fame is due, fame of the sort that recognised local artists like Horst Janssen and Paul Wunderlich have long enjoyed.

Right, the Kunsthalle hosts regular exhibitions.

Hamburg's major landmarks are built of red bricks; especially St Michael's and all the other main churches, the Free Port warehousing the Speicherstadt, the new shopping arcades and even the gate in Hamburg's coat-of-arms.

"If you know Hamburg," wrote Fritz Schumacher, Hamburg's legendary chief architect, "you'll certainly have seen the gigantic redbrick facade of St Peter's mysteriously shimmering in the slanting rays of the late-afternoon sun. If you take a close look, you'll discover that this lifelike shimmer is caused by the fact that dull hand-molded bricks and dark, slightly shiny clinker bricks are mixed in such regular fashion that they almost look like a chessboard."

Redbrick architecture stands wherever you look in the city: upmarket city-centre shopping arcades, expensive Elbe suburbs, the Speicherstadt, office buildings, churches, large residential areas, garden cities and even entire districts such as Barmbek or Hamm, they all have this distinctive feature. Hamburg is a north German redbrick city, and has been since the 13th century. However, redbrick buildings had a long struggle before they completely ousted their half-timbered competitors.

The fact that not just Hamburg but the whole of North Germany became a redbrick stronghold is the result of specific characteristics of the region: climate and landscape on the one hand; the shape-retaining and damp-resistant qualities of these bricks on the other. Red bricks, fired in a variety of ways, proved to be the perfect building material. Other positive characteristics include their heat-retaining qualities, the virtually unlimited construction and decoration opportunities they offer and their colourfulness, a feature that has won the hearts of architects and builders over the centuries.

Preceding pages: Redbrick frontages on Deichstrasse. **Left,** Chilehaus is shaped to imitate a ship's bow.

Bricks have been used for building in Hamburg for over 700 years. When industrial manufacturing processes were introduced in the 19th century, bricks became the dominant feature of industrial and everyday architecture.

Genius with bricks: The appointment of Fritz Schumacher, the much-travelled son of a Bremen diplomat, was an enormous stroke of luck for Hamburg. Many Hamburgers are convinced that it was the town planner and architect Schumacher who put Hamburg on the international architectural map and finally gave the city an unmistakable architectural image.

One of Schumacher's greatest achievements was the passing of Hamburg's Preservation of Buildings Act, which also covered the issue of listed buildings. Despite the bitter opposition of Hamburg's bureaucracy, Schumacher succeeded in attaching an urban planning department to the building ministry. Fritz Schumacher's urban development model for Hamburg, with axes stretching out into the surrounding region, is still valid today.

The new and totally unmistakeable redbrick face of Hamburg was Schumacher's work. During his 24 years in office, he planned the majority of Hamburg's public buildings and gave them an almost human countenance through the redbrick architecture he perfected.

Wherever you go, there are traces of Schumacher's work – either as architect or urban planner: school buildings such as Johanneum grammar school, Meerweinstrasse comprehensive in Jarrestadt or Krausestrasse grammar school; the finance ministry building at Gansemarkt with Richard Kuöhl's ceramic decorations; the Davidswache police station in St Pauli with its glazed ceramic decorations; the Museum of Hamburg History at Holstenwall; Chapel 13 and the crematorium at Ohlsdorf cemetery; Holthusen swimming baths in Eppendorf; the fire station on Alsterkrugchaussee; the chamber of handicrafts at Holstenwall; and the three terracotta ornamented arches of Krugkoppelbrücke in Harvestehude. In Hamburg, it is fair to say that Fritz Schumacher's work is everywhere to be seen.

Schumacher also oversaw the planning of two whole districts, the famous Jarrestadt and Dulsberg urbanisations, both in the region of Barmbek; the housing in Veddel and Barmbek's Habichtstrasse; and last but not least, the huge Stadtpark with its redbrick buildings.

Fritz Höger: But Fritz Schumacher was not alone in his efforts to promote a redbrick renaissance. Fritz Höger was another of the architects who was convinced that this material alone could preserve Hamburg's buildings from the ravages of "fog and sea breezes".

Höger, the son of a master carpenter from the small village of Bekenreihe near Elmhorn, at first learned his father's craft. All his life he regarded himself as a mere master builder. He was the architect responsible for Hamburg's world-famous Chilehaus (Burchardplatz 1, close to the centre of the city), renowned for its daring design. Almost five million rough-surfaced reddish bricks were used to build this looming office building, one of Hamburg's most photographed attractions.

The Chilehaus stands "as if on a thin tongue of land". It was built between 1922 and 1924 for the shipowner Henry Brarens Sloman who had made his fortune in the saltpetre trade with Chile. Locals ironically refer to the building as the "Wing", "Trout", "Eagle" or "Devil's Tip" because of its shape – reminiscent of a ship's bows. The building's ground plan earned it the nickname "The Iron". The bricks used were actually rejects which Sloman had bought cheaply.

Fritz Höger also designed the redbrick facades of the Haus Neuerburg cigarette factory (Walddörferstrasse 103) in 1926–27, as well as the former Palast der Arbeit, built for a Hamburg newspaper (*Hamburger Fremdenblatt*), and the Turm der Presse (Broschek-Haus) in Grosse Bleichen. The facade of the latter was decorated with striking golden clinker-brick corners.

When rebuilding took place (it is now Hotel Ramada Renaissance), the architects responsible for constructing the Hanseviertel shopping arcade specifically added the Grosse Bleichen/Heuberg corner.

Fritz Höger was also responsible for Hamburg's largest office building, the Sprinkenhof (Burchardstrasse 6–14) which was built between 1927 and 1943. The three stages of its construction represent more than just architectural history. Höger had two colleagues to help him build the first stage, Hans and Oskar Gerson. He was forced to complete the last stage alone: Hans Gerson had died but Oskar was removed from the job because he was a "non-Aryan".

In 1926 Höger wrote to a young architect: "You have to look at, feel and stroke these red bricks until you've learnt to love them; and you've got to imagine the great redbrick city, the great redbrick Hanseatic city which does not exist yet but will be completed within three generations."

During the economic crisis of 1923 the architects Heinz Esselmann and Max Gerntke designed Villa Neumann in Gross-Flottbek (Cranachstrasse 27). With its unusually high hipped roof, it is one of the main works of Hamburg's redbrick expressionist period as well as one of the best-kept houses of those years.

In recent times, red bricks have made a comeback. The interior and exterior of the opulent Hanseviertel shopping arcade (Poststrasse/Grosse Bleichen) are a fine example of modern redbrick architecture. Just across the street from Alexis de Chateauneuf's famous Alter Post (Poststrasse) which was built in 1845–47, the Hanseviertel architects designed weighty redbrick blocks with deep-set windows.

Unfortunately, however, Hamburg's skilled craftsmen had forgotten how to work with these traditional materials. In the early 1980s the architects were forced to get bricklayers from Poland for the redbrick facades to this building. At least these Poles were still masters of their craft.

Red bricks are still in use in Hamburg. If architects appreciate their potential, the result can be truly impressive.

Right, **Krämeramtswohnungen, a downtown courtyard typical of 17th-century Hamburg.**

In circulation terms, more than 50 percent of Germany's newspapers and magazines are published in Hamburg. Although printing came relatively late to the city, it quickly grew in significance. In the 16th century it was the main centre for books published in Lower German. Hamburg's first newspaper was published around that time; *Nyge tydynghe*, produced in 1526 by Johann Wickradt the Elder, was, however, a flash in the pan. Nearly a century later, Johann Meyer was more successful as a newspaper publisher and his *Wöchentliche Zeitung*, first published in 1618, lasted until 1678. It was the breakthrough for the newspaper business in Hamburg.

In the last three decades of the 18th century, reading societies and clubs were founded in Hamburg. Studying books and newspapers was no longer merely confined to a privileged elite. Contemporaries even complained that "everyone wants to read – even wardrobe girls, coachmen and outriders". The leading German newspaper of the period was published in Hamburg, the *Hamburgische unparteiische Correspondent*. This paper, which even attracted favourable comments abroad, achieved the remarkable circulation of 36,000 copies early in the 19th century.

Hand in hand with the increasing popularity of newspapers and magazines came the growing significance of books. It is no coincidence that two outstanding publishing personalities wrote literary history in Hamburg. In the second half of the 18th century, Johann Joachim Christoph Bode published the works of Gotthold Ephraim Lessing, Friedrich Gottlieb Klopstock and Matthias Claudius, the literary avant-garde of the period. Fifty years later, Julius Campe collected the writers of "Young Germany" under his wing as publisher of the works of Heinrich Heine and Friedrich Hebbel.

Nowadays diversification typifies Hamburg's media landscape, a factor that has turned the city into Germany's media capital. A total turnover of 22 billion marks makes the media business Hamburg's third biggest industry and fourth biggest employer with a total workforce of 34,000. Hamburg's owes its rise to fame as Germany's leading media centre (with Deutsche Press Agentur and *Die Zeit* founded here) to the liberal attitude displayed by the British occupying forces at the end of World War II.

Publishing houses: The publishing industry has remained the main arm of the media business. Of every two media deutschmarks, one is made in publishing, an industry which also leads in the media employment statistics with a workforce of 15,000.

Europe's best-selling tabloid *Bild* (with a circulation of over 4.4 million), Germany's top-selling general-interest magazine *Hör Zu* (over 3 million), Germany's leading Sunday newspaper *Bild am Sonntag* (over 2.5 million), Europe's most successful news-magazine *Der Spiegel* (over 1 million) and Germany's best-selling weekly newspaper *Die Zeit* (500,000) are all produced in Hamburg. The news for most of Germany's papers comes from Hamburg too, since the country's biggest news agency, *Deutsche Presse Agentur* (dpa) is located in the city. Three leading training centres for journalists are also based in Hamburg: the Akademie für Publizistik, Henri-Nannen-Schule and Journalistenschule Axel Springer.

There are two Hamburg publishing companies in Europe's top 10: Axel Springer Publishing with a turnover of DM1.6 billion (in 4th position) and Heinrich Bauer Publishing with DM 1.1 billion (9th). Five of the top six German publishers are Hamburg companies: Springer, Bauer, Gruner & Jahr, Jahreszeitenverlag and Spiegelverlag.

Three of these giants have also made a startling impact on the European media scene. In the late 1980s Gruner & Jahr and Bauer shook up the women's magazine market in the UK by launching three magazines which became instant best-sellers (*Prima*,

Left, Hamburg headquarters of the German news-magazine *Der Spiegel*.

Bella and *Best*). Along with Springer, this trio of Hamburg publishers have a number of successful publications or joint-venture projects in several other western European countries and, with the opening up of eastern Europe, in the former eastern block as well.

With some 80 publishers launching around 2,500 books a year, Hamburg is a leading light in the German book business. Rowohlt-Verlag revolutionised the book market with rotary press novels. Gruner & Jahr has just completed a new DM 300 million publishing house near the Elbe, Springer is investing DM 220 million in its city-centre site and Hoffmann and Campe is building new offices near the Alster. When Hamburg occasionally casts a longing glance in the direction of Munich or Frankfurt, this is only because no national quality newspaper is published in the city on the Elbe.

Electronic media: But consolation comes in the form of Germany's most popular TV news programmes, *Tagesschau* and *Tagesthemen*. Both are produced in and broadcast from Hamburg. The fact that Germany's favourite news programmes come from Hamburg is no coincidence. After all, this was where German TV really got going. On 12 July 1950 the first TV pictures were broadcast from Hamburg – a test card. In September that year the first West German TV channel, Nordwestdeutscher Rundfunk (NWDR), went on the air from an air-raid bunker at Heiligengeistfeld in Hamburg.

In 1953 NWDR (forerunner of today's NDR) moved to studios in the Hamburg suburb of Lokstedt, the first purpose-built TV studios anywhere in Europe. Now 18 percent of the TV programmes for Germany's ARD channel are produced in Lokstedt. NDR is the second-largest station within ARD, the network of state-owned regional broadcasting companies. Over 2,500 people are employed by NDR in Hamburg alone, a further 1,100 at the NDR studios in neighbouring Schleswig-Holstein and Lower Saxony.

Commercial media: In recent years, NDR has lost its cosy monopoly of the airwaves with the emergence of several commercial TV and radio stations. In one respect, however, the NDR slogan ("The Best of the North") will remain true for quite a while yet. Its commercial rivals employ only around 400 people at present. Although the three largest commercial TV companies (RTL plus, SAT 1 and Tele5) are represented in Hamburg, they mainly produce regional programmes.

Hamburg would dearly like to expand its electronic media base but its efforts have not met with too much success up to now. The commercial TV station SAT 1 already has a regional programme and its main news studio in Hamburg, and further plans for expansion have recently been scrapped. A production centre planned for a site near Hamburg's

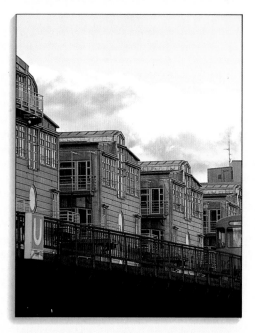

port is now to be built in Berlin. With the state-owned TV company ZDF, Germany's second national channel, not everything has gone according to (Hamburg's) plan either. For years ZDF has had a regional studio in Hamburg but was recently accused of "a bias towards the southwest" by Hamburg's mayor Henning Voscherau. He accused ZDF of increasingly neglecting its northernmost outpost.

Commercial radio is a story in itself. The smaller stations are having a difficult time, a fact even newcomers such as Premiere and Klassik Radio cannot hide. By far the most successful commercial station is Radio Hamburg, a company set up by Springer, Ufa, Bauer, Morgenpost and Lühmannsdruck. After only two years on the air, Radio Hamburg had already repaid its debts.

It has been a very different story for two other Hamburg stations, Radio 107 and OK Radio. The former faced a prolonged crisis in 1988–89 when RTL and Holtzbrick withdrew their support. Finally, the remaining shareholders, three businessmen, decided to go it alone.

OK Radio also found its Prince Charming. When the leading shareholder Klaus Schultz threw in the towel in autumn 1988, Frank

Otto (whose father founded the Otto mail-order empire) invested a good deal of his own money to keep Hamburg's smallest radio station on the air.

Record companies: With good reason Hamburg claims to play the tune in the music business. Fifty percent of German records and music cassettes are produced in Hamburg. Five of Germany's biggest recording companies – Polygram, Deutsche Grammophon, Teldec, WEA-Musik and Ariola RCA

Left, new offices for Gruner & Jahr, publishers of *Stern* and *Geo* as well as many others (above).

– are based in Hamburg, as are well-known music publishers such as Hans Sikorski, Chappell & Intersong and Peer as well as numerous sound studios. Boosted by the boom in commercial radio, the sound sector increased its turnover by more than 50 percent in the 1985–88 period to over DM 1.5 billion. However, the number of employees remained stable at around 1,500.

Film studios: Greater turnover but virtually constant levels of employment – this situation also applies to Hamburg's cinema industry. Some 2,900 employees in around 300 production and distribution companies recorded a total annual turnover approaching DM 900 million by the end of the 1980s. Figures that prove the health of the film city of Hamburg is better than its reputation would actually have us believe.

However, in contrast to Munich or Berlin, not many movies have been made in Hamburg, though a certain trend in its favour is evident. Film producers such as Hark Bohm, Doris Dörrie or Reinhard Hauff have discovered Hamburg's charms as a location. For TV films and specialist productions Hamburg has long been up among the leaders. The most important company is Studio Hamburg, one of the biggest of its kind in Europe. Here, TV films are produced at a 75,000 sq.-metre (18-acre) site with more than 10 recording studios, and state-of-the-art technology.

Hamburg's advertising business need not worry about its image. In recent years many a lucrative account has been won by city-based agencies. Even Germany's two most renowned automobile manufacturers, Stuttgart's Mercedes-Benz and Munich's BMW, have come to Hamburg to have their image (and therefore their sales) polished up.

With a turnover of nearly DM 6 billion and 6,700 employees Hamburg's advertising industry is now the third biggest in Germany. Over 27 percent of the German advertising industry's total turnover is accounted for by local businesses. Nine of the top 50 German agencies are based here, including Germany's No.1 agency, Lintas. In all, more than 1,000 Hamburg agencies are working to present their clients' interests in the best possible light.

Woods, marshes, heathland, parks, gardens, fields and meadows: Hamburg is Germany's greenest city. Nearly half of this entire city-state is made up of green areas. The 28 parks alone account for almost 10 percent of its area. But if stately gardens are what you're looking for, Hamburg is not the place for you. In contrast to many other German cities, Hamburg's parks and gardens are a reflection of the city's bourgeois-republican past and not of some princely desire for representative greenery.

Alsterpark: Hamburg owes a debt of gratitude to one of its former mayors, Max Brauer, for a unique parkland landscape right at the heart of the city. As early as 1910, the director of Hamburg's Kunsthalle (Art Gallery), Alfred Lichtwark, had demanded that the private gardens running down to the Outer Alster in Harvestehude should be turned into a public park. In 1952 Max Brauer ordered the implementation of this idea and the seignorial lakeside villas lost the lion's share of their front gardens. Brauer had them turned into a spacious park stretching along the west bank of the Alster – just in time for the International Horticultural Exhibition in 1953.

Although the 70 hectares (173 acres) of Alster parkland have lost some of their original spaciousness through newly planted trees and shrubs, the people of Hamburg dearly love "their" Alsterpark. What could be more pleasant than to stroll along the banks of the Alster on a warm summer afternoon while sailing boats glide past, dogs play on the grass and ducks and swans battle for crumbs in the shallows? Winter often offers a completely contrasting but equally stimulating experience when half of Hamburg makes its way on skates across the frozen expanses of the Alster, warmed by mulled wine.

Jenisch park: Jenisch borders the Elbe and is to the river what Alsterpark is to the Outer

Alster. Though the 43-hectare (106-acre) landscaped park does not quite reach down to the riverbank, the views it offers over the river are quite magnificent. A rich merchant and philanthropist, Caspar Voght, had this splendid park in Klein-Flottbek created at the end of the 18th century. The park was part of a model farm with meadows, fields, houses and farm buildings which Voght had designed, with English ornamented farms in mind, as a combination of parkland and farmland. The natural landscape of the Flottbek valley could not have served his purpose better. At the present-day junction of Hochrad and Baron-Voght-Strasse (Voght was one of the few Hamburgers to take a peerage) you can still see the manor house, the old farm buildings and the houses Voght had built for his farm workers.

There were four parks around Voght's estate. Parts of them still remain: Derbypark to the west, Grossflottbek golf course to the east and the botanical gardens to the north. Jenisch park to the south is the only one to have stayed virtually intact. Over the years Mother Nature has regained some of the ground "lost" to man-made landscaping and the lower part of the Flottbek valley is now a nature conservation area. However, this park landscape has lost none of the musingly dreamy character that first inspired Caspar von Voght. Though Senator Jenisch bought the park in 1828 and had some changes made, they were carried out in consultation with the former owner.

In 1831–34 Jenisch had a manor house designed in the classical style by the famous Berlin architect Karl Friedrich Schinkel and his young Hamburg colleague Franz Gustav Forsmann. Right at the heart of this almost rectangular building in the north-west corner of the park is a broad staircase. Visitors to Jenisch park cannot fail to notice several eye-catching features of the house's neatly structured facade: four Doric sandstone columns and the golden railings on the windows, balcony and roof.

Nowadays, the house and park belong to

Preceding pages: the domed Planetarium in the Stadtpark. **Left,** going walkies.

the city of Hamburg. Max Brauer was again instrumental in this. From 1924 until he was removed from office by the Nazis, Brauer was mayor of Altona (then part of Prussia). In 1927 he prevented the park from being split for allotments and building land by taking the entire Jenisch park, including the house, on lease and turning the villa into a museum. And that is what it has remained to the present day – apart from a 10-year interlude after World War II when the buildings housed bombed-out families and the city's horticultural department.

Whereas the ground floor of Jenisch-Haus reflects haute-bourgeois life in the 1840s, the two upper floors portray the development of urban middle-class life in Hamburg from the late Renaissance period to the turn of this century (represented by art nouveau). The view from the Garden Room across the park and Elbe across to the Harburg hills is truly magnificent.

Since 1962 there has been a second museum in Jenisch park to the northeast of the house: Barlach-Haus. Hermann F. Reemtsma, who made his fortune in cigarettes, had the small white building built to commemorate the work of Ernst Barlach, an artist born in Wedel near Hamburg in 1870.

The building, designed by the architect Werner Kallmorgen, was purposely kept as simple as possible to form a fascinating counterpoint to the Jenisch-Haus. The rooms where over 100 of Barlach's sculptures and more than 300 of his drawings are on view are grouped around a bare courtyard. One of northern Germany's greatest expressionists, Barlach was banned by the Nazis. The most important work of an artist who preferred wood to all other materials is also on show here: the *Fries der Lauschenden* which he completed between 1931 and 1935.

New botanical gardens: In 1979 the Botanical Gardens opened their gates on a site

formerly occupied by Voght's northerly park. It would be more accurate to refer to them as the New Botanical Gardens since Hamburg already had its Alter Botanischer Garten in the city-centre Wallringpark. The old gardens near Dammtor station were laid out as early as 1821. A stroll through their greenhouses is like stepping out into some foreign land where lianas, fig trees, palms, banana trees, coffee shrubs, orchids and rare cacti thrive. There is also a special collection of overseas plants that provide foods, spices, medicines, rubber and textiles. The new gardens are less exotic. Here the main emphasis is on domestic flora though there are the occasional trips to far-away continents, e.g. the impressive Japanese garden with its lakes and pools or the Chinese garden which boasts a splendid temple from Shanghai, presented by Hamburg's twin city in 1988.

City park: Hamburg's biggest park is its Stadtpark, created in the district of Winterhude in 1912–14. As was the case with the Alsterpark, the inspiration for the creation of this, Germany's largest public park, again came from Alfred Lichtwark. The realisation of his idea was entrusted to Hamburg's inspired chief architect Fritz Schumacher. The result of his efforts was a 180-

concerts featuring pop and rock stars liven up the parkland atmosphere during the summer months and various sports fields attract more (physically) strenuous activities all the year round. For those with an eye for celestial matters, the Stadtpark also has its own Planetarium.

The artistic design of the Stadtpark was just as revolutionary as was its functionality. Fritz Schumacher broke away from the delightful landscaped gardens of the 19th century to come up with a rigorous architectural concept of axial, symmetrical and geometrical features. A 1.4 km (1 mile) east-west axis cuts through the Stadtpark with a

hectare (444-acre) park where social and aesthetic aspects are united in perfect harmony with recreation, sport and entertainment. Schumacher's plan for a broad range of leisure activities has survived through all the turbulent years since the Stadtpark was first laid out. The large grassy areas are ideal for ball games, lazing around or barbecues. There are small gardens for relaxation and a lake for swimming. Other bodily needs can be met in a restaurant and café. Open-air

wreath-shaped collection of functional areas on either side. The east pole of this axis is a lake (Stadtparksee) with the Stadthalle, the west pole a water tower and Planetarium.

At the very heart of the park is a 30-hectare (74-acre) rectangular expanse of grassland enclosed by avenues of lime trees. Originally, Schumacher designed specific buildings for each of the large grassy areas but during World War II the Stadthalle, Stadtcafé and other buildings were destroyed by bombs. When the post-war reconstruction period began, none of the destroyed buildings were rebuilt.

Left, springtime in the Alsterpark. **Above**, Japanese-style boathouse in Stadtpark.

To bring some semblance of administrative order into the chaos of modern Hamburg, imaginary boundaries have been drawn (some of which are even historically justifiable), dividing this city of 1.6 million inhabitants into 104 districts, which in turn form seven "boroughs". Many of these districts are derived from ancient tribal areas. But if, 1,000 years or more ago, the inhabitants were called Friesians, Angles, Abotrites or Saxons, today's tribal distinctions are between yuppies, skins, teds or "poppers". Now it's difficult to say whether the image of some particular district has attracted people to live there or whether they themselves have shaped that district's image.

However, the fact is that the city centre sees itself as the heart of this cosmopolitan city, St Georg regards itself as the man in the street's district, and Wandsbek and Barmbek still look on themselves as working-class areas. A Pöseldorf address is virtually synonymous with a Porsche in the front drive whereas Elbchaussee inhabitants prefer an air of distinguished reticence. The people who don't need to move to an Elbchaussee villa live in Uhlenhorst, while St Pauli flirts with sin. Which brings us to the Reeperbahn. The days when travel agents and city trippers booked Hamburg only for its sex shows are definitely over.

Water is the central theme of this multicultural city, both in the port and in the Inner and Outer Alster. These two shallow lakes, which cover 180 hectares (444 acres) and are surrounded by parkland, are the result of a miller damming the river Alster back in 1235. Together the lakes, the ports and the canals combine to produce more city bridges than Venice – and earn the city the title of the Venice of the North.

The number of tourists visiting Hamburg every year has reached two million. They have discovered that Hamburg's weather is a lot better than its reputation (suitably run down by the city's Bavarian competitors) and that, despite the size and extent of the city, its immediate surroundings are remarkably rural.

Those visitors' most pleasant discovery, however, is likely to have been the people of Hamburg themselves. Whatever their reputation, Hamburgers are anything but cool or unfriendly.

Preceding pages: multicultural Hamburg; shoppers on Wandsbeker Chaussee; Atlantic Hotel on the Outer Alster; the Dom, an annual fair, in full swing at Heiligengeistfeld. <u>Left</u>, the steps of the Alster by the Rathaus.

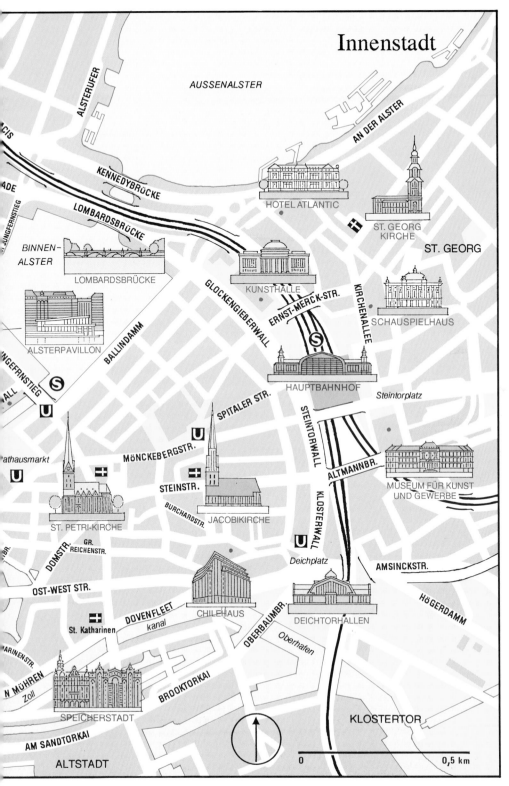

Innenstadt

AUSSENALSTER

ALSTERUFER

AN DER ALSTER

KENNEDYBRÜCKE

LOMBARDSBRÜCKE

ST. GEORG KIRCHE

ST. GEORG

BINNEN-ALSTER

LOMBARDSBRÜCKE

HOTEL ATLANTIC

JUNGFERNSTIEG

GLOCKENGIEBERWALL

KUNSTHALLE

ERNST-MERCK-STR.

KIRCHENALLEE

SCHAUSPIELHAUS

ALSTERPAVILLON

BALLINDAMM

HAUPTBAHNHOF

Steintorplatz

GEFRNSTIEG

SPITALER STR.

STEINTORWALL

ALTMANNBR.

MÖNCKEBERGSTR.

athausmarkt

STEINSTR.

BURCHARDSTR.

JACOBIKIRCHE

KLOSTERWALL

MUSEUM FÜR KUNST UND GEWERBE

AMSINCKSTR.

ST. PETRI-KIRCHE

GR. REICHENSTR.

DOMSTR.

OST-WEST STR.

Deichplatz

HÖGERDAMM

CHILEHAUS

OBERBAUMBR.

DEICHTORHALLEN

DOVENFLEET

St. Katharinen

kanal

Oberhafen

MARINENSTR.

N MÜHREN

Zoll

BROOKTORKAI

SPEICHERSTADT

KLOSTERTOR

AM SANDTORKAI

ALTSTADT

0   0,5 km

CITY CENTRE

For a place that has been described as fairly dead, Hamburg's city centre is pretty lively. The streets around the Inner Alster (the smaller, southernmost lake) form the pulsating heart of a cosmopolitan city. People meet for coffee at Jungfernstieg, stroll through the many shopping arcades, listen to street musicians, go to film premieres in downtown cinemas or simply enjoy view of the Alster with its elegant backdrop of pre-1914 buildings.

Life in Hamburg's city centre was not always like this. As recently as the 1970s, booming districts had a throttling effect on neglected downtown Hamburg. When the shops closed early in the evening, emptiness hung like a pall over the city centre. Dead was certainly the right word. The turning-point came in the early 1980s when the **Rathausmarkt** was revamped and a prestige shopping arcade, **Hanseviertel**, opened. The square in front of the **Rathaus** (city hall) was then closed to traffic and once again became the centre of city life. Hanseviertel proved to be the model for almost a dozen more shopping arcades.

But the renaissance of the western half of the city centre left the traditional shops along **Mönckebergstrasse** gasping for breath. In both halves of the city centre little remains of Hamburg's past. Apart from the main churches whose towers still shape the city's characteristic silhouette, most of the heart of Hamburg is a product of the past 150 years. But that does not make it any less beautiful.

Around the station: The best place to start any walk round the city centre is probably the **Hauptbahnhof** (main station). This building, which was completed in 1906, has the largest cantilever steel-and-glass station hall in Germany. All Hamburg's suburban and underground railway lines as well as numer-

Preceding pages: map of the city centre. **Below**, the centre, with the Rathaus in the left foreground.

ous bus routes pass through it. Right next to it, enclosed by the railway lines and six-lane Glockengiesserwall, is the so-called art island with the Kunsthalle, Kunstverein and Kunsthaus.

The **Kunsthalle** is a redbrick construction built between 1863 and 1868 in the Italian Renaissance style. A limestone extension was added in 1912–21. It contains one of the largest art collections anywhere in the German-speaking world. Exhibitions in the **Kunsthaus** concentrate on contemporary Hamburg art. However, this changed in 1992 with both the Kunsthaus and Kunstverein moving to new premises to make room for a new building to house the Museum of Modern Art.

Opposite the main entrance to the Hauptbahnhof is Germany's largest theatre, the **Deutsches Schauspielhaus**. In this splendid building, opened in 1900, Gustaf Gründgens made theatre history from 1955 till 1962.

To the south of the Hauptbahnhof, at Steintorplatz, the wealth of unique exhibits in the **Museum für Kunst und Gewerbe** (Museum of Arts and Crafts) is an added attraction. There are over 200,000 exhibits from Europe, Asia and America in the ochre-coloured building completed in the 1870s.

Nourishment is also available not far away in the **Markthalle** on Klosterwall. At present there are exotic restaurants and antique shops on the ground floor but soon visitors will also be able to satisfy their appetite for modern art here. Upstairs, in the communication centre, concerts, discussions and exhibitions are held. In the wholesale flower market to the south (Blumengrossmarkt) there is little of the market atmosphere left but **Deichtorhallen**, stylishly redesigned with the financial backing of Hamburg patron Kurt A. Körber, is the venue for a variety of art exhibitions.

An impressive example of the revival of north German redbrick architecture initiated by Hamburg's former chief

You can buy anything in Hanseviertel arcade.

architect Fritz Schumacher is the neighbouring **office-block area** between Steinstrasse and Messberg. One of these buildings, **Chilehaus**, designed by Fritz Höger and built between 1922 and 1924, has become internationally famous. Its walls on the corner of Burchardstrasse and Pumpen converge like the sharp bows of a ship. It is regarded as one of the finest examples of expressionist architecture.

Opposite this area of offices is the powerful-looking **Jacobikirche**, one of the five main Lutheran churches in Hamburg. The first historical record of this church was in 1255 but the present redbrick building was basically designed in the 14th and 15th centuries. It was severely damaged in a bombing raid in June 1944 but valuable features had already been brought to safety, in particular the organ built by Arp Schnitger between 1689 and 1693. This is considered to be north Germany's largest surviving baroque organ.

The oldest church: A few yards further down the street, between Möncke-bergstrasse and Speersort, you can see Hamburg's oldest church, **St Petri**. The first church on this site was probably built in the first half of the 11th century. The larger 14th- and 15th-century church was destroyed in the Great Fire of 1842 and shortly afterwards replaced by a neo-Gothic redbrick church on the same site. A 132.5-metre (434-ft) copper-covered tower was added in 1878.

Petrikirche miraculously survived World War II bombing raids relatively undamaged. One of the oldest surviving works of art in Hamburg, a bronze door knob featuring a lion's head and made in 1342, can be seen on the left-hand wing of the door at the west portal. Inside there are numerous medieval works of art. However, the best-known feature, Meister Bertram's high altar erected in 1383, is now on view in Hamburg's Kunsthalle.

When digging the foundations of the parish hall next door in 1962, workmen discovered what turned out to be Ham-

St Petri, miraculous survivor of wartime air raids.

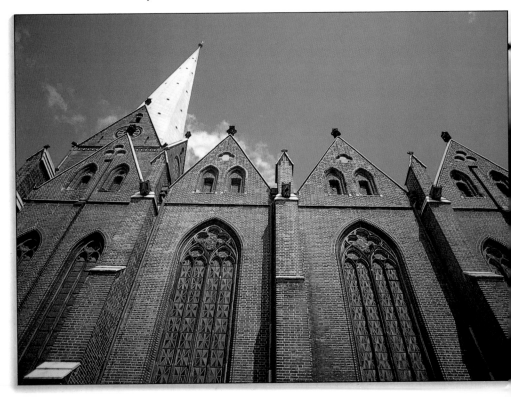

burg's oldest surviving historical remains: the natural stone foundations of a bishop's tower erected for defensive and residential purposes in 1040 for Archbishop Bezelin Alebrand. The remains are now on view in the basement of the parish hall (at the corner of Speersort and Kreuslerstrasse).

Shopping mile: Hamburg's main shopping street, **Mönckebergstrasse**, was built where the maze of alleys and slum-like tenements known as Gängeviertel stood up to 1908. This street, linking the Rathaus and Hauptbahnhof (main railway station), carries Fritz Schumacher's signature. However, the original street was considerably more expressive than the current product of postwar rebuilding. But this is still a fine place to be – for retailers *and* shoppers. Several large department stores have taken advantage of this prime location. Along with a parallel precinct, **Spitalerstrasse**, these two streets account for over half the city centre's shopping area. From Mönckebergstrasse you can stroll over Gerhart-Hauptmann-Platz, past Thalia-Theater erected in 1843, to **Ballindamm**, a distinguished street with typical Hanseatic flair.

Rathaus: But nothing is quite so typical of Hamburg as its Rathausmarkt and splendid Rathaus (city hall). Inside the duality of Hamburg's constitution becomes apparent in spatial terms: to the right the governing Senate and to the left the Bürgerschaft (parliament). Designed by a team of architects in the German Renaissance style and erected between 1886 and 1897, this Rathaus is actually Hamburg's sixth. It had to be built on 4,000 piles to surmount the problems caused by boggy land.

The number of rooms, 647, is said to exceed even those in Buckingham Palace. Though not all of them are as magnificent as the **Kaisersaal** and **Grosse Festsaal** on the first floor, visitors encounter marble, gold, precious stones, valuable paintings and distinguished carvings in wrought-iron work on any of the regular guided tours through the

Sprinkenhof, an office building opposite the Chilehaus.

building. Mythological and historical figures decorate the facade, crowned by a 112-metre (367-ft) central tower.

Behind the Rathaus is Hamburg's **Stock Exchange** (Börse) erected in 1839–41. Actually its origins go back to 1558 and as such is the oldest exchange in Northern Europe. If you want to see Hamburgers acting without their usual reticence, go around lunchtime and watch the goings-on from the gallery.

Between the Börse and Rathaus is the Ehrenhof with its **Hygieia fountain**. The dragon on which the goddess of health is riding stands for the catastrophic cholera epidemic which hit Hamburg in 1892. Another symbolic figure stands at the entrance to the **Ratsweinkeller** – Bacchus with a cup in his hand. Here, you can enjoy a glass of wine to go with Hamburg specialities served in pleasant surroundings.

Hamburg's **Rathausmarkt** was created after the Great Fire of 1842. Occasionally it is compared, not unfavourably, with St Mark's Square in Venice.

The original square was the work of Alexis de Chateauneuf but there have been several alterations in the meantime, the final one in the early 1980s. Since then concerts, open-air cinema, festivals and markets have attracted crowds to the square in front of the Rathaus. One of the new design elements is a tree-lined glass-and-steel arcade. At the point where Mönckebergstrasse turns into Grosse Johannisstrasse there is a statue of a pensive-looking Heinrich Heine. The poet has good reason to be sceptical. The original statue in Hamburg's Stadtpark was melted down by the Nazis.

Kleine Alster: To the north the square ends in the so-called Kleine Alster, with steps down to the water's edge, a favourite spot for tired tourists to take a break. An simple but impressive monument to the dead of World War I, designed by Ernst Barlach and featuring a mourning mother, overlooks the square on the edge of the water.

Beyond the Kleine Alster, the elegant

The Kleine Alster, favourite place for tired tourists.

colonnaded **Alsterarkaden**, one of Chateauneuf's masterpieces, emphasises the Venetian character of Hamburg's Rathausmarkt. Unfortunately, a fire recently tore an ugly hole in the centre of this building but it should not be long before this beautiful row of shops, offices and surgeries is restored to its former glory.

To the south of the Rathaus, Hamburg's oldest citizens' action group, the **Patriotische Gesellschaft von 1765**, is based in a neo-Gothic building erected in 1847 on the site of the old Rathaus which burnt down in the Great Fire of 1842, a fact which guests of the restaurant **Zum alten Rathaus** are reminded of. The ground on which the building stands is also full of history.

The neighbouring **Trostbrücke**, erected in 1881–82, was originally the first link between the episcopal Altstadt built around St Petri and the Neustadt around St Nikolai with the Nikolaifleet as a harbour. Only a few yards further on, one bridge erected in 1633, **Zollen-**

brücke, has survived the tempestuous centuries in-between. Hamburg's oldest surviving bridge crossed the Gröningerfleet, a canal that was later filled in.

Nikolaikirche, at the end of Trostbrücke, was the first church to be built for inhabitants of Hamburg's Neustadt in the 11th century. Now only the blackened 147-metre (482 ft) tower is left. The last church on this site, designed in the neo-Gothic cathedral style by the English architect George Gilbert Scott, was built in 1846–82 to replace the redbrick church destroyed in the Great Fire. The bombed-out nave of this 19th-century building and the blackened tower have been purposely left as a memorial to the victims of the war and Nazi repression.

Another dark chapter in Hamburg's recent past is recollected by the so-called **Stadthauskomplex** at the Fleetinsel. Originally the building was a baroque Görtz-Palais erected in 1710 (Neuer Wall 86) but the complex which stretches from Stadthausbrücke to Axel-Springer-Platz was where Hitler's Gestapo had its headquarters. The other side of Stadthausbrücke was a desolate piece of wasteland until recently. Now construction work is under way on the banks of the Alsterfleet and Herrengrabenfleet. The aim is to create a harmonious transition from the city centre to the port. However, the planners will have to overcome the **Ost-West-Strasse** hurdle. In the 1960s this motorway-like link between Millerntorplatz in the west and Deichtorplatz in the east was hewn through the old heart of Hamburg without the slightest respect for existing structures.

Half-timbered houses: This is particularly regrettable since most of what is left of old Hamburg is concentrated to the south of Ost-West-Strasse. Robbed of its natural environment, this area can give only a faint impression of what life must have been like for Hamburg's working class and bourgeoisie in pre-industrial times. Some small half-tim-

Breakfast at Herbie's.

bered houses and warehouses built in the second half of the 18th century have been restored in **Reimerstwiete 17–21**. A hundred years ago, Hamburg's city centre was full of similar tiny lanes or alleys lined by narrow-fronted but deep tenements.

Another typical example of what old Hamburg looked like is found in **Cremon 33–36** along **Nikolaifleet**. These buildings contained offices, warehouse space and living quarters under one roof. Ships were loaded and unloaded on the waterside and the goods then transferred onto horse-drawn carts on the street side. In **Deichstrasse**, on the other side of Nikolaifleet, you can best see how these multi-purpose buildings functioned. This street, which existed as far back as the 13th century, represents the only surviving complete group of buildings from old Hamburg. It is now a popular place for eating out.

Some of the buildings are from the late 17th century. A plaque in the en-trance to No. 42 recalls the fact that the Great Fire of 1842 started here. From **Hohe Brücke** there are good views of the canal side of the Deichstrasse houses, which were threatened with demolition not very long ago.

Another attraction in the neighbour-hood is **Katharinenkirche** on Zoll-kanal. First mentioned around 1250, the present church, a longish building built as a kind of basilica with no transepts, was erected between 1350 and 1450. The baroque spire with its so-called Störtebeker crown was designed by Peter Marquardt in 1656–57.

After severe bomb damage in World War II, in which the church's richly decorated interior was lost for good, the building was restored to its original (ex-ternal) splendour in 1950–55.

One example of a style common in old Hamburg is the **Krämeramts-wohnungen** (Krayenkamp 10). This last surviving 17th-century courtyard construction was erected in 1676–77 when the grocers' guild extended the

The Stock Exchange, or Börse.

existing building by adding two wings, half-timbered houses designed for the widows of their guild.

In the early 1970s the courtyard was restored and now houses an art gallery, antiques shop, souvenir shop and cosy restaurant. The historical furnishings of the **Museumswohnung** in House C prove how confined life was, even for the middle class, in those days.

City symbol: On the other side of Krayenkamp **Michaeliskirche** leaves one with a completely different impression. There are far-reaching views from the 132-metre (433-ft) tower and the white-and-gold nave with its self-supporting ceiling also gives visitors an impression of lightness. St Michael's, affectionately known as "Michel" by the people of Hamburg, has had an eventful history.

Built in the 17th century, the first building was struck by lightning and burned down in 1750. The replacement baroque church, designed in the form of a cross by Leonhard Prey and Ernst Georg Sonnin, burned down when roofing repairs on the tower caught fire.

The third Michel, a faithful copy of its predecessor, was erected in 1907–12 but suffered severe damage during World War II, later repaired. Since 1983, however, work has been going on Hamburg's most famous landmark in whose vaults Sonnin and Carl Philipp Emanuel Bach are buried. The top of the tower has been restored to former glory but it will be some years before all the work is completed. Despite the scaffolding and repair work, visitors can still enjoy the views from the platform 82 metres (269 ft) up, above Germany's biggest tower clock. Every day at 10 am and 9 pm, and at noon on Sundays, the warden of the tower continues a centuries-old tradition by playing a chorale in all four directions.

A little further up Ost-West-Strasse there is another historic church, the Anglican **St Thomas à Becket**. It was in 1611 that the city of Hamburg gave the guild of Merchant Adventurers a char-

Old Hamburg, as seen in Nikolaifleet.

ter permitting them to hold religious services in English. When British traders returned to Hamburg after the Napoleonic Wars, the city provided the present site and the current church was built. The congregation on an average Sunday is very mixed with people from the many English-speaking countries represented.

Neustadt: Not far away from Michel and the Anglican church, on Alter Steinweg, you might hear the notes of a trumpet coming from Hamburg's best-known jazz cellar, the **Cotton Club**. Here, at the heart of the old Neustadt, a number of attractive pubs and restaurants have established themselves around **Grossneumarkt**. Several of them offer live music.

To the northwest of Grossneumarkt, on Neanderstrasse and Peterstrasse, another Hamburg patron, Alfred Toepfer, paid for old redbrick and half-timbered houses which once stood in the slums of Gängeviertel to be relocated here. **Beyling-Stift** on the south side of Peter-strasse is a collection of original half-timbered houses erected in 1751 and restored in the 1960s. A memorial to the romantic composer Johannes Brahms, born in Hamburg, was erected some years ago on the first floor of the foremost building.

History museum: The history of Hamburg from the earliest days to modern times is graphically displayed at the **Museum für Hamburgische Geschichte** (Museum of Hamburg's History) on Holstenwall, the inner ring-road. The building, designed by Fritz Schumacher and built in 1914–23 is a museum piece in itself. Schumacher had parts of old Hamburg houses and historical sculptures built into the exterior of this redbrick building. Inside, the three storeys present a vivid exhibition of Hamburg's past. Models of the city, a 17th-century merchant's home and Europe's biggest model train layout are three highlights.

Slowly making one's way back to the Alster, past the baroque **Musikhalle**

Post-modern architecture on ABC Strasse.

built at the beginning of this century at Karl-Muck-Platz, you pass the last remains of Hamburg's **Gängeviertel**: a complete terrace of simple half-timbered houses built between the 17th and 19th centuries.

Inner Alster: At **Gänsemarkt**, a square completely redesigned in recent years, is the Lessing statue. Gänsemarkt empties into Hamburg's most exclusive shopping street, **Jungfernstieg**, which borders the Inner Alster along with Ballindamm, Neuer Jungfernstieg and the 1868 **Lombardsbrücke**.

Jungfernstieg, Hamburg's most famous promenade, was created in the 13th century when a miller built a dam across the Alster which was then a river, and used the water to drive his mill. Originally known as Reesendamm after the said miller, it was later renamed Jungfernstieg "because the ladies often went there for pleasure", as it says in one old chronicle. Heinrich Heine enthused about this promenade, which is still one of Hamburg's prettiest streets.

The **Alsterpavillon** was one of his favourite spots. He would sit there and enjoy watching the girls go by. It has lost none of its attractiveness, but the numerous shopping arcades are new, making a popular area even more so.

You might think that today's shopping arcades were modelled on **Colonnaden**. This link between Jungfernstieg and Stephansplatz, built in 1876–78, was an early forerunner of the principle of weather-free shopping. Nowadays, the whole street is a listed monument because a complete row of late 19th-century buildings with splendid apartments has been preserved in virtually pristine condition.

Tradition also plays an important role around the corner at Neue Jungfernstieg 9-14. In the legendary luxury hotel, **Vier Jahreszeiten**, the world's high society enjoys princely comforts.

Central park: Relaxation free of charge is offered in **Wallringpark** which stretches along the ring road from Stephansplatz to Millerntor in the south

Street musician on Jungfernstieg.

and the TV Tower in the north. This popular inner-city park landscape is made up of Planten un Blomen, the old Botanical Garden and Kleine and Grosse Wallanlagen.

The whole complex was created some 170 years ago when the fortifications that had surrounded the heart of the city since the Thirty Years' War were taken down. Their course is still evident on any map. The old Elbe Park on the other side of Millerntordamm was also part of these fortifications. Hamburg's tallest statue now stands on what was the Casparus Bastion – a 34-metre (111-ft) high figure of Bismarck.

Half-way up this park, the colossal buildings of the so-called **Justizforum** (Ziviljustiz, Oberlandesgericht, Strafjustiz and Untersuchungsgefängnis – Hamburg's main courts and remand prison) were built around Sievekingsplatz between 1879 and 1932.

The most famous part of the Wallringpark is **Planten un Blomen** which has already hosted three major horticultural exhibitions. The main attraction is a display of illuminated fountains which transforms the large lake into a sea of light every summer evening at 10.

To the southwest the park borders on Hamburg Exhibition Centre, to the northeast on the Congress Centrum Hamburg (CCH), the neighbouring 32-storey Plaza Hotel and Dammtor Station. This elegant glass-and-steel construction in art nouveau style, recently renovated at a cost of DM 22 million, has every chance of maintaining its reputation as Germany's most beautiful station. Alfred Hrdlicka's **Memorial for the Victims of War and Fascism** next to the station is likely to remain an uncompleted work. Intended as a counterbalance to the memorial to the dead of World War I erected by the Nazis in 1936 to glorify war, Hrdlicka abandoned the project after a dispute with Hamburg's arts department. The disagreement was about money – a sum going into the millions.

Downtown street music.

SHOPPING ARCADES

A few oysters at the gourmet snack bar, an espresso in the café opposite and on the way home a smart designer jacket in the boutique next door: in Hamburg's shopping arcades you can find everything the consumer's heart is likely to desire – providing you don't just talk about money but have got plenty of it. The shoppers' paradise on the Alster is not exactly cheap. Hardly surprisingly, therefore, most Hamburgers enjoy window-shopping in the arcades but prefer to purchase things elsewhere. But 20,000 visitors a day mean that enough money does get spent in all these shops and upmarket catering establishments.

Wind and weather cannot diminish the joys of window-shopping through Europe's largest collection of shopping arcades. Since 1971, 10 covered centres have emerged between Hamburg's Rathaus and State Opera House. What's more, each one has succeeded in uniting commercial and town-planning interests into true harmony, a rare enough achievement. Previously unused inner courtyards were transformed into some 300 boutiques, restaurants, art galleries, speciality stores and cafés selling everything from caviar to kitsch with a total retailing area of nearly 40,000 sq. metres (10 acres).

The shopping arcade era began with the Alte Post in Poststrasse. The Chateauneuf building erected in 1845-47 used to house Hamburg's four postal services in the days before Germany's postal reforms. In 1971 Hamburg's first shopping arcade with exclusive fashion shops and exquisite art galleries was established in the redbrick building with a corner tower that would seem more at home in some Italian palace. Around the corner, between Grosse Bleichen and Bleichenfleet, Hamburg's most original shopping arcade, Galleria, attracts shoppers with a purposely cool atmosphere. A few yards further on is Kaufmannshaus, in pre-1914 days Hamburg's biggest office block and now another city-centre shopping attraction. From here the footbridge across Bleichenfleet canal takes you to Neuer Wall and on, via a narrow passageway, to Alsterarkaden. The section beyond the bridge over the Alster lock is particularly pretty. Here the same Chateauneuf arcade has been drawing shoppers for a pleasant stroll for over 150 years.

Hamburg's newest shopping arcade is back in Grosse Bleichen. Bleichenhof offers an attractive ambience of glass, steel and marble. World-famous names such as Dunhill, Gucci and Harry's New York Bar underline Bleichenhof's appeal to Hamburg's upper crust. However, the most elegant and largest shopping arcade is still Hanseviertel between Grosse Bleichen and Poststrasse. Under glass barrel roofs shoppers stroll from one temptation to another past nearly 200 metres (650 ft) of shops, cafés and restaurants: art supplies, stationery, shoes, porcelain, antiques from England, dolls, lingerie, fashion and food. Every Saturday morning there is a particularly entertaining spectacle. Hamburg's would-be celebrities relish their oysters and champagne at the stand-up bar gawped at by guests at the café opposite. Here you can examine the truth of the old German saying that you have to suffer to be beautiful; even though the arcade is pleasantly warm, the latest fur coat just has to be paraded. But despite all the dire prophecies of economic ruin for Hanseviertel shopping arcade, it has become a big-selling success.

Crossing Poststrasse you reach Gerhofpassage and the neighbouring Neuer Gänsemarkt, which offer a broad range of culinary delights. A little further on, between Gänsemarkt, Colonnaden and Büschstrasse there is Gänsemarkt-Passage with a sports shop to add to the usual offering of fashion, jewellery and knick-knacks. Walking on through the late 19th-century Colonnaden, you come to Jungfernstieg where another shopping arcade has been established on several floors of what used to be a hotel, Hamburger Hof.

There is another covered shopping arcade near Mönckebergstrasse. Opened in 1974, the Landesbank-Galerie links Gerhart-Hauptmann-Platz and Spitalerstrasse. There are even plans to glass over the whole of Spitalerstrasse, now a pedestrian precinct which runs down to Hamburg's Hauptbahnhof or main railway station.

ST PAULI

"Oh, *St Pauli…* " Anyone who comes from Hamburg knows that suggestive smile on people's faces when they say where they're from. But apart from the fact that only one in 64 Hamburgers actually lives in St Pauli, the picture they have of the place is pretty distorted anyway. It's not just a red-light district of sex shows, sensuality and vice. Of course, the night life is pretty important in St Pauli but around the so-called "sinful mile" there are quite a few stretches of innocent amusement.

Beyond the glaringly colourful shows or shady pubs there's plenty going on and lots to talk about, in that other St Pauli where, besides some 450 pubs and clubs, 25,000 people live. These are ordinary folks and out-of-the-ordinary characters, manual workers and merchants, do-nothings and workaholics. These are the people who have given this district its particular ambience – but not at night. It is then that non-Hamburgers traditionally outnumber the locals, and up to 40,000 a night come to experience the Reeperbahn's attractions during the high season.

"St Pauli is booming!" That is how Hamburg tourist board sums up such statistics. Never before has St Pauli attracted so many visitors from all over the world. But the district's problems are increasing, too. There is high unemployment, drug problems are worsening and social tensions growing. This is partly a result of the fact that 30 percent of the locals are foreigners. Above all, there is a growing fear locally that in the short or long term St Pauli will be a victim of gentrification. The plans hatched by rich investment companies to redevelop and upgrade properties have aroused fears that soon there will be nothing left of the uncomplicated lifestyle of this red-light district – nothing, that is, but the stories old folk have to tell.

But forget about the property developers or lost romanticism. St Pauli was always a district that didn't give in easily. A look at its past will suffice to prove the point.

History: From the end of the 17th century, small summer-houses and country houses began to appear in what was then known as Hamburger Berg, a small "hill" outside the city walls. Seamen and boatbuilders, liver boilers and publicans settled down along the old high road to Altona. In 1682 the inhabitants of Hamburger Berg even got their own church, St Paulus. It was from this saint that,150 years later, the district got its name.

During the French occupation in autumn 1813, the haphazard settlement to the west of Millerntor was razed to the ground because the French needed an open field of fire for their attempts to repel the allied forces. They failed. So in 1814, after Napoleon's defeat, dwellings and pubs soon began to reappear. In 1830 Hamburger Berg was given suburban status and in 1833 received the title St Pauli. As mentioned above, it was named after the local church. The original building was a beautiful half-timbered construction which unfortunately the French destroyed as well. In 1819–20 a new red-brick church was built to the south of Hein-Köllisch-Platz, a building still surrounded by an idyllic green square.

Nightlife district: With the growing importance of the port and the arrival of steam ships St Pauli began to enjoy boom years as an amusement area. Thousands of sailors flocked into this suburb close to the river looking for entertainment and accommodation. The lengthy period needed for unloading and loading ships in those days meant that sailors had plenty of time for the attractions this port district had to offer. And the people of St Pauli were only too glad to accommodate their guests' wishes – after all, many of them were closely linked to the port anyway.

It is no coincidence that two streets

Preceding pages, and left, the Reeperbahn's attractions.

are known as Reeperbahn and Seiler-strasse. They acquired their names in 1887 when the rope-making business was booming. In long hallways ship's rigging, lines and ropes were manufactured from oakum. In 1894 St Pauli officially became part of Hamburg.

In the last quarter of the 19th century, splendid concert halls and beer palaces, magnificent theatres and operetta houses were built around Spielbudenplatz and along the Reeperbahn. One last relic of this era is the popular St Pauli Theater, built in 1841. It is actually Hamburg's oldest surviving theatre. The others fell victim to World War II bombing raids and the postwar tidy-up, generally known as reconstruction and redevelopment.

But despite these losses, entertainment still reigns on the Reeperbahn. With gas lamps and glittering music-halls a thing of the past, today's Reeperbahn draws the crowds with neon lights, strip clubs and never-ending shows like *Cats* (a box-office success since 1986).

Reeperbahn: Two colossal edifices catch the eye outside the St Pauli underground station: the **Bismarck monument** to the left and the **Millernplatz skyscraper** to the right. Neither of them has much to do with Hamburg or St Pauli. The Millernplatz bock is hardly a popular place; contaminated with asbestos, it is virtually empty. Otto von Bismarck is said to have eaten oysters at Johann Cölln's but otherwise he had little time for Hamburg.

So you can safely turn your back on both of them and devote yourself to less elevated matters – for example, bars, sauna clubs, erotica shops and topless (and bottomless) dancers, all of which St Pauli offers in abundance. It would be boring to list them all and visiting them all would be both expensive and exhausting. Anyone who fancies more detailed information about the various shows should get hold of a book available in any Hamburg bookshop entitled *Freizeitführer Hamburg von 7 bis 7*.

But sex isn't everything in St Pauli.

Map of St Pauli.

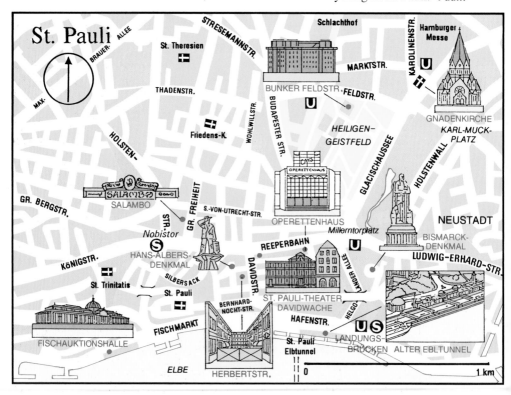

No. 19 on the Reeperbahn, for example, is a very respectable house. Since 1950 **Café Keese** has been inviting guests to join a "paradoxical ball" where ladies still invite gentlemen (preferably wearing suit and tie) to dance. Just a few doors further on, fine clothes are superfluous. In contrast to other **casinos**, the Reeperbahn's establishment lets you in with jeans and leather jackets. Further up, a golden statue of liberty shines out in front of an amusement arcade – hardly a sign of good taste but certainly an original idea. The entertainment palaces on the right-hand side are garishly colourful; on the left-hand side, around the Spielbudenplatz, they are generally more upmarket.

Spielbudenplatz has existed longer than St Pauli and the Reeperbahn. As early as 1798 it was populated by dealers, artists and gamblers. Hamburg did not tolerate them within the city walls but Hamburgers were glad to visit them outside. After the old pleasure palaces had disappeared from round the square,

Tugs moored in St Pauli.

somewhat temporary looking gambling dens and clubs were built in the middle. In the 1970s and 1980s increasing numbers of dealers and thieves frequented the spaces between the pavilions so in 1988 the decision was taken to demolish all but three of them. Since then, the bleak spaces left behind have been waiting for bright ideas from the town-planning department.

If three bus loads of *Cats* visitors don't happen to be blocking the street, you can't miss the **Panoptikum**, Hamburg's version of Madame Tussaud's, at the top end of Spielbudenplatz. You can also enjoy satirical shows, revues, comedy and cabaret at Spielbudenplatz – in **Schmidt's** and in all probability quite soon in **Zillertal**, which used to be a beer hall.

Schmidt's is extremely popular with Hamburgers and pretty plush, too, but in terms of pure plushness you can't beat the **St Pauli Theater**. Besides off-Broadway plays and light entertainment there is a good deal of popular

theatre, including plays in the local dialect, Missingsch.

Next door is Hamburg's most famous police station, **Davidswache**. The first station was built on the street of the same name back in 1854. Its purpose was to keep an eye on the turbulent goings-on around Spielbudenplatz. In 1913 Hamburg's industrious and talented chief architect designed a new domicile for St Pauli's police. Distinguished by its tall red-bricked gables, bay window, clock and ceramic decorations, the building underwent a complete renovation in 1990.

Off limits: Just around the corner is Hamburg's most famous "closed shop", the legendary **Herbertstrasse**. When day trippers and gaping groups of school kids began to get on the nerves of the busy ladies of that street, they simply closed it to women and under-age visitors. But there's pleasure a-plenty for everyone in the pubs, bars and discos elsewhere in the neighbourhood.

The new St Pauli: One of the centres of local amusment is **Hans-Albers-Platz**, named after Hamburg's most famous singer and film star. A monument to this great personality by the sculptor Jörg Immendorff stands in the square. With his pub La Paloma, Immendorff was also one of the first to turn this red-light district into an "in" place for Hamburgers from more respectable areas. From the mid-1980s **La Paloma** (formerly a pub for arty types), **Mary Lou's** across the square and **Mitternacht** in Gerhardstrasse began to attract people to St Pauli who had previously avoided the place like the plague. Corner pubs and dingy dives suddenly became "in" places and the archaic ambience became chic. Fine restaurants mingle with Turkish snack bars. Upwardly mobile ad men, journalists, intellectuals and creative types discovered the district as a new night-time pleasure ground.

This trend, the locals fear, will some day wipe out the what is left of the unique atmosphere, charm and milieu of this dockland. Rich investors have

The Panoptikum, Hamburg's Madame Tussaud's.

smelt the potential profits from the new pleasure-minded populace and have bought up whole rows of houses. Of course, this is not the yuppies' fault but they did start the ball rolling. Smooth, cool marble-lined entrances, however, have not yet replaced all the dingy doorways and St Pauli is still a bit of both – new, often novel pubs and music clubs with a pinch of the old St Pauli.

Tour of the joints: But not every place where one has to have been (and been seen) is a newcomer. The **Top 10 Club** (Reeperbahn 136), a survivor from the legendary Star Club era, still draws the crowds with rhythmic delights. The time to be there, however, is between 4 and 9 am. When the night is somewhat younger, music lovers go for the concert and cinema centre **Docks** (Spielbudenplatz 7), the Latino club **Sam Brasil** (Silbersackstrasse 27), **Molotow** (Spielbudenplatz) or **Grosse Freiheit 36**. Most of these clubs stage frequent live concerts. If you prefer a beer at the bar, there are plenty of fashionable pubs

The red light district.

(but, fashion being what it is, there's no guarantee they'll all still exist when this book goes to press): the plushy **Prinzenbar** behind Docks (Kastanienallee), the scruffy **Sparr** (Hamburger Berg) or the friendly atmosphere of **Geier** (Hein-Köllisch-Platz) where a contemplative cappuccino can be enjoyed during the daytime or even outside.

Once this round is finished, drop into **Gun Club** (Hopfenstrasse), **Nachtclub** (Schmuckstrasse) or Tempelhof – providing, of course, you know that everyone refers to them as such; there's actually a different name over the door. Nachtclub is known as **Cool**, Tempelhof as **Camelot** and Soulkitchen II is actually **einer geht noch**, a tiny and extremely loud cellar bar in Bernhard-Nocht-Strasse. In contrast to all these, **Meyer-Lansky's** (Pinnansberg) is more chic and shiny but not unpleasant.

But a daytime stroll around this area is worthwhile, too. Shops on and around the Reeperbahn sell leathers, punk accessories or extravagant lingerie and

HANS ALBERS

When Hans Albers was born on 22 September 1891 in the St Georg district of Hamburg, his father was already well known as "handsome Wilhelm". But the master butcher who lived in Lange Reihe 71 never dreamed his son would make it to anything grander than sausages. The head of the Albers family was far from pleased about Hans's dreams of becoming an actor, especially when he started practising his autograph on the wallpaper of his room at the age of 13.

Father Albers finally lost patience with Hans when his son seemed more concerned about winning the swimming club championship than doing well at school. Hans was persuaded to do an apprenticeship with a chemicals and paints dealer in Grosse Bleichen but secretly attended drama classes. His first audition, however, was a flop. His auditioner was straight to the point: "Young man, you haven't an ounce of talent in you. Just forget all your hopes!" Luckily the subsequent star of German stage and cinema did not follow this advice.

In 1911 Albers got his first part. During the next two years he did the rounds of provincial theatres: Güstrow in Saxony, Bad Schandau in Mecklenburg and Helgoland, the island off the North Sea coast. Then he was back in Hamburg. His first engagement was at the Schiller Theater in Altona, but then a year later came German mobilisation and the outbreak of World War I.

Hans Albers was engaged by the Thalia Theater to play heroic parts and at the same time kept a promise made to his mother: "I'd told her that if I didn't manage to become an actor in my hometown within three years, I'd return to some commercial job." Albers was saved from this fate – but not from military service, where he was severely wounded on the Western Front. At the end of the war, he moved to Berlin where he stayed for the rest of his life.

He was given a five-year contract as a character actor and operetta buffoon to appear at three Berlin theatres. "Our Hanne", as he was soon known, did well in a variety of parts of every genre: comedies, dialect comedies, dramas, operettas and numerous shows. He not only had an athletic body, now well recovered from war wounds, but also considerable acting talent. Many women fell for him but one in particular was his constant companion, Claire Dux, prima donna of the Berlin State Opera. She knew everyone in Berlin and soon Hans Albers was a nobody no longer.

Now a stage star, Albers was enthusiastically received by audiences and critics alike. Charlie Chaplin visited him in his dressing room and Gustaf Gründgens repeatedly watched plays in which he starred. In those years the cinema was gaining in popularity and significance but although Albers acted in over 100 silent films, his filmography lacks any parts which would now be termed "classic". But he successfully managed the transition from silent films to talkies, a hurdle many of his colleagues failed to clear. This popular actor was one of the first stars of modern-day German cinema – an overnight leap to stardom which brought him fame all over the German-speaking world. As a blue-eyed charmer and hard-drinking ruffian, he played his way into the hearts of millions. Albers, often referred to as "big blond Hans from the Reeperbahn", made his most famous film, *Große Freiheit Nr. 7* (a film about St Pauli and the Reeperbahn), in the face of Hitler's disapproval. Even so, he was later criticised for continuing to make films in Germany under the Nazis. Actually, his common-law wife, Hansi Burg, was Jewish, a fact the Nazis knew full well. Only Albers' tremendous popularity saved him during that time. Interestingly enough, not a single photo exists which features Albers in the company of any prominent Nazi.

After the war he bought a house at Starnberger See in Bavaria where he used to close his eyes and listen to the tape-recorded sounds of ship's sirens. But as he himself once said, "Your home is where you die, not where you live".

"Bavaria," he went on, "is a wonderful place but I don't want to end up as some old Otto in a cemetery in Tutzing. When it's my turn to go, it's going to be Hamburg." He was buried at Ohlsdorf cemetery in Hamburg in July 1960.

there's no need to worry about the restrictive German shop-opening hours. In St Pauli's red-light area the shops stay open until well after 6.30 p.m. Ferret out curiosities, antiques and erotica in the labyrinth of **Harry's Hamburger Hafenbasar** (Bernhard-Nocht-Strasse). Get yourself a life-long souvenir of St Pauli in **Tattoostudio Dänemark** or any of the numerous tattoo shops around Grosse Freiheit.

A side street off the Reeperbahn, **Grosse Freiheit** is the temple of permissiveness. But that's not the reason for its name ("great freedom"). There was freedom of religion and trade in this street, formerly a border route to Altona, earlier than in the rest of Hamburg. Nowadays, the freedom takes the form of innumerable strip shows with promising names such as Tabu, Regina, Tanga Club or Lady Lyn. It is also the home of René Durand's legendary **Salambo**, one of Hamburg's oldest sex shows, and old-fashioned St Pauli pubs such as **Grethel und Alfons**. At the

Curiosities at Harry's Hafenbasar.

northern end of Grosse Freiheit, the Catholic church of **St Joseph's** with its baroque facade (1718–23) overlooks the colourful goings-on. Across the road from the church, **Schmuckstrasse** branches off Grosse Freiheit.

This was the centre of St Pauli's Chinese community until May 1944 when all the Chinese living in Hamburg were rounded up by the Nazis. Since then, there has not even been a single Chinese restaurant to remind people of what was Chinatown. After the war, the remaining side of this street was commandeered by transvestite clubs.

Going on from Schmuckstrasse you can hardly avoid ending up on Simon-Utrecht-Strasse, which is scarcely a pleasurable experience in view of the high density of traffic. Ironically, it was because of its "quiet location" that Heinrich Heine's uncle Salomon had the German-Israelite hospital built here. The present building was renovated in 1843. At the heart of the hospital, from which Jews were banned in

1939, there was a synagogue. There are now plans for it to be rebuilt.

Northern St Pauli: This part of St Pauli is mainly residential – and (relatively) inexpensive. Lots of the inhabitants are elderly and have lived here for decades, but there are also newcomers and students, who love the rough and ready charm of St Pauli, the ease with which people get on first-name terms and stop for a chat in the street. Behind the many multi-storey apartment blocks there are plenty of examples of the terraced housing so typical of Hamburg. These backyard terraced houses are considered to be the oldest form of subsidised housing. One particularly early example of such settlements is Jägerpassage (Wohlwillstrasse 28) which was built in 1866. In the early 1980s, there were plans to demolish these backyard terraces but these schemes were later shelved thanks to the determined opposition of residents and squatters. If you keep your eyes open while strolling through the area, you're sure to discover several more specimens of these half-hidden terraces.

Pleasure park: To the north-east of this residential area, as a kind of buffer between St Pauli and the city centre, lies **Heiligengeistfeld**, a huge area of land that has always been used for pleasure purposes. Originally Hamburg's annual funfair was held next to the city-centre cathedral, hence the local name for the fair, "**Dom**". After the cathedral was demolished in 1806, the stalls and stands of the showmen and travelling people moved to various sites in the city before finding a regular home at Heiligengeistfeld. They have been congregating here and at Spielbudenplatz since 1899.

North Germany's biggest fun fair, the Dom is held three times a year (in March/April, July/August and November/December). In 1900 Barnum & Bailey staged performances on this site and ever since, circuses, travelling shows and other great events have taken place here.

The rough and ready charm of St Pauli.

But Heiligengeistfeld also has a long tradition as a venue for political events. When the 1918 revolution reached Hamburg, the first mass rally was held here. Later the Nazis were to use the "field" as a venue for mass meetings. In 1986, 50,000 demonstrated against what had become known as the "Hamburg encirclement", when police surrounded a crowd of several hundred opponents of nuclear power stations.

Today there's only one building on Heiligengeistfeld but it's certainly a prominent feature of the landscape. This **air-raid shelter** was built in 1942, partly to provide protection for the local population and partly as a suitable site for flak batteries. Nowadays, laboratories, photographers, artists and fashion designers populate this "creative bunker" on Feldstrasse. There have been repeated plans to blow up the bunker but the explosive force required to break up the concrete colossus would probably cause the underground railway tunnels running beneath it to collapse, and so

The "creative bunker" on Feldstrasse.

the schemes have all been abandoned.

Another prominent feature to the west of Heiligengeistfeld should not be forgotten. When Hamburg's soccer stars from FC St Pauli are playing at home, a visit to Millerntor is an experience not to be missed. Take the time to watch St Pauli, join the crowds before and after the game and you'll see something of the "other St Pauli". Football has got a lot to do with the area itself and the people who live here.

Southern St Pauli is dominated by the river Elbe and the port. If you chose the best way to arrive in Hamburg – by ship up the Elbe – you are sure of a fitting landing at **St Pauli Landungsbrücken** – a 700-metre (2,296-ft) long, pontoon construction topped by monumental cupolas. The first of the nine landing stages was built in 1839, and only port vessels and river boats can tie up at them now, the only exception being the ferry to Harwich in England.

The tower at the eastern end, which looks like a clocktower, actually indi-

cates the depth of the water in the Elbe under which the old Elbtunnel, built in 1907–11, passes at the western end. Under the magnificent cupola of the tunnel entrance a lift transports cars down to the two, nearly 450-metre (1,476-ft) long tunnels connecting the northern bank of the Elbe with the ship-building island of Steinwerder. Although a revolutionary construction in its day, the old tunnel has long been outdone by the (relatively) new Elbtunnel which escorts the A7 autobahn under the river. But despite that, or maybe for that very reason, visitors find it interesting to take the iron steps or lift down to the cool shaft under the Elbe and marvel at the tiles and decorations on the walls.

Above the river: Back above ground, the impressive buildings on the heights above the river and the steadfast **Hafenstrasse** houses to the left catch the eye. The latter have become a synonym for political unrest and strife between the state and left-wing militants.

They were originally occupied, illegally, in 1984. Then came the enforced evacuation, re-occupation and bitter and often violent struggles. Since 1986 the occupants of these few houses on Hafenstrasse were given rental contracts for a fixed period of time but, as yet, no long-term solution has been found for those buildings earmarked for demolition.

The magnificent frontages up on the ridge include what used to be a home and hospital for seamen built in 1853–63. Now the posh **Hotel Hafen Hamburg** has found a home there. Of course, several floors have been added and the interior done up quite considerably. Behind the hotel is the huge **Hafenkrankenhaus**, a hospital built at the turn of the century.

Another piece of the Elbe panorama is the **Navigation college** built in 1903–05 with a Dutch Renaissance facade crowned by gables and towers. Though not as beautiful, its next-door neighbour is certainly more famous – the **Bern-**

Sunday morning crowd at the Fischmarkt.

148

hard Nocht Institute for Tropical Diseases. The only relic of the old vantage-point pubs along the ridge is **Bavaria Blick**. Stop here for a rest and a great view, not as far as Bavaria but certainly across the port.

Fischmarkt: In spite of the splendid view from the ridge above Landungsbrücken, it is well worth climbing the steps down towards the river again – especially if it happens to be early on a Sunday morning. That's when Hamburg's famous **Fischmarkt** takes place – a mixture of weekly market for non-claustrophobic St Paulians, tourist attraction and end-of-the-road for more or less steadfast night-owls. In earlier times (around 1703), when everything was more genuine, idyllic and of course better, the Fischmarkt meant what the name suggested. Freshly-caught fish were smoked, marinated, salted, cooled, packed and sold by hordes of busy fishermen, dealers, workers and merchants.

Nowadays, early on Sunday morning coaches convey curious tourists down to the Elbe before congesting the side streets; sleepy Rhinelanders tumble out of hotels and locals, mostly the worse for drink, stagger from all-night pubs. Hangovers abound but pickled herrings offer hoped-for relief. The crowds jostle past innumerable stands, some actually selling fish. Coffee is in great demand and many are glad when they finally reach the end.

In winter when it rains, it's not quite so full and the professional barkers who draw in as many spectators as buyers with their flowers, bananas or fish are worth seeing. Maybe you'll manage to fight your way into the **Fischauktionshalle**, a highly-decorative cast-iron construction built between 1895 and 1896 and renovated in 1982–84. It seems strange to hear jazz or rock bands playing in this ecclesiastical-style building during the Fischmarkt hours – on Sunday mornings from 5 to 9 am. The exterior and interior of this redbrick hall are certainly worth seeing.

The market doesn't just sell fish.

Working class stronghold: Tiny but tenacious, a bit dingy but still very much alive, **Karolinenviertel** is a small area in St Pauli but it has a great big heart. Only about 400 metres (1,300 ft) in length and width at the northern end of the district, it is caged in by the Television Tower, Exhibition Centre, the slaughterhouse and Heiligengeistfeld.

Nowadays, around 7,500 people live in what used to be a working-class stronghold. Nearly half of them are foreigners. The housing may not be upmarket but it certainly has tradition; some 90 percent was built before 1900. Karolinenviertel has some of Hamburg's most beautiful facades and no other district has such a labyrinth of terraces, lanes and passageways. There are cobbled yards with rows of houses and factories, and even multi-terraced complexes such as Karolinenpasage.

Back in the 1960s there were plans to have the whole area demolished, but fortunately they were never carried out. Now such destruction would be impossible. The struggle against gentrification has traditionally been particularly bitter in Karolinenviertel. This was where Hamburg had its first punks, squatters and organised opposition to property developers and demolition threats. Not always peaceful, it was nearly always successful. Squatters are still moving in to "save" run-down property and the battle for cheap accommodation continues. So Karolinenviertel is a pretty turbulent place and visitors may well feel a little uneasy, especially at night, in what the locals (somewhat exaggeratedly) call "Hamburg's Bronx".

However, it's certainly more fun to visit Karolinenviertel during the daytime, e.g. on Saturday afternoon for a stroll through the colourful market. Secondhand shops, fashion designers, junk shops, popular pubs, oriental snack bars and novel breakfast cafés reveal the charming side of this district. In summer there's washing hanging across some streets, people stop for a chat in the courtyards and hordes of screaming kids charge through the passageways.

It is this very charm that attracts old people and the creative types who reside in the **Vorwerkstift**, built between 1866 and 1867. Originally flats for the poor at Vorwerkstrasse 21, they are now used by artists as apartments, ateliers or exhibition rooms. In earlier, less picturesque times the district was bordered by cesspits and cemeteries though the plague is no longer a problem. Only the chapel on Jungiusstrasse, well away from the heart of Karolinenviertel, reminds one of the old cemeteries.

Another church marks the southern boundary of Karolinenviertel, the turn-of-the-century **Gnadenkirche**. Next to it, a half-timbered former school has also survived. A commemorative plaque and the inscription "Israelische Töchterschule" reminds passers-by of another ex-school at Karolinenstrasse 35. A private Jewish girls' school was opened there in 1884 and then closed

Some of the local housing is now occupied by squatters.

down by the Nazis. From 1939, Hamburg's remaining Jewish schoolchildren were rounded up and deported to the concentration camps.

The neighbouring neo-Gothic power plant was Hamburg's first large-scale electricity-generating station when it was built in 1894. Three other reminders of the district's working-class past are the factory in Glashüttenstrasse 78/79 and a chimney behind No. 36. "Warner's Corsets", the factory at No. 38, is well worth seeing.

When the visibility is good, you can get the ultimate overview from the TV Tower. Named after the famous physicist, the **Heinrich-Hertz-Turm** is 204 metres (669 ft) high (271.5 metres/890 ft if you count the antenna) and thus easily the highest building in Hamburg. Built between 1965 and 1968 under the supervision of Fritz Trautwein and Fritz Leonhardt, the TV Tower also offers a slowly rotating restaurant with unrivalled views of the city from 132 metres (433 ft) up.

Like Karolinenviertel, only a bit of the neighbouring **Schanzenviertel** is part of St Pauli but it has much more in common with the latter than with Eimsbüttel, to which it, strictly speaking, belongs. Lots of foreigners live here, too; rents are still relatively low and battles to preserve this cheapish accommodation have been fought in the recent past. Here, too, there are numerous back courtyards, many with touches of classicism. Between Sternstrasse and Neue Pferdemarkt you find some particularly beautiful examples of terraced housing, e.g. Beckstrasse or Augustenpassage. Around bustling Schulterblatt, with its novel shops, pubs, corner shops and grocer's, there are more of these backyard houses, nicely known as "St Pauli Garden Flats" in bygone times.

Another example of the search for new forms of accommodation was the so-called **Boarding House des Westens** at Schulterblatt 26–36. The original idea for a "one-kitchen house", combining living in your own four

Fine facades in Karolinenviertel.

walls with the communal service and facilities of a hotel, came from Berlin. When the experiment failed in 1930, the building was turned into a normal block of rented flats. Now a business operates behind the grey stone front.

Slaughter quarter: The western boundary of Schanzenviertel is dominated by the **Schlachthaus** (slaughterhouse) in Sternstrasse. Since the smaller facilities were closed, 95 percent of Hamburg's slaughtering is done here. Formerly a cattle station, together with the cattle market at Heiligengeistfeld and Sternschanze, the slaughterhouse plays an important role in the meat-supply business. Built between 1889 and 1892, it still dominates the surrounding area – many businesses depend on it, including restaurants such as the **Schlachterbörse** in Kampstrasse where not very long ago slaughtermen in their blood-splattered overalls could get meals around the clock. Plans to construct a residential estate on part of the slaughterhouse grounds were shelved in 1986, so the old buildings and "dying ox" statue are safe for the time being.

There is also a strong cultural tradition in Schanzenviertel. To the south of Pferdemarkt you can marvel at the circular steel skeleton construction of the **Schilleroper**, home of the Busch circus from 1888 onwards. Around the turn of the century, it was re-opened as the **Schiller Theater**. During the 1920s and early 1930s the German labour movement organised performances there. Hans Albers and Asta Nielsen also appeared and shows or vaudeville were on the programme. After the war, the arts had no chance at all in Schilleroper. It became in turns a garage, emergency accommodation, hotel and warehouse – now in a state of decay.

Flora drama: The **Flora Theater** on Schulterblatt met with a similar fate. Built as a concert hall in 1888, it was the home of popular theatre and variety shows. Later it became a cinema before a store selling household supplies moved in. In 1988 this once splendid

house of entertainment fell victim to the plans of musical marketing man, Fritz Kurz. He wanted to stage his second Andrew Lloyd Webber spectacle here and all but the entrance with the house number 71 was demolished. However, the locals took to the streets fearing dire consequences for the area if an up-market cultural palace was built here.

Only after numerous demonstrations, negotiations and some violent street battles did Kurz relent, taking his *Phantom of the Opera* to a purpose-built building at Holstenplatz. Now the old theatre is known as "Rote Flora" and there are plans to turn it into a community cultural centre.

This is only a recent episode in a long tradition of strife in Schanzenviertel. Back in 1682, what is now Sternschanze park with its former water tower was built as a fort to protect Hamburg from the Danes. And in 1930 Nazis and communists fought what became known as the Battle of Sternschanze. Certain traditions die hard.

Worker in the Schanzenviertel Schlachthaus.

GOAL, GOAL, GOAL!

For football fans Hamburg has two big attractions. One club is well known throughout Europe, Hamburger SV (HSV); the other less so, FC St Pauli. HSV is a club with a long tradition, celebrating its centenary in 1988. FC St Pauli was founded in 1910 and only developed into a top North German club after the last war. In those days, the manager of West Germany's 1974 World Cup winners, Helmut Schön, turned out in the traditional brown-and-white St Pauli strip.

HSV has won numerous German championships and Cup Finals over the years and recently been successful in European competitions; by contrast, St Pauli has been happy simply to avoid relegation from the Bundesliga (second division of the national league) – in which it was successful until recently.

When it was set up in 1963, the German Football Association (DFB) even refused St Pauli admission to the top flight. But the DFB's criterion was a club's sporting achievements and not its likeability rating. St Pauli fans are sure of one thing: "HSV might have better players but ours are nicer!"

Another difference between the two clubs is their grounds. Whereas HSV plays its home games in the vast Volksparkstadion, there is no running track between the St Pauli players and the crowd at Millerntor, their tiny ground. If you shout loud enough, one of the players might shout back. Nowadays the DFB insists on fences to prevent crowd trouble, but after St Pauli's home games they sometimes open the escape gates onto the pitch to celebrate an (unexpected) home win.

One thing is certain – wins are fought for and celebrated by spectators and players alike. When the team loses, everyone is sad. After home games, players and fans meet in the totally packed clubhouse bar. The big attraction of St Pauli is that there is no them-and-us situation between highly-paid professional footballers and spectators who merely pay to get in. "When you see how the fans are glad or sad, you'll do everything you can so as not to disappoint them." That's how midfield star

Peter Knäbel describes his experiences after moving to St Pauli from Bochum. At first he couldn't believe that a bad pass was not greeted with boos but encouraging shouts of "Try better next time!"

Every post-match press conference includes a ritual thank-you to the fans. The atmosphere at Millerntor is always one of cautious optimism and often one of delirious delight. It is typical of the spirit that ex-president Otto Paulick's wife sells home-made cakes to support the youth teams.

When asked recently whether the club's left-wing image disturbed him, Paulick countered that St Pauli had always had its roots in working-class sport. There was nothing wrong with this tradition, he said, and even the anarchist Hafenstrasse (a quarter occupied by squatters) fans with their

skull-and-crossbones flags had never behaved badly. His successor as president, Heinz Weisener, has similar views. Even right-wing Social Democrat Hans Apel, currently vice-president, doesn't worry about left-wing extremists – providing they're real St Pauli fans and pay for their tickets.

St Pauli has remained unscathed by the hooligans who masquerade as fans of other clubs in the country. St Pauli's tiny ground probably offers these right-wing thugs too little anonymity. There are even banners like "No more fascism, no more war, no more 2nd Division" at St Pauli home games (unfortunately the latter protest has been in vain). And when fans initiated a unique campaign against racism and violence at football grounds, the players and manager were quick to voice their support.

Though HSV and St Pauli fans are not exactly friends, they do not hate each other in the way many "divided" cities' fans do. For St Pauli fans the away games at Volksparkstadion are a severe test of loyalty. Robbed of their natural surroundings, they seem to wilt and die; the St Pauli team frequently does no better.

St Pauli fans only feel really at home in their own tiny ground. When 20,000 fans start the famous St Pauli roar at Millerntor, their encouragement – uniquely expressed with the longest final "i" in European football – has been known to spur their team on to that goal in injury time which can topple top teams from their thrones.

ST GEORG

When a district of Hamburg is named after a saint, the innocence of its inhabitants is invariably nothing to write home about. St Pauli, for example, is known all over the world for its bars and sleazy nightclubs, but St Georg is no less sinful. This small chequered district, to the south-east of the Alster and by the side of the Hauptbahnhof, is the city's melting-pot.

St Georg is where Hamburg's one-and-only Catholic order of nuns co-exists with streetwalking under-age drug addicts offering their bodies to pay for the next shot. Here, the early-morning dole queue lengthens in front of the employment office only yards from a gay bar where the last of the late-night strip shows is just coming to an end. While top stars like Michael Jackson stay in the traditional Hotel Atlantic, once Hamburg's best and still one of its top-class establishments, less-famous newcomers – immigrants from the East and those seeking political asylum or their fortune in Hamburg – vegetate in any of 100 cheap hostels that were brothels only a few months before.

Levantine St Georg: More than half of St Georg's 9,713 inhabitants (down from 21,500 in 1953) are foreigners. More than 100 nationalities are represented here. Most are from Turkey so it is hardly surprising that there is a high concentration of Turkish businesses: five snack bars, 16 travel agencies, nine food shops and seven import and export firms. These Levantine traders keep their shops open till late in the evening. The concept of closing time is foreign to St Georg.

Relatively few old people live here. Who, at the sunset of their life, would want to weave their way through whores and cars on the way to the grocer's? Or share the few trees with nearly 10,000 others? St Georg belongs to its foreigners, artists and, in recent times,

increasing numbers of yuppies buying their way into this unsophisticated district and driving up rents. And so St Georg is home to Hamburg's young rich and poorest poor.

Within less than two square miles, there are lakeside Alster villas and slums in which flats are still being let without running water. St Georg has reached a crossroads – one path is "gentrification" with big firms buying up property with the help of front men; the other "slumification".

Hovels in history: In 1192 Count Adolf III of Schauenburg and Holstein founded a home for lepers on a site that is now St Georgskirchhof at the corner of Alstertwiete. The lepers were glad to live near the Alster, which was then outside the city walls, partly to avoid infecting the healthy citizens, partly to enjoy the privileges of such proximity to Hamburg. Returning crusaders brought generous gifts to support the home, which soon began to look after old women as well.

The home was named after the patron saint of travellers and the sick, St George, a name that even nowadays proves admirably suited to an area bounded on the one side by Hamburg's largest hospital and on the other by the main railway station. With the city of Hamburg bursting at the seams as its population grew in the 14th and 15th centuries, traders and skilled craftsmen moved into the suburb of St Georg. In fact, it housed everything for which there was no room within the confines of the walled city: gallows, bleaching fields and brickworks.

Landed and stranded: Everyone arriving in Hamburg by train gets out in St Georg. Most hurry to the western exits of the main station, anxious to get to work on time. Those who turn eastwards are immediately confronted by the district; the scantily dressed bodies of drunken prostitutes decorate the way; young males in much too tight trousers wait for a pick-up and a Peruvian band adds their version of *El Condor Pasa* to the babble. And through it all wafts the cozy smell of hot chestnuts.

The construction of the **Hauptbahnhof** (main station) brought life to a sleepy suburb. In 1906 work on the daringly designed main hall with its conventionally built towers was completed. The horse-drawn omnibuses on the Wandsbek-Altona route had been stopping in St Georg since 1839 but it was the beginning of this century when the district finally became the main stopping-off place for the travelling public.

The Hauptbahnhof today is the meeting place of a tangle of railway lines, above and below ground. More than 300 long-distance trains leave the station every day, with international destinations such as Copenhagen, Stockholm, Moscow, Vienna, Oslo, Milan, Zurich, Geneva, Paris, Brussels and Amsterdam. The station has a thriving shopping arcade, particularly good for buying guide books, and also houses a tourist office which opens long hours.

Outside, the main **tourist office** (which opens normal office hours) is across the square, beyond the large taxi rank. Buses for the airport leave from here.

Competition for St Pauli: The many emigrants who came to Hamburg to collect their papers before embarking for the New World looked for temporary accommodation near the station. St Georg was thus turned into a district of lodgings. Major hotels were built to cater for this transit traffic – in 1909 the Hotel Atlantic next to the Alster and the Reichshof, in baroque-like art nouveau style, on Kirchenallee. Only four years later, the latter had to be extended to cope with the visitors.

Excited emigrants were keen to while away the time before departure for the promised land and so the entertainment business blossomed in St Georg. This small district grew to rival St Pauli, the well-known red-light area next to the port. Most of the 40 cinemas that existed in Hamburg in 1910 were located in St Georg. The Hansa Theater was opened **Map of St Georg.**

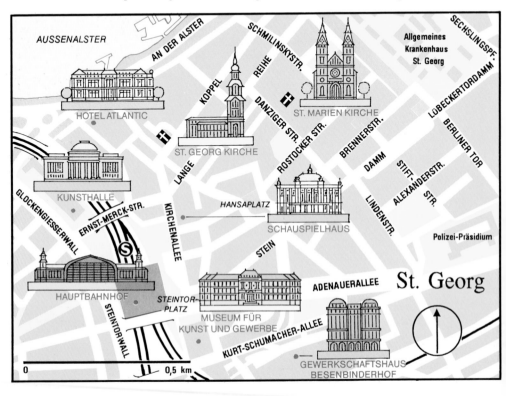

here on 5 March 1894, followed by the opening of the Deutsches Schauspielhaus on 15 September 1900.

The crowds of people milling through St Georg increased apace. After the opening of Hamburg's (partly overground) underground railway in 1912, the district round the main station was soon bursting at the seams. Over 80,000 people a day got off or changed trains here. St Georg had become one of the world's busiest districts.

When you leave the station in the direction of Kirchenallee, you can still feel this cosmopolitan flair. On warm summer days, there's even a touch of southern Europe when the street cafés are filled with travellers enjoying cappuccinos. Above their heads, neon lights publicise the offerings of a hard-porn cinema.

Only a few yards away stands the **Deutsches Schauspielhaus**, Hamburg's most prestigious theatre, which was first established in Gänsemarkt in 1765. One of the company's earliest

productions, Shakespeare's *Othello*, was so gruesome that it caused members of the audience to faint and provoked several premature still-births, according to newspaper reports.

The Schauspielhaus's present building was completed in 1900 on the site of the English Tivoli, a dance hall with a garden and stage where small-scale plays were sometimes performed. Since then the venue has achieved worldwide renown under its directors Ivan Nagel, Peter Zadek and Michael Bogdanov. Huge posters advertising the current plays have even included actors dropping their pants, a gesture well suited to the quarter.

A few paces to the north of the Schauspielhaus lies the **Spadenteich**, St Georg's main square where six roads meet. A choice spot for the prostitutes who weave their way through the rows of cars before negotiating terms with the drivers and disappearing into one of the vehicles.

The traditional-style pub **Max &**

On-house advertising.

Consorten has been tempting guests to a glass of wine or beer ever since 1894. At the bar a punk is likely to be talking to a pin-striped gentleman at the bar and next to the piano, a prostitute is probably resting from her night shift.

St Georg has traditionally been the place for entertainment. Back in 1912 there were 219 pubs and bars here. That makes today's total seem modest: 148 pubs, 27 amusement arcades, 12 sex shops, 8 striptease shows and 49 sleazy hotels. A hundred years ago, these venues had names like Old Flute, Iron Pavilion, Trumpet or Tivoli; today's names are no less cheerful: Frau Möller (Lange Reihe 96), Cheerio, All The Best (Lange Reihe 86) or La Strada (Lange Reihe 57).

St Georg: Beyond Spadenteich is **St Georgskirchhof**, with a sculpture of St George fighting his dragon. This sculpture by Gerhard Marcks is as hidden away as the church belonging to the Kirchhof, which is known as Holy Trinity and not St George's. Its architect was Johannes Leonhard Prey, one of the men who designed St Michael's Church (the famous Michaeliskirche). After the war it was rebuilt along with the baroque facade of its tower.

Only a few yards from the church lies St Georg's best-known "secret" attraction – a backyard with an almost rural ambience. An inconspicuous gateway between houses 3 and 7 in St Georgstrasse leads to a conclave of low, two-storeyed, redbrick houses, built in the first half of the 19th century to provide emergency accommodation and now the home of artists and intellectuals trying to escape to the anonymity of big-city life.

At the end of St Georgstrasse, Rautenbergstrasse leads down to Holzdamm where the magnificent **Hotel Atlantic** stands out in pristine white, a building completed in 1909 in late-baroque palace style. Its lordly splendour will impress any guest staying at the hotel or merely enjoying a cup of coffee. The Atlantic has many rooms with a

Greengrocer in Lange Reihe.

view – usually across the Alster or towards the neighbouring girls' home, Holzdamm Convent.

A stroll along the banks of the Alster, or to be more exact the **Outer Alster**, offers rest for the eyes after the jigsaw jungle of houses in St Georg. Yachts criss-cross the lake under the blue skies of summer while winter sometimes draws thousands of skaters on to its frozen wastes. The road along the lake is skirted by romantic-style villas and three- to four-storeyed residences in the classical style – the home of advertising agencies, undertakers and even the YMCA. Between them, and in the streets away from the lake, the prostitutes have also set up shop.

Prostitution and drugs: The oldest profession in the world (prostitution) can look back on 150 years of tradition in this district. After the Great Fire of 1842 which destroyed large parts of the old city, many of the whores who used to live there moved to St Georg, which had been spared by the flames. This reloca-

Antique market in Lange Reihe.

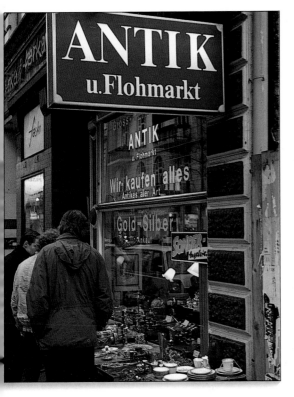

tion annoyed some of the residents, as indicated by the caustic comments in one St Georg diary: "It is possible that genuine privation has driven these females to take up residence here and it is really pleasing to see how full the apartments of these needy persons are with young men who come to alleviate their hardships; this must give strangers a good impression of the charity of Hamburg's young men."

Nowadays, we are a bit more realistic about the genuine distress in which prostitutes live – forced to sell their bodies by a dependence on pimps or drugs. **Café Sperrgebiet**, run by a church charity, tries to help them find a way out of prostitution. Hamburg's noblest representative of the oldest profession, Domenica, is the café's most popular helper.

Away from the speeding traffic along An der Alster, the main road link between the city centre and Hamburg's northern districts, there are two streets where the pace of life has not changed for 30 years: Gurlittstrasse and Schmilinskystrasse.

Famous residents: Brigitte, a poodle coiffeur with a shop in Koppel, takes her own dog out for a walk and meets "hen-killer Hermann", who for years had a poultry shop in Lange Reihe. They stop for a chat, as they have done for decades. At Koppel 100, milk is still sold straight from the churn. "Sutje" is the Low German word they use to describe life here: it translates roughly as "nice and slow."

Koppel, a street whose name originates from the time when prosperous Hamburgers put their horses out to pasture here, is one of the diversions for cars stuck in the morning rush-hour jams along the Alster. There are four garages and car dealers in a street where there's hardly ever a parking space free. Anyone coming here by car is in a difficult predicament but some help has been provided by a multi-storey car park behind the Schauspielhaus which is open 24 hours a day.

The Hamburg journalist Carl von Ossietzky, who was murdered in a Nazi concentration camp, lived here for years – in Schmilinskystrasse 6 and Koppel 106. Von Ossietzky, who was awarded the Nobel Peace Prize while in the concentration camp, had been the publisher of *Weltbühne*, one of the best-known left-wing magazines during the Weimar Republic. Since February 1990, a square (formerly known as Greifswalder Platz) has borne his name. As the site of St Georg's weekly market, it is also the place where farmers from the surrounding region come to sell their fruit and vegetables.

The long row: The real heart of St Georg is **Lange Reihe**. "A dash of Prussia laced with two splashes of Paris, three drops of the Balkans and four pinches of poetic charm." That was how author Hansjörg Martin described the atmosphere in St Georg, a mixture most accurately reflected in Lange Reihe. Approximately 10,000 cars a day weave their way down this narrow street, their speed somewhat reduced by traffic schemes of recent years. Twenty years ago, when trams were still running, they sometimes had to push cars out of their way to get through.

Lange Reihe is a mecca for actors and journalists, in fact for anyone attracted by St Georg's shady flair. Strolling past the desperately young streetwalkers, you make your way to the acting community's favourite haunt, a basement wine bar known as "**Dorf**" (don't look for a sign – there isn't one; it's under the chemist's at No. 39). Or **Café Gnosa** with its coffee-house atmosphere, planned as a gay bar with top cuisine by owner "Effi" Effinghausen but now the Eldorado of Hamburg's creative scene, not just for homosexuals. It's a favourite dining spot for playwright Heiner Müller, actor Ulrich Tukur and journalist Peggy Parnass, but if you want to get a seat in Café Gnosa, you need to be there early.

A decade ago, Hamburg's alternative scene discovered St Georg as one of the few city-centre districts where rents were still low. Lots of students and artists moved into bed-sits or shared apartments. They took their art into St Georg's backyards and enriched a whole district. The best example is the **House of Handicrafts**, a former machine factory in the backyard between Lange Reihe 75 and Koppel 66 where 13 businesses ranging from an art gallery to a goldsmith have set up shop. On the ground floor, **Café Koppel** serves as a meeting place for artists and craftsmen, numerous guests and customers. Vegetarian lunches and home-made cakes prove a big attraction.

St Georg's oldest house is **Lange Reihe 61**, a half-timbered, gabled building built in 1640 when St Georg was still the place where urban Hamburgers had their summer residences.

Around the turn of the century, "Handsome Wilhelm" Albers made a name for himself in St Georg. His butcher's shop was at Lange Reihe 71. In 1912 his son Hans was born. Hans

The district's patron saint.

Albers didn't want to spend his life making sausages so he went onto the stage instead. The quintessence of the seafaring spirit of adventure, Hans Albers' blue eyes and melancholy voice still cause hearts to flutter when his films have their umpteenth re-run. As a successful movie star, he always lived in Room 208 of the Atlantic when in Hamburg. A plaque on the wall marks the house where he was born.

Across the road, undertakers advertise their services with his name. While "hen-killer Wilhelm" still had his poultry shop, he ensured that Hans Albers' music sounded out along Lange Reihe each year on 22 September, the dead star's birthday. But the record player has been silent ever since rent increases forced butcher Wilhelm to close down and retire.

At the end of Lange Reihe, Hamburg's largest hospital, a 1,000-bed institution established in 1823, forms the boundary of St Georg. It was built on the site of a protective wall which the City constructed in 1680. Nowadays, the greenery between Lange Reihe and Steindamm is the only park in the whole of St Georg.

Dealers and addicts: But an evening stroll through this particular park landscape is not to be recommended. Over 5,500 crimes a year are reported in St Georg alone. A fifth of all Hamburg's drug victims are found here, and 130 police officers patrol the area in four shifts round the clock.

The main problem is drugs, which the addicts acquire in increasingly sophisticated ways. Even children earn extra pocket money by running errands for the dealers. With the drugs hidden in the pockets of their anoraks, they stroll past patrolling police officers on their way to waiting customers.

For years now, citizens' action groups have been fighting for better protection for these kids. Numerous groups have been formed – for women, gays or parents. All work closely together. Back in 1830, more than 300

Spadenteich, St Georg's main square.

citizens of St Georg got together to sign a petition demanding more rights from the city council.

In 1987 the St Georg Inhabitants' Association was set up to support all the other organisations. Its predecessor, the St Georg Citizens' Association, is 100 years older. The owners of the businesses that the Inhabitants' Association represents, however, have mostly long since left the district to live in one of the city's greener suburbs.

One of the Inhabitants' Association's main concerns is the plight of children in St Georg. The building in which the day-care centre was once located has since been sold to some conglomerate. Many kids therefore had no choice but to play on the streets or one of the three playgrounds. But even these are dangerous places in St Georg. Parents are constantly finding used needles thrown away by heroin addicts, in all probability a potential source of AIDS.

Promenades: Nowadays, heavy traffic thunders its way along Steindamm and Adenaueralle but back in the 18th century Hamburgers liked to stroll down these promenades. Turnpikes barred the way, but for a toll of four shillings, the bars would be lifted and privileged 18th-century Hamburgers could enjoy one of their favourite pastimes, a Sunday cab ride.

Steindamm, or Steinstrasse as it used to be known, was one of Europe's first paved roads. It led from the city to the St Georg hospital. In the 1950s the character of this road was altered as the bombed parts of St Georg were rebuilt. Hamburg's city planners wanted to restore the old mixture of residential and business premises but the Steindamm property owners got their way. The result was a predominance of business premises. Initially, the hotels and office buildings were fairly low-storeyed affairs but in the 1970s tall blocks shot up well above the previous skyline. Now, Turkish snack bars and travel agencies are located next door to office blocks and porn shops in Steindamm.

Kirchenallee, with its theatres, hotels and restaurants.

Variety entertainment: No. 17 is still the most popular address for more sedate tastes. This is where the **Hansa Theater** has been amusing audiences with an extraordinarily good variety programme since 1894. Spinning plates on bamboo sticks, doves flying out of magician's hats or clowns falling all over the place – "never on TV, only here" is the small theatre's slogan, proud of the fact that, on the first of each month, a host of new artistes awaits an eager audience. Only Heidi, who announces each new number, has been on the programme for many years.

Squares and streets: Stralsunder Strasse leads down to what was the heart of St Georg, **Hansaplatz**. The limes and maples rustle in the wind in a square surrounded by multi-storey apartment houses, architectural relics of the building boom of the 1870s. Up to a few years ago, Hansaplatz was where the people of St Georg met to chat or go round the market. In the afternoons kids played in the shadow of the huge trees or dashed on their bikes round the groups of older folks passing the time of day. In the evening young lovers exchanged their first kisses under the 20-metre (65-ft) high statue of Hamburg's patron saint, Hammonia.

But Hansaplatz has lost its innocence. Children are quickly dragged past what has become a main local dealing place for drugs, where figures are always lurking in the shadows. In brief exchanges the prices are fixed before the actual handover is made in the less conspicuous surroundings of neighbouring streets. The buildings round the square now house knocking-shops, sleazy bars or basement rooms for those seeking political asylum.

The south-eastern part of St Georg belongs to the gays, the Muslim community, the unemployed and the world of art. In Pulverteich, one of the streets off Steindamm, there's **Pulverfass** where the plushy, powder-puff gay scene meets. Next door, in **Crazy Boys**, there are shows every night at which the compère asks his standard rhetorical question: "Man or woman? No-one really knows."

The next turning off Steindamm, Böckmannstrasse, takes its name from a large park set out in the early 18th century when prosperous Hamburgers had their weekend residences in St Georg. Now, Böckmannstrasse is almost like a Muslim enclave. Its inhabitants understand Turkish better than German. Men in traditional dress and veiled women regularly make their way to house number 41, the **Ar-Raudhah**, Hamburg's largest mosque.

Stronghold of trade unions: Every morning, dole queues stretch out along the other side of Adenauerallee and Kurt-Schumacher-Allee where the **employment office** was built in the 1950s. A few buildings further on, at **Besenbinderhof 57/58**, the trade unions have their home. The powerful-looking building, completed in 1906, was meant to symbolise the strength of the trade union organisation.

Peruvian musicians by the railway station.

As August Bebel, the leader of the SPD party at the time, said at the official opening ceremony, "this building is not only a sign of our solidarity and the willingness to make sacrifices but also of our self-confidence. I am not exaggerating when I say that, besides the city hall and the main railway station, our trade union house is Hamburg's third architectural attraction."

Unfortunately, much of the building was destroyed in the war and nothing more than the polished red marble columns, now part of the glass facade of the Bank für Gemeinwirtschaft, bear witness to its former glories.

At the main bus station in front of trade union house you can catch a coach to destinations throughout Europe. To the west of the station, where the Museum for Art and Handicrafts now stands, there used to be a lamb market. On the Friday before Whitsun, there were roundabouts, fire-eaters and lambs changing hands here.

The second big festival was the

"Waisengrün" in summer when orphans went begging through the streets, passing other more fortunate children waiting for them with their parents. "Gotteslohmidan" (a popular abridgement of "God's reward my thanks") was the traditional cry of thanks uttered by the orphans when coins clattered into their tins.

The neo-Renaissance **Museum für Kunst und Gewerbe** (Arts and Crafts) was opened in 1875. Its courtyard contains a Renaissance facade from the Kaiserhof of 1619 and inside there is a mirror room decorated in the style of the late Historical period. Other memorable features of the museum are its Jugendstil and Far East collections and the Japanese tea ceremony which takes place in the Far Eastern rooms.

Threats: St Georg is still a conglomerate district with an astonishing capacity to integrate foreigners. But its inhabitants are always on their guard. The sword of Damocles hung over the district in 1966. Its city-centre location, with favourable transport links, tempted the union-owned Neue Heimat Group to come up with their Alsterzentrum Project. Everything between the Hauptbahnhof and Lohmühlenstrasse and the Outer Alster and Rostocker Strasse was to be torn down – with the exception of the churches and Hotel Atlantic.

Under the plan, a huge multi-storey skyscraper complex with housing for 20,000 people, jobs for 15,000 and parking for 16,000 cars was to be constructed. Its supporters referred to it as a "large-scale, spacious and modern plan" for this district but the inhabitants of St Georg feared rising rents and destruction of a deeply rooted community. Their protests were successful. The planned Alster Manhattan was relocated to become City-Nord, a grim labyrinth of office blocks to the north of the Stadtpark. That time, at least, the district of St Georg managed to fight off radical change. Nevertheless, its days may well eventually be numbered.

Left, St Georgskirchhof, and right, the Hotel Atlantic: both safe from developers.

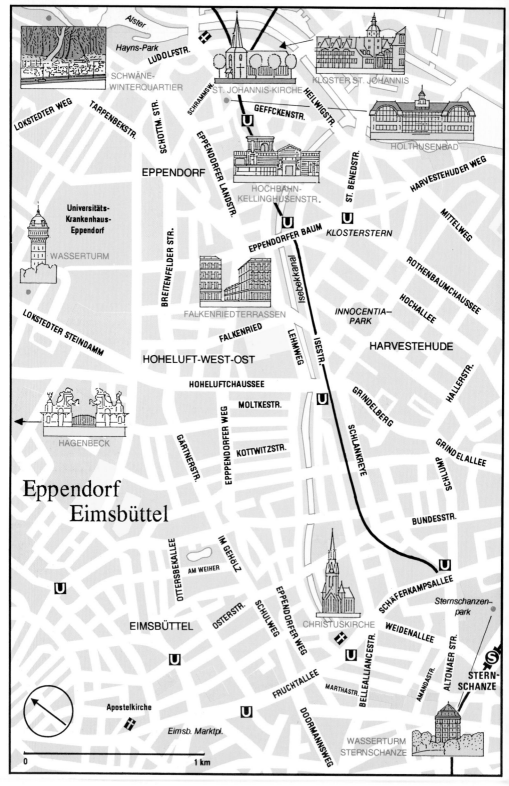

Alster

Hayns-Park

LUDOLFSTR.

SCHWÄNE-
WINTERQUARTIER

St. JOHANNIS-KIRCHE

KLOSTER ST. JOHANNIS

LOKSTEDTER WEG

TARPENBEKSTR.

SCHOTTM. STR.

SCHRAMMSW.

GEFFCKENSTR.

HEILWIGSTR.

HOLTHUSENBAD

EPPENDORF

EPPENDORFER LANDSTR.

HARVESTEHUDER WEG

Universitäts-
Krankenhaus-
Eppendorf

WASSERTURM

HOCHBAHN-
KELLINGHUSENSTR.

ST. BENEDSTR.

KLOSTERSTERN

MITTELWEG

BREITENFELDER STR.

EPPENDORFER BAUM

ROTHENBAUMCHAUSSEE

HOCHALLEE

Isebekkanal

INNOCENTIA–
PARK

FALKENRIEDTERRASSEN

FALKENRIED

LEHMWEG

ISESTR.

HARVESTEHUDE

HALLERSTR.

LOKSTEDTER STEINDAMM

HOHELUFT-WEST-OST

HOHELUFTCHAUSSEE

GRINDELBERG

GRINDELALLEE

HAGENBECK

EPPENDORFER WEG

GÄRTNERSTR.

MOLTKESTR.

KOTTWITZSTR.

SCHLANKREYE

SCHLUMP

Eppendorf
Eimsbüttel

OTTERSBEKALLEE

IM GEHÖLZ

AM WEIHER

BUNDESSTR.

SCHÄFERKAMPSALLEE

Sternschanzen-
park

EIMSBÜTTEL

OSTERSTR.

SCHULWEG

EPPENDORFER WEG

CHRISTUSKIRCHE

WEIDENALLEE

AMANDASTR.

ALTONAER STR.

STERN-
SCHANZE

Apostelkirche

FRUCHTALLEE

MARTHASTR.

BELLEALLIANCESTR.

Eimsb. Marktpl.

DOORMANNSWEG

WASSERTURM
STERNSCHANZE

0   1 km

EPPENDORF AND EIMSBÜTTEL

Both these districts have the same postal address, Hamburg 20, but that's where the similarity ends. Eppendorf and Eimsbüttel present a picture of contrasts. Eppendorf has nearly 22,000 people in an area of 271 hectares (669 acres) whereas nearly 54,000 are concentrated in an area of only 323 hectares (798 acres) in Eimsbüttel. But although the latter was decried as a "desert of bricks and stones" only a few years ago, it has now developed into a popular residential district within easy reach of the city centre. But it is still nowhere near as chic as Eppendorf.

Eppendorf: This district, to the north of the centre and west of the Alster, is for many the quintessence of good living. Everything a person might need is available, at a price, here. Watercress soup with turkey liver for dinner tonight? No problem, the supermarket round the corner has it. And if not, there's always the open-air market in Isestrasse. This **Isemarkt** on Tuesday and Friday mornings is one of Hamburg's most colourful – and most noisy, since the stalls are located right under the arches of Hamburg's "underground" railway.

There's no shortage of fine boutiques here, either. And if you don't want to pay designer prices, there are also two department stores, several second-hand shops and perfectly normal clothing shops. Feeling like eating a pakora and biriyani, or would you prefer pizza and pasta? No problem in Eppendorf. There's an Indian at Eppendorfer Marktplatz and Italian restaurants on virtually every corner.

Eppendorf is a fine place to live but by no means over-fine. In contrast to neighbouring Pöseldorf, Hamburg's chic clique hasn't completely taken over the area around Eppendorfer Baum and Eppendorfer Landstrasse. However, increasing numbers of traditional shops are being forced to close down to make way for boutiques and rents are shooting up. Largely spared from the bombs of World War II, Eppendorf basks in the glory of turn-of-the-century urban architecture. The five- and six-storey apartment houses with their magnificent facades have been renovated and now bear ornamental plasterwork featuring angels, blossoms and laurels.

History: In 1990 Eppendorf celebrated its 850th anniversary in style. It was first mentioned in 1140, when Archbishop Adelbero confirmed in a deed that the cathedral chapter of Hamburg owned a farm in "Eppenthorp". Eppendorf is actually thought to be even older. However, there is no proof for the theory that its name goes back to Archbishop Ebbo of Reims who set about converting the population of northern Germany in the 9th century. The name can also be derived from the old word for water: *ap* or *ep*. Whatever its origins, Eppendorf remained a rural community until the 17th century.

The only bit of Eppendorf to make a name for itself in those years was **St Johannis Kirche** (Ludolfstrasse 62) at the Alster crossing to Winterhude. Its parish included Eppendorf and 16 other villages. The church is first mentioned in 1267, but the current building, Eppendorf's oldest landmark and Hamburg's most popular venue for weddings, is a half-timbered construction built in 1622. The Romanesque field-stone tower is older but that is now hidden behind brickwork put up in 1751 when it was also crowned with a cupola.

Rich nuns: Only a few yards further on, in Heilwigstrasse 162, **St Johannis convent** stands as a reminder of the centuries-old links between Eppendorf and Herwardeshude convent (in what is now Harvestehude). In 1343 this monastery acquired the village of Eppendorf and all its inhabitants from Count Adolf VII of Holstein for 239 pieces of silver. The nuns of Herwardeshude, who were capable businesswomen and not averse to the pleasures of the flesh, bought up one village after another: Othmarschen, Ohlsdorf, Eimsbüttel, Borstel and Rissen were all in their hands.

It was not until 1832 that the city of Hamburg acquired Eppendorf from the nuns who had themselves been forced by the Reformation to move into the city centre. In 1914 they moved back to Eppendorf to reside in the convent's wonderful group of buildings right next to the Alster. The clock tower with its lantern-crowned copper cupola is visible from far away. However, any hopes of closer acquaintance with the convent and its nuns are dashed by tall wrought-iron railings.

From village to town: Very little remains of what was the heart of Eppendorf. Traffic now roars past the church and through **Eppendorfer Marktplatz,** where in the 19th century a popular groceries and cattle market took place every June. The last remaining farmhouses were demolished to make way for cars in 1970. So the small half-timbered house at the corner of Mar-tinistrasse and Eppendorfer Landstrasse seems almost anachronistic. In 1887 a cab driver named Kunkel established an inn and beer garden where the horses could be unharnessed. Nowadays, it is an Italian restaurant.

All but one of the "pleasure yards" (*Lusthöfe*) built by Hamburg mayors, senators and merchants between the farmhouses from the 17th century onwards have disappeared too. Now the **Willsche Haus** in Ludolfstrasse 19 is the sole reminder of the days when Eppendorf was a summer attraction for rich, urban Hamburgers who used to spend their leisure time in houses like this half-timbered building built in 1728. Other reminders of these bygone days are street names likes Kellinghusen-strasse, Knauerstrasse, Schrammsweg or Haynstrasse and some wonderful gardens which were saved from housing development and opened up to the public in the early 1930s.

What is left of the **Seelemannscher Park** next to St Johannis Kirche gives

Heilwigstrasse on the Alster.

some idea of Eppendorf's past splendour. A bronze statue commemorates Samuel Heinicke who as a sexton in Eppendorf established Germany's first deaf-and-dumb school where pupils were taught by the phonic method. Beyond Eppendorfer Marktplatz and between Eppendorfer Landstrasse and the Alster, what used to be a senator's garden, **Hayns park**, is another good place for a stroll. A columned temple built in the classicist style for the senator to enjoy his cup of coffee still stands.

Am Mühlenteich: Beyond Hayns park, to the right, is **Meenkwiese**, a meadow created in 1914 when the Alster was canalised and widened to form a basin upstream from Winterhude quay. Its purpose was to save Eppendorf from flooding. To the left, between Erikastrasse and Salomon-Heine-Weg, is the idyllic Mühlenteich, a small lake that is probably as old as Eppendorf itself. As early as the 13th century there was mention of a mill at the spot where the Tarpenbek had been dammed. Nowa-

days, Hamburg's swans have their winter quarters here, lovingly cared for by swan-keeper Harald Niess.

A memorial at the corner of Tarpenbekstrasse and Lokstedter Weg is reminiscent of Eppendorf's more recent past: the **Ernst Thälmann Gedenkstätte**. The secretary-general of Germany's Communist Party (KPD) in the 1920s and 1930s and former member of the Reichstag and local parliament, Ernst Thälmann lived in the ground floor of this Eppendorf house. He was seized by the Nazis in 1933, taken to Buchenwald concentration camp and murdered there in 1944. Now, the life, work and death of this legendary labour leader are documented here.

To the west of Tarpenbekstrasse a number of charity foundations were set up between the late 19th century and the 1920s. Their detached buildings in park-like surroundings have shaped the character of this area. To the south west is the **Universitäts-Krankenhaus Eppendorf (UKE)**, a hospital origi-

St Johannis
Convent.

nally built between 1884 and 1889. A collection of pavilion-style buildings in a spacious park, UKE became a model for many other hospitals in Germany and abroad. It is still one of Germany's leading clinics.

Eppendorfer park, in front of the hospital, is actually the only park in the district which was established by the municipal authorities.

But now back to **Eppendorfer Landstrasse**, where the urbanisation of Eppendorf began in the first half of the 19th century. The small houses built in those years were demolished from 1880 onwards to make way for the now characteristic apartment houses built for Hamburg's *haute bourgeoisie*. A few demographic statistics show the speed with which Eppendorf developed; in 1811 Eppendorf had only 708 inhabitants; but by 1900, six years after it officially became a district of Hamburg, the population had shot up to 29,200.

What are probably the most beautiful apartment houses are located between Eppendorfer Landstrasse and the railway. Even their courtyards have got quality, a fact illustrated by the terraced housing built on **Schrammsweg** around the turn of the century. A masterpiece of this architectural genre is the art nouveau building at **Eppendorfer Landstrasse 98** where richly decorated four-storey houses are grouped around a courtyard.

Splendid villas: On the other side of the railway, between Isebekkanal and the Alster, Eppendorf's villa district was erected on what used to be the village meadow. The buildings in **Heilwigstrasse** are particularly elegant but their true charm is only revealed to anyone who takes a boating trip along the canals. This desirable residential area was opened up with the building of **Kellinghusenstrasse Station** in 1912. Its architectural counterpart on the opposite side of Goernstrasse is found in the redbrick swimming baths, one of Fritz Schumacher's many contributions to Hamburg's cityscape.

Now integrated and totally revamped

Brahms-Stuben on Ludolfstrasse.

inside, **Holthusenbad** (as it is properly known) is one of Hamburg's finest swimming baths. Across the road is Kellinghusen park.

In the old days Eppendorf was full of garden cafés and dance halls, with a particularly high concentration at the junction of Eppendorfer Baum and Eppendorfer Landstrasse. The place where Al Jarreau began his career and Udo Lindenberg came to fame, **Onkel Pö** on Lehmweg, has long since gone but Eppendorf is still an excellent place for a pub crawl.

Terraced housing: Almost idyllically located at the heart of Hamburg, **Falkenried** is Hamburg's largest collection of terraced houses. Originally, this small estate to the west of Lehmweg was built for workers and their families. Now it is the home of a wide variety of people – young and old, drop-outs and *petit bourgeoisie*. The flats in these three-storey terraced houses are cheap, tiny and pretty much in need of repair. But they have nothing in common with dark,

dreary and badly ventilated slum buildings. Anyone who has strolled through the narrow car-free precincts between the terraces and taken note of the Mediterranean-like lifestyle of their inhabitants will see why residents fought so fiercely against plans to have the houses demolished.

Eimsbüttel: The recent history of Eimsbüttel, south-west of Eppendorf and west of the Alster, has been completely different from that of its neighbouring district. However, things began in a similar fashion. The first historical record of the little village beyond the gates of Hamburg was in 1275.

In 1339 those self-same nuns from Herwardeshude convent bought the entire village along with all the buildings, cattle and serfs for the grand sum of 300 pieces of silver. In 1830 it was sold to Hamburg. In 1874 it became a suburb and in 1894 an official district.

In the 17th and 18th centuries wealthy Hamburgers began to build their country residences outside the city walls.

Restaurant in Holthusen swimming baths.

Eimsbüttel, too, had its proud-looking houses with well cared-for gardens and parks. But only street names such as Alardusstrasse, Doormannsweg, Lappenbergsallee, Lastropsweg and Lutterothstrasse remain to remind us of that period; at the turn of the year 1813–14 French troops burnt down Eimsbüttel to open up a clear field of fire on Hamburg's Sternschanze. The only building to survive was a top-class inn known as Heuhof. It was saved because the French appreciated its excellent cuisine and well-stocked cellar.

Pretty Marianne: When Napoleon's troops left, Eimsbüttel made a name for itself as a destination for day-trippers. The most famous inn belonged to a certain "pretty Marianne", whose reputation drew men from near and far to Eimsbüttel. Such crowds arrived that the police had to hold back the masses. Even Heinrich Heine enthused about her and went as far as to erect a literary monument to her in his book *Memoiren des Herren von Schnabelewopski*.

Just as in Eppendorf, the abolition of the ban on settling beyond the city gates at the end of 1860 brought about Eimsbüttel's change from rural village to metropolitan district. Whereas it was mainly the middle classes who settled in Eppendorf, many working-class families moved to Eimsbüttel from 1870 onwards. They had been driven out of their traditional areas by the construction of Hamburg's Free Port and the demolition of the much-decried Gängeviertel slums.

Hovels and villas: The first urban housing was erected in the southern part of **Schanzenviertel** between Kleiner Schäferkamp/Altonaer Strasse and Bellealliancestrasse. There was a noticeable contrast between the spaciously designed front apartment houses for wealthy tenants and the simple backyard housing with tiny, dark flats for working-class families.

The schizophrenic character of this housing is best seen in **Weidenallee 22–30**, built in 1881. Behind the splendid

Eimsbüttel, with the Planetarium in the far distance.

town villas there is a four-storey backyard block of housing where little daylight can penetrate. During a second building boom around the turn of the century, the speculators and sharks had a field day here. More and more houses (and people) were crammed into smaller and smaller spaces. But instead of basement housing in backyards, fortunately banned from 1882 onwards, there were workshops for skilled craftsmen or small factories.

Weidenallee 6–12 is a good example of Eimsbüttel's typical mixture of residential and industrial buildings. Behind the two posh art nouveau apartment houses there are terraced houses with small front gardens and a factory. Now the factory has been converted into studios with the ground floor occupied by the **Künstlerhaus** with its regular programme of art exhibitions.

From Schanzenviertel the late 19th-century urbanisation of Eimsbüttel spread out in a northerly and northwesterly direction. Apartment houses were built between Eichenstrasse and Eimsbütteler Marktplatz, once the heart of the old village, but most were destroyed during World War II. Though a district with little industry, 50 percent of Eimsbüttel's houses were destroyed.

After the war, 25 million bricks and 4,000 tonnes of scrap and pieces of iron were collected at Eimsbütteler Marktplatz for use in rebuilding. By 1951 Eimsbüttel was completely free of ruins, the first district in Hamburg to be so. All the rubble was taken to a site between Volkspark and Eidelstedt cemetery, so the fans of Hamburg's leading football club, HSV, now watch their team on the remains of prewar Eimsbüttel.

The fact that HSV now plays on such foundations is particularly ironical in view of Eimsbüttel's prewar prowess in German football. The **Victoria ground** (Lokstedter Steindamm 87) was the venue for four international fixtures between 1907 and 1923. Cup finals and political rallies were held here. When Hitler spoke during the 1932 election

Men talking in Eimsbüttel.

campaign, policemen with machine guns sat on surrounding roofs. The ground is still one of the prettiest in Hamburg but the days when crowds of 35,000 came to HSV-St Pauli games (in the 1947–48 season) are definitely over.

Since World War II, functional post-war architecture has dominated though there are still some streets with late 19th-century charm – for example **Emilienstrasse**, in the part next to Wehbers Park. Nobody could claim this is true of **Osterstrasse**, however, Eimsbüttel's main shopping street, and the six-lane "motorway", otherwise known as **Fruchtallee**. Functional aspects were also the dominant influence when Eimsbüttel's largest communal building, **Hamburg-Haus** at Doormannsweg 12, was built in 1965.

The area between Eichenstrasse, Heussweg and Unnastrasse presents a completely different picture. Splendid-looking town houses and apartment blocks line the streets around the picturesque Eimsbütteler park. The most beautiful buildings are in **Otterbeks–allee** and **Am Weiher**. Hardly surprisingly, there are also some fine pubs and restaurants in the neighbourhood. **Café Strauss** with its beer garden (at the corner of Eichenstrasse and Heussweg) and **Maybach**, across the road, are two of the most fashionable places.

On the other side of the park, in Unnastrasse, the firm of Beiersdorf has its headquarters. Eimsbüttel's biggest employer has made a global name for itself with sticking plasters, cosmetics and medicines. When the chemist Paul Beiersdorf got a patent for "manufacturing coated plasters" in 1882, he could not, in his wildest dreams, have thought that his invention would one day be part of every first-aid box.

Generals' quarter: North-east of the Beiersdorf complex, there is another relatively well preserved area of late 19th-century housing known as the "generals' quarter" because all the streets were named after generals from the Bismarck era. The cobbled streets, old trees and nicely restored facades of the houses give the area its special flair.

Another sight worth seeing is the turn-of-the-century block of housing at **Hoheluftchaussee 95**. The inner courtyard contains an impressive factory building. In 1984 this former tobacco factory was turned into studios and offices with a popular pub and restaurant, appropriately known as **Factory**, on the ground floor.

The area between Isebekkanal and Schlankreye was developed at a relatively late stage of Eimsbüttel's urbanisation process. From the turn of the century onwards a number of municipal buildings such as **Emilie-Wüstenfeld-Gymnasium** (1919–23) and the ever-popular **Kaiser-Friedrich-Ufer open-air baths** (1934) were erected here.

Two particular attractions are located just outside Eimsbüttel: **Hagenbeck's Tierpark** (Hamburg's zoo) and, just opposite on Gazellenkamp, **NDR TV studios**. Visits to the latter can be arranged via the NDR press office.

The Herzog bar in Landstrasse.

HAGENBECK TIERPARK

Hamburg hasn't got a zoo, it's got Hagenbeck. Hagenbeck is different. It always has been. At a time when other zoos still kept their animals cooped up in cages, Hagenbeck's had well cared-for, spacious areas for them to live and move in. Here even the lions are not kept behind bars.

Hagenbeck is also different from most other zoos because it is a self-financing enterprise. It is run by a sixth-generation family firm which does not receive any state subsidies. The spacious areas in the Hamburg district of Stellingen, where 360 kinds of animals and birds now live, was bought by Carl Hagenbeck in 1907.

His Tierpark in downtown Neuer Pferdemarkt had become too small. The purchase of the Stellingen site and construction of the zoo cost millions, a vast sum which had to be financed solely from gate receipts.

Since then nothing has changed – a fact that shouldn't be forgotten when walking round the zoo. Consider the huge quantities of meat, fish and plants fed to the animals and birds day after day: a ton of hay and straw, 180 kilos (369 lbs) of fish, 130 kilos (286 lbs) of meat, 65 kilos (143 lbs) of fruit and vegetables and 350 kilos (771 lbs) of concentrated feedstuffs. Add to all this the cost of heating, lighting and wages and you have a daily bill of some DM 25,000.

Another special feature of Hagenbeck's, the cage-less enclosures, may not seem so surprising nowadays. But when the zoo was opened, this was indeed a revolutionary step. It was Carl Hagenbeck's idea to offer the animals a much more natural habitat, merely separated from the public by a ditch, moat, low wall or fence. Over a period of many years, he had very carefully studied the behaviour patterns and habits of his animals. He was thus able to determine how far they could leap or climb. Consequently, he was able to restrict their desire for unlimited movement by natural means. In 1896 he even got his "panorama" enclosures patented by the Imperial German patent office. They were unique in that there was a total absence of any restraining bars.

The whole story began with just six seals which the fishmonger Gottfried Clas Carl Hagenbeck put on show at St Pauli fish market in 1848. Four years later, the first live polar bear joined the seals. A flourishing trade in animals developed from these modest beginnings. In 1866 the fishmonger's son, Carl Hagenbeck, took over the business. Soon trappers were travelling the world to look for animals on Hagenbeck's orders.

The animals they caught found new homes individually or as entire menageries in the zoos of Europe and America. Hagenbeck himself went on exhibition tours, presenting his animals to delighted crowds. Later on, they were joined by Eskimos, Kalmucks and other representatives of "exotic" tribes for the amusement of astonished audiences.

You can still see documents and photos of what appears to modern eyes to be a rather disturbing spectacle in the bird house at Hagenbeck's. The last of these "Peoples' Shows" (as they were known then) took place in 1931.

Nowadays, Hagenbeck's chief concern is to keep the animals and birds in the most suitable conditions, i.e. the most natural habitat, for each particular species. The zoo's successes in breeding speak for themselves. Even animal-protection activists recognise the role which zoos now have to play in preserving threatened species.

If you really want to see everything Hagenbeck's has to offer, you'll need a whole day to get round. Even arriving at this zóo is a striking experience – entering the fine art nouveau gate with its famous elephant heads. You can easily lose track of time when watching Antje the walrus, now a famous mascot used for publicity purposes by north Germany's public broadcasting corporation (NDR).

At the elephants' enclosure, the beasts gracefully stretch their trunks towards the public's edible gifts. Coins (or even notes) are simply passed on, as quite inedible, to their keeper standing nearby. At feeding times, the Polar Panorama is also a great attraction, particularly for children, as sea-lions and seals perform acrobatics in return for a welcome meal of fish.

Hamburg has few attractions that are as popular with children as Hagenbeck's are.

HARVESTEHUDE AND ROTHERBAUM

Nowhere in Hamburg has more water or greenery. Harvestehude, Rotherbaum and Pöseldorf undoubtedly form one of the most beautiful urban residential landscapes anywhere in Germany. **Hamburg 13**, the district's postal code, is thus one of the city's finest and most desirable addresses. Anyone who can afford a home here, on the western shores of the Alster, benefits from one of the most prestigious middle-class residential areas in Hamburg.

The proximity to the city centre, a desirable location near the river, streets lined by splendid rows of trees and extensive gardens, the decorative facades of 100-year-old houses, a total absence of any industry or trade and the presence of Hamburg University are all dominant features of Hamburg 13.

Here you can stroll through the incomparably attractive villa landscape of Harvestehude on the Outer Alster, between the *haute bourgeois* apartment houses, villas and university institutes of Rotherbaum and through fashionable Pöseldorf; here you'll soon realise why Hamburg 13 has become the place where the city's slightly reserved patrician class prefers to live.

You'll also see why it has recently been infiltrated by yuppies and turned into the home of the lifestyle avant-garde, and why more and more publishing houses, doctors, lawyers, brokers, boutiques, art galleries and half a dozen advertising, photo and model agencies have settled in the area.

Pöseldorf: Not surprisingly, there are many Hamburgers (particularly those who cannot afford such a lifestyle) who do not have such positive feelings about Hamburg 13. If you want to get a concentrated dose of Pöseldorf, you only need to walk up **Milchstrasse** (between Harvestehuder Weg and Mittelweg): here are Jil Sander fashions, exquisite English-made men's clothes, restau-rants, interior design, antiques and, of course, beautiful people.

Estate agents, insurance companies and consulates have now taken over the urban palaces of bankers, merchants and shipping magnates whose gardens stretched right down to the water's edge up to World War II, and who liked to travel to their city-centre offices by Alster steamer. Hamburg has more consulates than any other city in the world apart from New York. This is hardly surprising. What better office site could one find than the lakeside Alsterufer and Harvestehuder Weg?

Architectural moods: When, around the turn of the century, Hamburgers were building their houses in what is now Hamburg 13, there was ample opportunity for every kind of taste, style and architectural mood. There are half-timbered houses next to neo-Renaissance buildings, neo-Classicist next to purest art nouveau, or modern designs next to neo-Gothic palaces. Many of the villas with their decorative Gothic facades or

Classicist plasterwork fronts were built during the first wave of settlement after the Great Fire of 1842 and the subsequent removal of the ban on the building of housing beyond the city walls at the end of 1860.

Some of these villas are semi-detached or form small, exclusive terraces. There are entire streets of late 19th-century houses built in the neo-Renaissance or neo-baroque style or turn-of-the-century homes in the art nouveau or *heimat* style (e.g. Heilwigstrasse, Hochallee, Feldbrunnenstrasse and Oberstrasse). Along **Alsterufer** and **Harvestehuder Weg** are magnificent mansions with opulent facade decorations and extensive gardens. Traditional and expressionist redbrick buildings are along Alsterufer, Sophienterrasse and Fontenay. In the late 1960s the facades of many of these 19th-century houses were lovingly restored and delightfully painted – some white, others quite colourful.

Harvestehuder Weg: This is still Hamburg 13's finest showpiece street with many remarkable houses: Nos. 5 and 6 in the English Castellated Gothic style, or the neo-Renaissance Nos. 7a and 8. Nos. 12 and 14 were built by Rathaus architect Martin Haller. No. 12, known as the **Budge Palais**, is particularly worth seeing. It was built for the banker Henry Budge (1840–1928), who made his fortune in America.

The most magnificent part of the Palais, the **Hall of Mirrors**, had to move to make way for extensions to the College of Music (now resident here), but it was reconstructed in the Museum für Kunst und Gewerbe in 1987. The Palais had one less than reputable past occupant: in 1937 it became the official residence of Nazi *gauleiter* (district officer) Karl Kaufmann.

Another villa built in 1878 by Martin Haller (No. 41) now houses the publishers **Hoffmann & Campe**. In 1963 a plaque commemorating the poet and writer Heinrich Heine, whose works were published by Campe, was placed **Map of Harvestehude and Rotherbaum.**

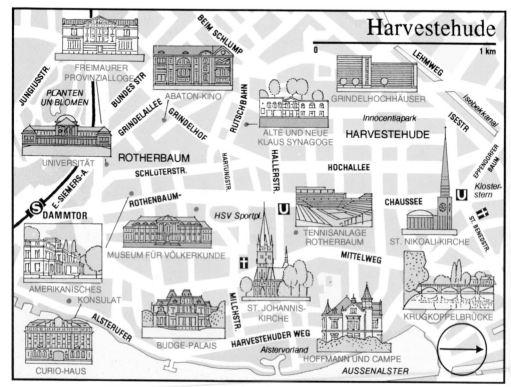

184

in front of this house. The plaque was originally located at the publishers' old building in the city centre.

The Anglo-German Club opposite has long been characterised by its traditional exclusive British atmosphere. Women, for example, are not allowed onto the premises before 6 pm.

Two villas further up the road from the Hoffman & Campe building is a redbrick house designed and erected in 1928 by the Bauhaus architect Emil Fahrenkamp.

On the opposite side of the road, to the north of Krugkoppelbrücke, is the **Eichenpark** on the banks of the Alster. This was Friedrich von Hagedorn's favourite place and a bronze statue commemorates the poet (1708–54) who enthusiastically praised the landscape of Harvestehude in his ode of the same name: "Here in vaulted airs, the sun rises most pleasantly, and smiles on the flowery paths and looks with delight on the Alster's course." Hagedorn could even have written these lines today –

Magnificent mansion on Alsterufer.

especially at **Bobby Reich**, opposite his favourite park.

From the pontoon patio of the restaurant and landing stage, always crowded in the summer months, there's a magnificent panorama view of almost all the Alster with the towers of Hamburg's city centre reaching skywards in the distance. The neighbouring **Krugkoppelbrücke**, a splendidly restored redbrick and reinforced-concrete construction with three arches, is the work of Fritz Schumacher and Gustav Leo (1927–28).

Between **Rothenbaumchaussee** and **Mittelweg** many university institutes, lawyers' offices and galleries are now housed in the tall apartment houses. In pre-war days, Jews liked to live here but now doctors and lawyers have taken their place. In the terraced courtyards between Rothenbaumchaussee (101– 103 and 71–73) and in Schlüterstasse (82–84) where once the craftsmen and messengers lived, there are now university lecturers, students and writers.

The most striking building is **Curio-Haus**, erected in 1910–11 for the oldest German teachers' association (Rothenbaumchaussee 13–15). Now it is the head office of the Hamburg branch of the German teachers' union. The house was named after the man who founded the original association, Johannes Carl Daniel Curio, and became the venue of legendary Hamburg artists' parties in prewar days. Up to 1950 it was also where the "Curio Haus trials" were held, a tribunal on the Nazi crimes committed in Hamburg.

Further up the road (No. 64) you cannot miss the monumental **Museum für Völkerkunde** (Ethnological Museum). It was erected in 1907–11, designed by Albert Erbe, financed by Hamburg merchants and filled with exhibits collected by its director Georg Thilenus (1868–1939). His motto was quite simple: "The whole world under one roof". The exhibits include the costumes, everyday articles, arts and crafts of peoples all over the world: from Eskimo kayaks to a Maori assembly house from New Zealand. The entrance hall and the great hall are art nouveau masterpieces.

Jewish Hamburg: No. 38 Rothenbaumchaussee served as an office for Hamburg's Jewish community from 1916 onwards but it was taken over by the Gestapo in 1939. It was here that the persecution and extermination of Hamburg's Jews was systematically planned. In Oberstrasse 116–120 the architects Felix Ascher and Robert Friedmann designed the new **Temple Synagogue** in 1930–31. It was considered to be one of the most modern and impressive ecclesiastical buildings constructed during the Weimar period, with room for 1,200 worshippers. Only the cost of its destruction saved it from the same fate as many synagogues destroyed by the Nazis.

The school and young people's rooms were located at the back of the synagogue. The seven-branched candlestick or minorah of the temple is represented in the front window. Recently, the Hebrew inscription was uncovered: "My house shall be called a house of prayer for all peoples" (*Isaiah 56.7*). After the war the building was extended to serve as a concert and broadcasting hall for the Northwest German Broadcasting Corporation (NWDR). Now its successor, NDR, stages highly-regarded concerts in the former synagogue. The memorial on the outdoor flight of stairs was designed by Doris Waschk-Balz and erected on 9 November 1983 to commemorate the desecration of the synagogues in the Third Reich.

Further up Rothenbaumchaussee is **Hamburger SV's** traditional football ground. This was where the renowned team played its home games up to the introduction of the national Bundesliga in 1963. Now only the HSV amateurs play here.

Tennis is the game next door. With Steffi Graf and Boris Becker heading a tennis boom in Germany, the Rother-

The Rotherbaum tennis court, where Boris Becker plays.

baum courts needed to be extended and modernised to stage the German Open. Now the days when back-row spectators had to stand on tip-toe to see anything are definitely over. The annual championships attract record crowds and takings year after year.

At the top end of Rothenbaumchaussee, at the roundabout known as **Klosterstern**, stands the excellently restored underground station of the same name. The entrance with its red-brick columns and copper-covered roof leads down to the 1930 station designed by Walter Puritz.

The next exit from the roundabout, itself encircled by magnificent apartment houses, leads to the Lutheran church of **St Nikolai** on Harvestehuder Weg. It was designed by Gerhard Langmaack and built in 1960–62. An Oskar Kokoschka mosaic has adorned the bright, asymmetrical interior of the church since 1974. The crucifix on the altar and the bronze reliefs on the pulpit are the work of Fritz Fleer. There are more striking examples of haute bourgeois housing in the neighbouring Abteistrasse and Nonnenstieg.

The geographical centre of Harvestehude and Rothenbaum is in Heimhuder Strasse: the neo-Gothic church of **St Johannis** designed by Wilhelm Hausers and erected between 1880 and 1882. One modern idea included in the church was the extension of a transept to form a main room. On the north side there is a replica of Giovanni da Bologna's famous *Scourging of Christ*.

Ballin's villa: At the top end of Feldbrunnenstrasse (No. 58), the architects Werner Lundt and Georg Kallmorgen had the splendid **Ballin Villa** built in 1908–09 for Albert Ballin (1857–1918), the then director of HAPAG, the Hamburg cargo line Amerika-Packetfahrt-Aktiengesellschaft. However, with his life's work ruined by World War I, this Jewish shipping magnate and friend of the Kaiser committed suicide in mysterious circumstances.

The exterior of the villa with its clas-

Grindelberg high-risers, the first such blocks in Germany.

sical columns is a good example of turn-of-the-century reformist architecture. After World War II, Hamburg's arts department was housed here for some years but since 1978 it has been the seat of the UNESCO Institute for Pedagogics (the theory of teaching).

University and Grindelhof: Within sight of the copper-covered cupola of the main building of the **University** you can see Hamburg's oldest statue (1802). It commemorates a mathematician and scientist, Johann Georg Büsch (1728–1800), who was one of the founders of the Patriotische Gesellschaft.

In 1919 Hamburg's parliament decided to turn the Hamburg Colonial Institute, established in 1908, into a university – even though Hamburg's mercantile community still felt that commercial training was infinitely preferable to academic study.

The **General Lecture Hall** on Edmund-Siemers-Allee was erected in 1909–11 and presented to the city by the Hamburg merchant after whom the road was named. The technically avant-garde building is a monolithic reinforced concrete construction. At the side door to the entrance hall there is a bust of Senator Werner von Melle, a man who did much to promote research and science in Hamburg. The present bust is a rough copy of the Friedrich Wild original which was destroyed in 1977. The actual campus is behind the old Lecture Hall along Moorweiden-strasse and Schlüterstrasse. Some 40,000 students crowd into the lecture halls and faculties scattered around this neighbourhood.

The building in which the Frei-maurer-Provinzialloge Niedersachsen is housed in Moorweidenstrasse was erected in 1907–09. Its temple-like facade is similar to some of the oldest, and long demolished, freemasons' buildings in Hamburg.

Between Moorweidenstrasse and Edmund-Siemers-Allee the **Square of the Jewish Deportees** commemorates the place where the first deportees, over

Lunch break on the Outer Alster.

188

3,000 Hamburg Jews, were rounded up from October to December 1941 for deportation to Riga, Lodz and Minsk. In 1983 a monument designed by Ulrich Rückrien was erected to commemorate this event. On the way to the campus is the **Dammtor Palais**, a beautiful red-brick corner house erected in 1910–12 and now famous for its basement **Heinrich-Heine-Treff**, one of the most important literary clubs in Hamburg since the early 1980s.

The campus area: This student quarter, with its innumerable pubs and restaurants, bookshops and libraries, was almost moved to Gross Borstel in 1929 and again to Othmarschen in 1937. But in the postwar year the campus was modernised and extended with the Studentenhaus, the Auditorium Maximum (1957–59), the Philosophenturm (1957–62) and the Rechtshaus all completed. The Carl von Ossietzky State and University Library was rebuilt in 1980–82.

The first university building to be added to the one of Edmund-Siemers-Allee was actually a converted stables (Allendeplatz 1–3). Built in 1908 for 400 horses and 100 carriages (and reputed to have been Europe's largest luxury horse-and-carriage business), it was taken over for university purposes in 1929. It was here that the philosopher Ernst Cassirer and the psychologist William Stern held their lectures. Both were driven into exile by the Nazis. Frescoes by Constantin Hahm (1986) painted along the stairs of the building illustrate its eventful history.

In 1970 Hamburg's first cinema, **Abaton-Kino**, opened in the old garage later installed in what was the stables. With different films screened every night, Abaton has become a kind of institution in this area. It has even featured premieres of films by star directors such as Rainer Werner Fassbinder, Werner Herzog, Hans-Jürgen Syberberg and Wim Wenders.

In front of the stables there used to be the large **Bornplatz synagogue**, de-

Grindelhof has a large student population.

signed by Ernst Friedheim and Semmy Engel, erected in 1904–06 and then pulled down in 1939. A Hamburg art teacher, Margrit Kahl, has marked the ground plan of the synagogue with metal strips on an inlaid paved base. In 1989 the square where the synagogue stood was renamed Joseph-Carlebach-Platz after Hamburg's last chief rabbi, who was murdered in Jungfernhof concentration camp near Riga.

Next to the square, at Grindelhof 30, is the building which used to house the Talmud-Tora-Realschule, an Ernst Friedheim building erected in 1909–11. It was an Orthodox Jewish school that gained a reputation well beyond Hamburg's borders. Nowadays, the college of librarianship is housed here.

Students, writers and people young and old now live in the quiet side streets of this former Jewish quarter and photographers, bookshops and restaurants have set up their businesses here. Grindelhof leads into Hartungstrasse where a small but famous Hamburg theatre, **Kammerspiele**, is located. It chiefly owes its fame to Ida Ehre, for many years the leading light.

This was where Wolfgang Borchert's famous anti-war play, *Draussen vor der Tür*, a dramatic story of returning "war heroes", had its premiere on 21 November 1947. Its building, which has its own long history, was constructed by a merchant known as Pfennig at the end of the 19th century. In 1904 it was sold to the Henry Jones Lodge of Jewish Freemasons. It also housed the Society for Jewish Ethnology and the Logenheim charity.

In 1930 the building was sold to the Anthroposophical Society. When the latter was banned in 1935, it was taken over by the Jewish Cultural Federation and subsequently renovated. From 1934 to 1941 the Hamburg branch of the Cultural Federation worked here and the building's dramatic tradition began with a performance of Shakespeare's *Romeo and Juliet*.

Not far from the theatre, at Rutschbahn 11a, there was another Jewish place of worship which Semmy Engel had built in a backyard in 1905. It was known as the **Alte und Neue Klaus Synagogue** and was basically square with three axes, a rectangular extension for the Holy Shrine on the east side and a transverse entrance hall on the west. In 1910 a lecture hall was added on the west side. This synagogue had 140 seats for men and a further 40 barred seats for women. Nowadays, the building is used as business premises.

High-risers: Further to the north lies **Grindelberg**, a district that was badly damaged by bombing raids in World War II. The first high-rise flats in postwar Germany were built here – 12 blocks, each between 8 and 14 storeys, covered in pale bricks. They were actually designed in 1946 for the British occupation troops and completed in 1956. The grassy areas between them were purposely made into a traffic-free zone and several statues were erected here in 1956–58.

Abaton-Kino, Hamburg's first cinema.

JEWS IN HAMBURG

The history of Jews in Hamburg begins in the late 16th century when Sephardim, Jews of Spanish or Portuguese descent, were expelled from the Iberian Peninsular and made their way to Hamburg via the Netherlands. They settled down in the city to work as merchants, brokers, shipbuilders, ship owners or doctors.

In terms of their religious rites, language and social status, these Sephardim were very different from the German-speaking Jews, known as Ashkenazim, who arrived in Hamburg somewhat later. In fact the Sephardim represented a kind of imported economic elite who, as a self-confident religious and social minority, provided an additional stimulus to Hamburg's existing trade. With over 40 subscribers they were also among those who founded the Hamburg Bank in 1619, one of the first clearing banks in Europe along with those in Venice and Amsterdam.

Despite the key role they played in Hamburg's success, the terms under which the Sephardim were permitted to live in the city deteriorated to such an extent towards the end of the 17th century that most left Hamburg for Holland or Altona.

Not many buildings were erected by Hamburg's Portuguese Jews and, apart from the Königstrasse cemetery in Altona, hardly any have survived. The stones of over 2,000 graves in the cemetery are placed horizontally, in contrast to those of the Ashkenazim. It was not until 1854–55 that support from Sephardim outside Hamburg enabled a new Sephardim synagogue to be built (Markusstrasse 36–38). It was held in high esteem for its architecture and excellent acoustics.

Hamburg seems to have forgotten its Portuguese Jews. No street, no square and no memorial commemorate great Sephardim such as the gynaecologist Rodrigo de Castro whose books *De universa mulierum morbuorum medicina* (published in Hamburg in 1603) and *Medicus politicus* (Hamburg 1614) were many years ahead of their time and are still worth reading nowadays.

The German-speaking Jews known as Ashkenazim came to Hamburg from Westphalia and Hannover at about the same time as the Portuguese Sephardim. They settled in the Imperial Free City of Hamburg and in the neighbouring cities of Wandsbek and Altona where religious freedom was guaranteed. During the 18th century their numbers gradually increased. They administered their own affairs and exercised their own justice in internal and ceremonial matters. Their relations with the senate had been put on an orderly footing by the Jewish Regulations of 1710.

Around 1800 there were some 6,500 Jews in the city. Relatively speaking, Hamburg had the biggest Jewish population in Germany (6 percent of the city's population).

During the first half of the 19th century, the Jews' demands for equal status before the law and social recognition began to meet with success. Jews were accepted as pupils at Johanneum Grammar School and Akademisches Gymnasium. Jewish schools were established (Talmud-Tora-Schule in 1805 and Israelitische Stiftungsschule in 1815). An important step towards social acceptance was the Synagogue Reform of 1817 which led to the establishment of the Temple Association.

Men such as Gabriel Riesser, Isaac Wolffson, Isaac Bernays, Anton Rée, Salomon Heine, Salomon Ludwig Steinheim and Albert Ballin became famous in the fields of business, politics or the arts.

In 1931 Hamburg had 20,000 Jews among its 1.2 million inhabitants – the fourth-largest Jewish community in Germany after Berlin, Frankfurt and Breslau. In Altona 5,000 of the 190,000 inhabitants were Jews. But the post-1933 anti-Semitic measures which culminated in the desecration of synagogues and destruction of Jewish shops in November 1938 prompted many to leave. Of the 8,400 who were still in the city in 1939, 7,000 were murdered in the Nazis' extermination camps. Another 1,000 were deported to the gas chambers from European countries occupied by Germany.

Today the Jewish community in Hamburg is made up of some 1,500 members. Their spiritual home is the synagogue consecrated in 1960 at the corner of Hohe Weide and Heymannstrasse.

WINTERHUDE AND ALSTERDORF

In 1833 the author of a guide to the north German province of Holstein described how his party "left Alsterdorf to our right and hurried on to the heights on the slopes of which, to the right of the Alster, the laughing village of Winterhude is located."

This "laughing village" on the north east shore of the Alster has grown somewhat since then. In fact, little of old Winterhude is now visible. On the fields where farmers once worked for Harvestehude monastery there are now villas and residential homes, with highlights such as the architecturally progressive Jarrestadt, the less avant-garde offices of City Nord, Hamburg's ever-popular Stadtpark with its Planetarium, some of architect Fritz Schumacher's most beautiful school buildings (Johanneum, Meerweinstrasse and the former Lichtwarksschule) and the mecca of modern drama fans, Kampnagelfabrik.

When Hamburg lifted the ban on settlement outside the city gates at the turn of the year 1860–61, many prosperous citizens bought land from farmers for speculative purposes. Two decades later, Winterhude became one of Hamburg's most desirable residential areas and also one of its most flourishing industrial suburbs. Around the turn of the century, its population rose dramatically: 3,200 inhabitants in 1880, 11,000 in 1894, 33,000 in 1920 and some 50,000 in 1991.

The new residents naturally needed housing and so roads were built between 1895 and 1920. Adolf Sierich, then the most important property owner in Winterhude, took the opportunity to name numerous new roads after members of his family: Sierichstrasse, Maria-Louisen-Strasse (his first wife), Clärchenstrasse (his second wife), Dorotheenstrasse (his mother), Agnesstrasse (his second wife's sister) and Willistrasse (the son of his second marriage). A whole area of apartment blocks and splendid town houses was built along the new roads. Their art nouveau facades still dominate the cityscape.

The hub for traffic passing through is the recently redesigned **Winterhuder Marktplatz**. This was a controversial plan which has not been particularly successful – hardly surprising, considering the volume of traffic. The buildings surrounding the square were mostly built in the 1920s.

Along the Alster: Approaching from Eppendorf, a bridge over the Alster marks the beginnings of Winterhude. Up to World War I, the Alster to the north of this bridge was just a dreamy little stream with marshy banks reaching as far as Eppendorfer moor. Alster steamers sailed no farther than here.

From 1865 onwards **Winterhuder Fährhaus** became an extremely popular place for days out. In fact, it was never the ferry house that its name suggests because Alster steamers did not actually stop at the bridge. After the war, congresses, parties, balls and masquerades were celebrated at the Fährhaus. In later years it became a popular spot for young people to meet.

Nearly a century after it was built, the Fährhaus began to decay badly in the 1970s. With part of the building damaged by arson in 1977, the municipal authorities had the partly derelict building pulled down on 6 August 1979 – in the face of vociferous protests by numerous fans of the old building. Between 1986 and 1988 new buildings were erected on the site with apartments and offices and a new pedestrian bridge over the Alster.

A theatre, **Komödie im Winterhuder Fährhaus**, aims to re-restablish old traditions here with a programme of light dramatic entertainment. The matinees with poets' readings and concerts are particularly popular. After a performance, guests meet up in **Dell'Arco**, the theatre restaurant, or one of the two Italian restaurants in

Preceding pages: in the Stadtpark. **Left**, Leinpfad on the Alster: one of Hamburg's prettiest streets.

Hudtwalckerstrasse, **Fra Diavolo** and **Bologna**.

Famous street: Opposite the theatre is one of Hamburg's prettiest and finest streets, **Leinpfad**. Its name is derived from the fact that in the 19th century it was from this riverside path that barges were pulled up the Alster on lines. In the days when Alster steamers still stopped along Leinpfad, Hamburg businessmen could even reach their city-centre offices by boat.

Some of Hamburg's most famous contemporary personalities live in the expensive villas along Leinpfad: Gert Bucerius, publisher of *Die Zeit*, Rudolf Augstein, publisher of *Der Spiegel* and ex-Mayor Klaus von Dohnanyi. Some of these fine buildings have been turned into apartment houses or simply pulled down. There are more villas in neighbouring Agnesstrasse, Willistrasse and Bebelallee.

Not far from Winterhuder Marktplatz are several streets where individual houses represent important chapters in Hamburg's architectural history: Hudtwalckerstrasse 24–30 (Johannes Hansen, 1928–29), Olsdorfer Strasse 2–6 (built by Fritz Höger, the Chilehaus architect, in 1927–28) and Winterhuder Marktplatz 10 (Heinz Esselmann and Max Gerntke, 1927–28).

In Ulmenstrasse 23–27, 33–35 and 48 there are the so-called **bleachers' houses**, bungalow-style working-class apartment houses built in the 19th century. As the name suggests, Hamburg liked to have its clothes washed and bleached in Winterhude.

Homes for the poor: Middle-class Winterhude is also characterised by numerous residential blocks in which citizens in need or low-income families were able to live for a reasonable cost. Such homes have a long tradition in Hamburg but the buildings which shape the face of Winterhude today were mostly built this century.

The plans for the Winterhuder **Stifte** (as these residential blocks are called in German) between Braamkamp and

The Winterhuder Fährhaus, popular meeting place.

Ohlsdorfer Strasse were drawn up by Fritz Schumacher in 1922. He consciously chose a site near the Stadtpark. Some of the blocks are well worth a particular mention: Georg Buchecker Stift (Ohlsdorfer Strasse 53–55), the Detaillisten Kammer Parkheim (Baumkamp and Bussestrasse), the Stift in Baumkamp 81–97, Braamkamp 48–76, Efeuweg/Fiefstücken, Jacobi-Stift (Beim Jacobistift 6), Hamburger Heim (Krochmannstrasse 41–45) and Senator-Erich-Soltow-Stift (Krochmannstrasse 47).

Stadtpark: Going northwards from Winterhuder Marktplatz, you come to one of Hamburg's two most important green belts: one is the Stadtpark, and the other one is Europe's biggest cemetery, Ohlsdorfer Friedhof.

Meadows and woods, a water tower, a large playing area, an open-air stage, a lake, children's playgrounds and a bird sanctuary: the **Stadtpark** has them all. Over one mile long and half a mile wide, it is almost the same size as the Outer Alster. At weekends, thousands of Hamburgers stroll, jog, fly kites, flirt, play football, sail little boats, play rugby, train for American football, play with frisbees and boomerangs or have a go at mini-golf in the park. And if people in the neighbouring streets become aware of a considerable rise in the noise levels of not exactly idyllic Winterhude, it probably means that one of the regular open-air summer rock concerts is taking place in the park.

In 1901–02, the City of Hamburg bought the wooded land near Grasweg and Borgweg from Adolf Sierich, who used to hunt there. Between 1910 and 1914 Fritz Schumacher designed Hamburg's largest park, of 151 hectares (373 acres). Before working as a municipal architect in Hamburg, this much-travelled diplomat's son had studied England's most beautiful parks. His dream for the park was to create an "open-air house for the people" in which the urban masses could find relaxation and recreation at weekends.

Winterhuder Quay from Hayns Park.

Schumacher divided the land into smaller areas with functionally planned lanes and hedges. But unfortunately World War II destroyed the original concept. One of Hamburg's biggest flak defence units was located in the Stadtpark and so it was a natural target for bombs. Then the urgent postwar need for fuel was met by ruthlessly chopping down Stadtpark trees.

And so, in the 1950s, the Stadtpark was redesigned along more modern lines. The Stadthalle, where lectures and concerts had taken place, had been destroyed in the war and was not rebuilt.

Donations enabled remarkable sculptures to be erected all over the park: Arthur Bock's *Diana with Hounds* (1911) in the garden of the Brunnenhaus; two coquina sculptures by Georg Kolbe (1926–27) at the entrance to the largest playing area; *Diana with Hind* (1910) by Georg Wrba in the Dianagarten; and *The Bathing Woman* (*circa* 1870) by Reinhold Begas near the paddling pool. The fountain with its entertaining penguins was designed by August Gaul.

Seeing stars: If Hamburgers don't come to their Stadtpark for a bit of relaxation, they might well be intent on looking at stars – an attraction since 1930 when a **Planetarium** was established in what used to be a water tower. Up to 270 people can be seated in the domed building to enjoy the monthly programmes or one of the many special lectures. Nearly 20,000 visit the Planetarium each year. The projection dome is nearly 21 metres (68 ft) across, so large that the starry sky can be accurately projected on to it. The Planetarium has one of the world's most modern and versatile planetarium instruments, a Zeiss Model VI projector.

Visitors entering the Planetarium see a unique exhibit, the world's only cross-sectional planetarium instrument, illustrated and lit up to explain how such a complicated device actually works. The astronomy and astrology collection which art historian Aby Warburg cre-

Swans in Mühlenteich.

198

ated for the Planetarium was on view here until 1966, but now only some of those exhibits form part of the new exhibition.

The platform at the top of the 60-metre (196-ft) high water tower offers an interesting view of northern Hamburg. The building itself was renovated to mark the 60th anniversary of the Stadtpark and the fountains now function again.

Regional contrasts: To the north and south of the Stadtpark are two architecturally interesting areas. The park's northerly neighbourhood is dominated by the offices of **City Nord** where 40,000 people work by day; at night City Nord is a ghost town.

With office space becoming scarcer and scarcer in the city centre, Hamburg's chief architect in the 1960s, Werner Hebebrand, had the foresight to plan a new office district away from the centre. Hebebrand's conception saved Hamburg's virtually "unspoilt" city centre from the ravages of far-reaching,

and mostly negative, redevelopment.

The area to the north of the Stadtpark used to be the site of numerous small allotments before the heart of corporate Hamburg was transplanted to the 120-hectare (296-acre) site between Sengelmannstrasse, Hindenburgstrasse and the suburban railway station at Rubenkamp. The whole site was turned into an architectural showpiece with corporate headquarters vying for design honours.

The undoubted masterpiece is the **HEW** office (Überseering 12) which was designed by Arne Jacobsen and Otto Weitling in 1963–69. It is just one outstanding example of Danish architectural internationalism. The glass facades of the HEW headquarters reflect the glories (or otherwise) of their office neighbours.

Residential jewel: To the south of the Stadtpark is the residential district of **Jarrestadt**, a jewel in the town-planning history of municipal housing. With the chaotic conditions of Germany's industrialisation creating unexpected

Love-nest on the Osterbek Canal.

problems in the housing market, chief architect Fritz Schumacher came up with a visionary project. His idea was a radically new type of urban apartment-house estate, and to develop this idea he organised a town-planning competition in 1926.

With humane living conditions, children's playgrounds right next to the flats and benches in small parks for senior citizens, the area between Jarrestrasse, Semperstrasse and Grossheidestrasse and Glindweg was to become a model of modern urban housing.

Schumacher and Karl Schneider, a Bauhaus architect who died in exile in America in 1945, oversaw the work of several architects whose plans submitted in the competition had met with their approval. These ideas had one thing in common: cubically shaped redbrick buildings and horizontal windows – formal, functional architecture featuring four- or five-storey residential blocks which allowed lots of light and air into the apartments.

For many years, Germany's Social Democrats looked upon the Jarrestadt estate as a mirror of and means towards radical social change. In 1930 Meerweinstasse School, again the work of architect Schumacher, was opened in Jarrestadt, an example of progressive architecture and educational ideas. A local paper described it as "one of the most beautiful and modern schools in Hamburg, a so-called co-educational school for boys and girls... Light and air flood into this glass palace from all sides." Unfortunately, the Nazis were violently opposed to this "red hotbed of Winterhude" and terminated co-education in 1935.

Factory arts: On the eastern flank of Jarrestadt you cannot fail to notice a bunch of apparently derelict buildings which seem due for demolition. Signs of life, however, do brighten up the picture of decay. Hamburg, the cool, cosmopolitan capital of northern Germany, has a strange love for half-decaying remains of its industrial past as

Futuristic offices at City Nord.

in the legendary concert hall in Altona known simply as Die Fabrik; or the city-centre Deichtorhallen beautifully restored with a sponsor's money; or even in these Winterhude ex-factories known as **Kampnagel**.

The communist author Willi Bredel did his apprenticeship here, an experience he turned into a much-praised novel *Maschinenfabrik N & K* in 1930. Until 1968 Nagel & Kaemp manufactured iron cranes at this extensive site. After the company closed down, there were threats of demolition and redevelopment. But then in 1981, when Hamburg's main theatre, Deutsches Schauspielhaus, was being renovated and modernised, the stage was re-erected in one of the empty factories.

In 1982 an exhibition of working-class culture in Hamburg around 1930 was also staged at Kampnagel. Then Peter Brook produced *Carmen* here, and Thalia Theater staged Offenbach's *Ritter Blaubart*. To mark Rolf Liebermann's retirement after many years as

director of Hamburg Opera, his jazz opera *Cosmopolitan Greetings* was also staged at Kampnagelfabrik. From then on the arts centre has never looked back; drama groups, freelance artists, women's festivals, a circus, and even art exhibitions from the very official Kunsthalle have been established in this popular venue.

If Kampnagel is the temple of Hamburg's alternative muses, Winterhude's **Johanneum** grammar school is the establishment's place of learning. The list of former pupils contains the names of many Hamburg mayors and ministers. **Johannes Bugenhagen**, a friend and colleague of Luther's, after whom the school is named, played a decisive role in introducing the Reformation to Hamburg. He also helped found the school in 1529. In front of the present building (Maria-Lousien-Strasse 114) there is bronze statue of a boy. Created by Engelbert Peiffer in 1885, it was erected at this spot in 1929. The current building is on the third site: the school's

The villa splendour of Winterhude.

first home was in St Johannis monastery, and the second in the city-centre cathedral square (Domplatz).

Fritz Schumacher (who else?) gave the school its present three-winged building with entrance arcade in 1912–14. Although he designed 40 other school buildings for Hamburg, the Johanneum remained one of his favourites – and is also regarded as one of the most impressive examples of his skills. Famous former pupils include Heinrich Hertz, Harry Graf Keissler, Hjalmar Schacht, Hans Erich Nossak, Walter Jens and Ralph Giordano.

Not far away, in Graswed, was built what was then known as the **Lichtwark School**, which was again designed by Schumacher. But it was more the reformist educational concepts of young teachers and not the work of the architect which made this school's reputation in the interwar years.

Art and the arts were important subjects in the Lichtwark curriculum. Amongst its most famous former pupils are ex-chancellor Helmut Schmidt and his wife Loki. Both have often praised the progressive teaching they enjoyed at the Lichtwark school. The Schumacher building now houses Heinrich Hertz comprehensive.

The pupils attending these two schools still come from the catchment area along the Alster, and many of the more affluent are from the villas and fine town houses between Sierichstrasse and Leinpfad. These buildings are fine examples of the historical style of the late 19th century or the rural style of the Weimar Republic.

Grown-up village: The Holstein village of **Alsterdorf** was handed over to Hamburg by the Danes in 1803. It became a part of the city but was initially subject to the supervision of St Johannis monastery. Then in 1913 Alsterdorf became a fully-fledged district of Hamburg. Wilhelm Kaisen, Bremen's mayor from 1945 to 1965, grew up in Alsterdorf. In his memoirs entitled *My Work and Life*, he vividly describes his childhood in

Garden city residential area.

Alsterdorf during Kaiser Bill's rule. Of the many farmhouses still standing in those days, only one remains – at the corner of Rathenaustrasse and Alsterdorfer Damm.

The district is probably best known for its **Alsterdorfer Anstalten** (between Sengelmannstrasse and Alsterdorfer Strasse). This institution was established in 1860 by Pastor Heinrich Matthias Sengelmann because, as he said in his call for donations for its foundation, "Hamburg has not done anything for the poorest of the poor". Nowadays, the organisation continues to make a major contribution to social work throughout the city. The Alsterdorfer Anstalten's neo-Gothic redbrick church of **St Nicholas** (1889) is one surviving reminder of the age in which its work began.

After World War I, middle-class houses and rich bourgeois villas were built along the banks of the Alster and its canals. The river itself had been canalised in 1909 to prevent flooding.

One semi-detached pair of houses which was designed by Hermann Höger in **Brabandstrasse 1–2** is particularly worthy of mention since it successfully combines Expressionist and Gothic elements.

A further architectural highlight of Alsterdorf is the "garden-city" residential area (**Gartenstadt**) between Hindenburgstrasse, Sengelmannstrasse, Heilholtkamp and the railway. It was built in 1936–38 as a detached housing development with small gardens.

Not far away, there is a more modern development, typifying the best in modern urban housing. Between Brabandstrasse, Maienweg, Alsterkrugchaussee and Hindenburgstrasse is the Wolfgang Borchert estate, which was built in 1982–85.

Its name, that of Hamburg's distinguished anti-war poet and dramatist, and the names of its streets, all victims of the Nazi terror regime, is a clear reflection of the social democratic ideals of its founders.

Romantic picnic: flowers and wine.

UHLENHORST AND THE ALSTER

Standing at the corner of Hamburger Strasse and Winterhuder Weg in the shadow of the Mundsburg skyscrapers, having just emerged from the underground station, it's hard to identify what is usually described as "pretty" or even "splendid" about Uhlenhorst. It's fair to say that the district's beginnings are not very auspicious. The fact that postwar architectural monstrosities mark the outskirts is of little concern to true Uhlenhorsters, however, who know where the real attractions of this highly desirable residential area lie.

History: This north-eastern district between the Osterbek and Mundsburg canals, Winterhude and Eilbek, has a curious history for the simple reason that it has very little history at all. Around 1256 there is mention of a tiny place called Papenhude in this area but the only interesting feature was a mill for local farmers, and of course it was outside Hamburg's walls. When visitors to Hamburg hear the 164 hectare (360-acre) Alster lake described as the "most beautiful of Hamburg's ladies", very few of them will realise that this pretty stretch of water originally was anything but a lake.

The Alster is basically a small tributary of the Elbe. Both the Inner and Outer lakes are man-made. As early as 1200, the river flowing in from the north was dammed. In 1235 a miller had a larger dam constructed in order to catch the waters of the Alster after nearly 50 km (31 miles) of unrestricted meandering. In this way the Inner and Outer Alster were created over the centuries. And it is on the north-east banks of the Outer Alster that Uhlenhorst lies.

In the early 18th century Hamburg had a country house built for its guests on the Uhlenhorst estate it had leased, but it was not until after the Great Fire of 1842 that things began to liven up in this area. The water level of the Alster had been lowered by nearly 1 metre (3 ft) so that large parts of Uhlenhorst could be drained for development. But few people had the time or money to build houses some way outside the city walls. Uhlenhorst was still largely cornfields and meadows where cattle grazed and its farmers used the Alster to transport produce to Hamburg's markets.

Boomtown Uhlenhorst, which a syndicate bought up, didn't get going until the ban on settlement outside Hamburg's walls was lifted at the end of 1860. At last Hamburgers could go in and out of the city as and when they liked. Locks were built and the Alster was straightened out at several points to ensure that heavy rains did not automatically lead to flooding. With the conditions now good, a real exodus from the city began and within a few years the east bank of the Alster was populated.

Hamburg's "rococo poet" Friedrich von Hagedorn wrote about the Alster: "Elbe shipping makes us richer, the Alster teaches us to be social! The former fills our warehouses, on the latter foreign wine tastes good..." In his day Hamburg's social life was on the Inner Alster, especially along the noisy Jungfernstieg, the promenade along the water's edge. Soon, however, it moved out to the banks of the larger lake.

Schwanenwik and Feenteich (villages on the eastern shore of the Alster) did not possess any boulevards where the more prosperous folk could stroll up and down. But soon the leisured classes were enjoying themselves along the banks or laying out expansive lakeside gardens, preferably in the English tradition. Others came to the lake from further away for a day out on Sundays.

In those days the place to live was actually the west bank where Hamburg's long-established "good" families and wealthy upstarts had their homes in Harvestehude or Rotherbaum. Even as recently as the end of the 19th century, the "distinguished" families of the west bank still made sure that their sons and daughters did not flirt with someone from the "other side" where it was considered that the free-thinkers and some "lower classes" lived.

There was also a certain amount of jealousy evident when the west bankers eyed the overseas merchants on the east bank who had made their money from trade. But what kind of a lifestyle were the people of the east bank enjoying?

Whereas Pöseldorf on the west bank with its maze of small lanes was occasionally referred to as "Jigsaw-Village", the late 19th-century urbanisation of Uhlenhorst developed along very different lines: spacious streets, splendid villas with extensive gardens and turn-of-the-century or art nouveau-style apartment housing.

Almost all of this original structure has survived. The beauty of playful or aesthetically simple facades of houses such as Wikinger-Haus (Hofweg 7), Hofweg-Palais (Hofweg 51) or the Villa at the corner of Hofweg and Gustav-Freytag-Strasse, is mirrored in the apartments within – and not just in such exemplary streets as Hofweg or Schöne Aussicht.

Nowadays, Uhlenhorst is the address for people who aren't drawn to image-conscious areas such as Blankenese, Eppendorf or Pöseldorf – but these people have certainly got money! Although Uhlenhorst is part of "working-class" Barmbek in administrative terms, it is among the most expensive districts for housing or rented accommodation. Only Harvestehude, the estate agents say, is a bit dearer. In terms of property prices, Uhlenhorst has already overtaken such traditionally expensive areas as Othmarschen or Blankenese.

Outer Alster: When Hamburg's Ministry of Public Works sees fit to publish a brochure entitled *The Outer Alster – Development, Biology and Vegetation* to inform people of a conservation programme for the banks of the lake, nearly everyone in Hamburg knows what's behind it. The Alster is in trouble. Like

What's on offer at the Mühlen-kamper restaurant.

virtually every other lake or river affected by urban pollution and subjected to canalisation, which makes it even more slow-moving, the water quality of the Alster is deteriorating.

There has been a considerable drop in the variety of flora and, in particular, fauna in the river, with a resultant reduction in the self-purifying qualities of the water. After heavy rain, the combined sewers overflow and spew untreated sewage into the lake. The reeds growing on the edge of the lake used to protect the banks from erosion caused by waves from boats, but the weeds never lasted long. From the 1950s attempts were made to replant them and use this green fence to protect the flora and fauna from dogs and people. However, it was not until the late 1970s that the survival of these plants could be more assured.

This huge lake 2 metres (6 ft) deep, 1 km (0.6 miles) wide and 2.8 km (1.7 miles) long, with its surrounding greenery, is a unique recreation park, right in the middle of Hamburg. Yachtsmen, rowers and windsurfers compete on the water as joggers or cyclists go through their paces around its green circumference. Over 2,000 benches around the perimeter offer plenty of opportunity for a rest.

The Alster has always been used to transport people and produce. Now there are two railway lines tunnelling underneath it with the White Fleet steamers sailing across it. These popular boats, and the Alster swans, have one privilege in common; they enjoy right of way over leisure boats.

Swans have been kept on the Alster since medieval times. So as not to lose these valuable birds, strict laws were passed in the 17th century to ensure suitable punishment for anyone who "publicly annoyed this holy bird" or secretly stole one for the cooking pot. In the third largest German-speaking city after Vienna and Berlin, hunger was a constant companion, so stealing the swans was always a temptation.

Café Fiedler at Mühlenkamper Fährhaus.

Hamburg has long employed a paid swan-keeper with the job of breeding, feeding and caring for these protected birds. In late autumn he rounds up the swans before transporting them by boat to their winter quarters.

It is said that Hamburg is the only city in Europe, apart from London, to regard the royal swan as a sign of its patrician class. In 1953 Queen Elizabeth II kindly gave Hamburg two pairs of white swans from her own royal flock – a present which naturally delighted anglophile Hamburg. Now a considerable number of the swans on the Alster are descended from these British pairs.

The swans can't complain about a lack of water in the summer months. Hamburg has numerous canals and smaller lakes, a fact underlined by the city's proud claim to have more bridges – over 2,300 in all – than Venice. Ever since the east bank of the Alster was inhabited, visitors to Hamburg have enjoyed strolling through Uhlenhorst, praising the "most beautiful view in Germany". The American diplomat George F. Kennan was 86 years old when he confessed, in *Life Impressions*, to his secret love affair with this part of Hamburg: "How can you explain this attraction? I don't know the answer. But I profess to this part of the city as if to a goddess."

Beautiful views: Uhlenhorst's attractions on land are undiminished. The art scene is at **Atelier & Galerie auf der Uhlenhorst** (Averhoffstrasse 24). City sightseeing tours nearly always stop at Schöne Aussicht and at Feenteich admire the magnificent, late-classicist **Gästehaus des Senats** at No. 26 where the Queen of England and Charles de Gaulle have stayed. These tours may include a visit to the **Norddeutscher Regatta-Verein club house**, one of the oldest and most exclusive sailing clubs on the Alster (founded in 1868), or **Klipper Tennis and Hockey Club** where Hamburg's current mayor is said to swing a racquet from time to time.

Visitors can admire the exotic look-ing **Shiite-Iranian Mosque**, visit **Uhlenhorster Fährhaus** on the banks of the Alster or look enviously at the rows of magnificent apartment houses lining Hofweg or Papenhuder Strasse. There are Greek, Spanish, Chinese, Japanese, Caucasian or Indian restaurants but unfortunately, most unimaginative tourists usually end up eating at the beery, dreary **Friesenhof** at the corner of Winterhuder Weg and Hamburger Strasse.

Papenhuder Strasse offers plenty of evening entertainment with Hamburg's only real jazz cellar, **Dennis' Swing Club** (No. 25), the exquisite cuisine at **Rexrodt** (No. 35) or the jolly pub atmosphere opposite at Souterrain. Walking down Hofweg, some people spend most of their time gazing skywards. They are quite literally star-gazing, looking for Boris Becker's oft-quoted palatial penthouse apartment.

Boating on the Alster: A noticeable feature of Uhlenhorst is the many landing stages where various boat-hire firms

Goldbeker market.

offer their services. More than 200 boats of various shapes and sizes are available for hire. Then there are over 700 rowing boats and yachts belonging to the ten rowing and sailing clubs dotted around the Alster. Add to these the privately-owned watercraft and you end up with a splendid fleet moving to and fro across the lake. Where better to enjoy the view than from one of the spacious lakeside lawns or **Bobby Reich**, an overcrowded but highly popular landing-stage café at the northern end of the Outer Alster? And despite all that boating and pollution, an astonishing number of anglers are seated along the banks.

In fact, the conservation measures set in motion by the ministry of public works seem to be working. There are now said to be more than 20 different kinds of fish in the lake, including carp, pike, eel, bitterling, tench and even crayfish. They should by rights thrive in the three million cubic metres of dark brown water – coloured by the moors from which the Alster originates. Angling is permitted in the Alster providing you have got a licence to do so, but bathing is still forbidden. The last Alster swimming baths survived from 1846 until 1897 but for more than 80 years there has been a ban on (voluntary) bathing in the river.

The White Fleet: There are often more than 200,000 people around the Alster on the numerous warm sunny afternoons in Hamburg. Despite all rumours to the contrary, this is a drier place than, for example, Venice.

Many of these lakeside visitors enjoy a trip on one of the White Fleet steamers but have no idea of the boat fleet's chequered history. A merchant named Droege was so fed up with having to take a coach to get to Hamburg that he decided to charter a Rhine steamer for the Alster. But this boat's engine did not survive the trip via the North Sea and up the Elbe to Hamburg. Moreover, a leak caused it to sink in Hamburg harbour before even reaching the Alster.

Droege's second attempt failed as well, this time for the silliest of reasons. The paddle steamer he ordered was too wide to pass through the Alster locks! A ship's broker named Parrau came to the rescue and finally ensured that a boat suitable for the Alster and its locks reached Hamburg. The narrow, screw-driven *Alina* was a welcome addition to the city's transport fleet. But it was a long time before these steamers became less a method of getting to work and more a tourist attraction.

The Literature House: "I know no other area where a dead poet can lie there so well buried. But it's much more difficult to live there as a live one," complained Heinrich Heine while visiting Klopstock's grave in Ottensen. Since then, however, Hamburg has given the literary world, if not a home, at least a house. The house in question, the **Literaturhaus** in Uhlenhorst, sponsored by the Association of Publishers and Booksellers, is certainly splendid. After all, nothing should be too ex-

Fine houses, Papenhuder Strasse.

pensive for idealists – especially in Hamburg where it has been said that everything is lacking, except money. Thirty-two golden cherubs and a painting decorate the ceiling of the great hall of this Literaturhaus (Schwanenwik 38). Four million deutschmarks were spent on its renovation. The money was donated by one of Hamburg's media barons, Gerd Bucerius of *Die Zeit*, but his journalists are rarely seen within its walls. Only **Lit**, the literature centre, reminds visitors that this house could act as a meeting place for literary figures and not just for events about literature.

Should a writer visit the **Literaturhaus Café** in the hope of finding a contemplative place to pursue his calling, he'd more than likely flee for the nearby lakeside with his books or paper under his arm. The room has been wonderfully restored, having risen phoenix-like from the ashes of its former existence as a home for "fallen girls", but it has become exactly the opposite of what writers expected or hoped for: crowded with yuppies, coffee-drinking day-trippers, students and anyone who has read one of the many references to this café in the "where to go" press.

Munich, about to establish its own literary coffee house with the aim of bringing authors back to their coffee tables, needs no warning. The Munich-based newspaper *Süddeutsche Zeitung* has already got the gist of things: "The fact is that authors do not tend to sit around in beer-drinking surroundings to hear someone on the next table explaining how to play a certain suit at cards. They prefer quieter places.

"In fact, such a café does exist. There, authors can sit down without being bothered much. The rooms are magnificently decorated and the waiters suitably discreet. And not long ago the waiter used to bring pen and ink along with the coffee and a glass of water … All the rooms were pleasantly quiet."

Yes, there is such a place – but it is the Café Hungaria in Budapest.

So why not in Hamburg or Munich? As one critic put it, the Hamburg location is fundamentally flawed because "the interior (of the Literaturhaus) has the discreet charm of a draughty underground station and the hearty demeanour of the waitresses puts a premature end to any attempt to get nominated for a Nobel Prize."

Hamburg's literary circle can take heart from Gustav Wied, who passed on the following words of consolation to the editors of the Journalists' and Authors' Annual *Our Hamburg – For the Year 1911*: "Unfortunately, I am, as is well known, a satirist. But if I lived in Hamburg, I would be a lyric poet. Sailing across the Alster on a summer evening with the moon peeping out from behind St Mary's and thousands of glistening sparks of light reflected in the duskily veiled surface of the Alster is one of the most beautiful and poetic experiences one can have. Though naturally, even then, you need to keep your feet on the ground…"

Left, a place for discussion and **right**, for boating.

KONZERT - PROGRAMM

UHLENHORSTER FÄHRHAUS

RESTAURANT
SCHWEGLER
JNH. JOHS. SCHWEGLER

ALTONA

In earlier times, if you wanted to travel to Hamburg's western areas, you were on foreign soil as soon as you left St Pauli heading west. This, you see, was the border between Hamburg and Denmark, and Altona belonged to the Danish throne.

Danish town: In the late 16th and early 17th centuries Altona's economy enjoyed the patronage of the counts of Schauenburg. However, when Altona came under Danish rule, the King of Denmark tried to build it up into a serious rival for its more mighty neighbour, Hamburg. For a while this proved successful – much to the annoyance of the Hamburg "moneybags". The popular pronunciation of Altona, "All to nah" (all too near!), may well have its origins in this period.

The freedom of trade and religion enjoyed in Altona since Schauenburg days contributed to the immigration of Jews and various Protestant denominations, as well as of craftsmen who were prevented from settling in Hamburg itself by its strict guild laws.

Nowadays, you can still see evidence of this planned settlement of businesses at the far end of the Reeperbahn, an area that belonged to Altona in those times: **Grosse** and **Kleine Freiheit** are street names that refer to freedom of trade, not licentiousness, as you might suppose today. The Danes also introduced another kind of freedom in Altona – freedom from customs dues within the borders of the kingdom.

These three freedoms produced an economic upswing in Altona during the 18th and early 19th centuries that made the town the second-largest on Danish territory after Copenhagen. In 1800 Altona's merchant fleet was made up of 296 ships, a number Hamburg was only to reach some 45 years later.

There were several shifts of the customs frontier between Hamburg, Altona and **Ottensen** (Altona's suburb) during the 19th century. These alterations resulted in frequent changes in the concentration of industrialisation. But Altona was being transformed from a trading town into a city with a large working-class population, and the fact that housing was cheaper and the cost of living lower here than in Hamburg led to a rapid increase in the population.

It was not just the industrial working classes who appreciated Altona's advantages. Many people who worked in Hamburg commuted to work from homes in Altona, even though both belonged to different countries. As both cities expanded, the frontier between the two became less and less apparent. Altona's factories and working-class estates did not offer particularly good living conditions. The many cases of tuberculosis meant that the popular term for Ottensen became "Mottenburg" (moth-eaten) – because of the moths that were supposed to nest in sufferers' lungs. Not surprisingly, the new ideas of the socialist workers' movement found acceptance here and the town soon became known as "red Altona".

Nazi period: Today all that has changed. Red Altona, the factories and the concentrated working-class estates have disappeared. The Communist, Socialist and Social-Democratic organisations which dominated public life in Altona during the Weimar Republic were smashed by the Nazis when they took power, replacing the SPD that had ruled Altona city hall up to 1933. The often violent struggles between right- and left-wing forces reached a climax on 17 July 1932, Altona's Bloody Sunday, when 18 people died and over 60 were seriously injured.

In 1937 Altona lost its municipal independence when the Nazis' Greater Hamburg statute brought about an enforced incorporation. Hitler's plans for a model city of his new republic included a representative 250-metre (820-ft) high skyscraper on the banks of the Elbe in Altona. But they never got further than the drawing-board stage. Interestingly enough, the new tunnel under the Elbe takes almost exactly the same route as the huge bridge planned by Hitler's architects.

The oldest part of Altona, the Altstadt, was destroyed by World War II bombing, a fate shared by many neighbouring districts. You can still see the gaps in some otherwise intact streets.

Frontier town: Standing at the western end of the Reeperbahn, at **Nobistor**, it is hard to believe that late 19th-century three- and four-storey town houses were once the prevalent feature of the former border between Hamburg and Altona. Now you can only see them in old photos on view at Altona Museum. If you look west, with the Reeperbahn behind you, all you see of Altona are some skyscrapers and the roofs of buildings erected in the 1950s. This was the old frontier between Altona's Altstadt and Hamburg. In those days the way into the centre of the Altstadt led through narrow lanes to the station and the neighbouring district of Ottensen.

The present-day centre of Altona has shifted westwards away from the old Altstadt, a development which began with the erection of the first railway station on the site of what is now the Platz der Republik. A stroll from St Pauli to Altona does not offer much in the way of sightseeing delights. On the contrary, it is more of a lesson in how not to conduct urban redevelopment. It's better to start your trip round Altona and Ottensen from the railway station, the centre of modern Altona.

The only cultural monument in the area between Nobistor and Altona station is the old **Jewish cemetery** in Königstrasse where Heinrich Heine's father lies buried. However, it is not open to the public and some of the graves are in very poor condition.

The centre: The central axes of modern-day Altona are Neue Grosse Bergstrasse and its extension Ottenser Hauptstrasse on the one hand, and Max-

Map of Altona.

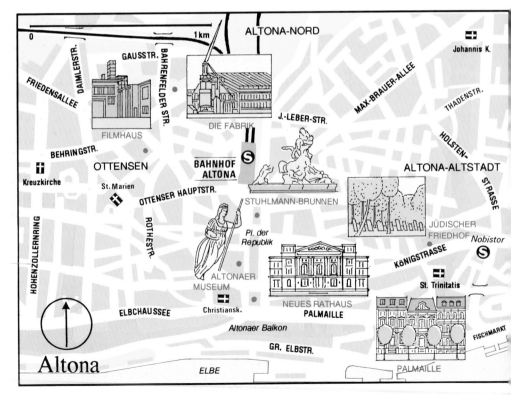

Brauer-Allee on the other. **Altona station** is at the junction of the two. This hub of underground, inter-city and suburban rail and bus traffic is a monstrosity which is still a thorn in the side of many older inhabitants of Altona.

South of the station there is a square with gardens, now known as **Platz der Republik** but once imperially named Kaiserplatz. A subway provides direct access to the square from the station. At the end of the subway, almost hidden from view by the subterranean site, there is the monumental **Stuhlmann-Brunnen**, a 1900 fountain which was moved to its present location during the redevelopment of the city centre. The two powerful-looking centaurs battling for a fish are meant to symbolise the rivalry between Hamburg and Altona.

At the southern end of the square is Altona's **Rathaus** (city hall), opened in 1898. Nowadays, several local administrative offices are housed here so the building is generally open to the public. As a young man, Ernst Barlach was involved in creating the sculptures which decorate the building. Also in front of the north face is Altona's monument to Kaiser Wilhelm, an example of how William II's loyal citizens liked to present themselves and their ruler.

The south face of the building is more interesting. It is partly composed of the late-Classicist facade of the very first Altona railway station built in 1844. From here you can look across to the so-called **Elbbalkon** (Altona Balcony), a patch of garden on the heights above the river offering a fine view down into the port and Kohlbrandbrücke, the new bridge across the Elbe.

Klopstockstrasse separates the Rathaus from the Elbbalkon, a short road linking highly desirable **Palmaille** with its magnificent Classicist buildings and the **Elbchaussee** along which rush-hour commuter traffic to and from the city's western suburbs crawls on weekdays. Less than 10 metres from this busy road, the poet Friedrich Gottlieb Klopstock and his family are buried in the

Palmaille: a splendid street of Classicist architecture.

nearby **cemetery of Christianskirche**.

North German museum: On the eastern side of the Platz der Republik are two of Altona's cultural highlights: **Altona Theater** and **Altona Museum**. The former offers a mixture of popular traditional plays and more modern light entertainment. Altona also has two other smaller theatres, both of the experimental kind: Theater in der Basilika and Monsuntheater.

The museum is not only dedicated to the history of Altona but also serves as a general museum of northern Germany. On the first floor are detailed models of a variety of north German farmhouses. A museum restaurant has also been opened in a fully restored rural cottage built in 1745. The role of Altona as a harbour town and trading city is very impressively illustrated by a collection of models vividly portraying the various methods of catching fish.

To the east of Platz der Republik runs Max-Brauer-Allee. The man the road was named after was the Social-Demo-cratic mayor of Altona during the Weimar Republic. He was later Hamburg's first postwar mayor. The road only really deserves the term "Allee" (avenue) in the section north of the station where it widens into a tree-lined arterial road. The high density of traffic hardly makes it an attractive place to stop for long, but there is one place worth visiting on its length: the **Theater für Kinder** (Children's Theatre).

Grosse Bergstrasse and Ottenser Hauptstrasse cross Altona's north-south axis at the station. Grosse Bergstrasse runs from St Pauli to the station with Neue Grosse Bergstrasse parallel. Shops and offices are concentrated along both of them.

Ottensen: Beyond the station this shopping street runs on as **Ottenser Hauptstrasse**, where there are quite a few older buildings and numerous small shops, a colourful mixture of delicatessens, natural cosmetics and tea shops, boutiques, supermarkets and electrical stores. But any stroll down **Altona graffiti.**

this road shouldn't go beyond Spritzenplatz where strange-looking punks may well try to extract a modern-day form of toll from passers-by.

Right at the far end of the road there is one of Altona's most attractive and original features, a seemingly unremarkable second-hand bookshop known as **Bücherwurm**. It may not have as many books as some of its larger rivals in Hamburg but the prices here are most reasonable.

Ottenser Hauptstrasse is a gathering place for colourful locals: punks, Turks, students, Greens, yuppies, labourers and office workers. Almost like the Kreuzberg district of Berlin, which is famous for being cosmopolitan.

You can't stop progress: But what is commonly referred to as progress is even making itself felt in leisurely Ottensen. The site of a supermarket, closed as a result of streamlining moves at head office, is to be redeveloped as a shopping arcade for "upmarket tastes". Developers hope to attract some of the big spenders from Blankenese, Wedel, Flottbek and Rissen to stop off on their way to or from Hamburg city centre.

It is doubtful whether such changes will pass smoothly. The public outcry that followed when the Flora Theater in Schanzenviertel was to be redeveloped is warning enough of the possible strength of local feelings. What's more, Ottensen has already seen similar conflicts and past experience does not exactly suggest that the district's many representatives of the so-called "subculture" are particularly tolerant of newcomers. Though they like to buy their fruit and veg at the Turkish corner shop or work for the development of a multi-cultural society in the local community centre, their tolerance doesn't necessarily stretch to yuppies.

A process of gentrification has started in Ottensen in recent years. It is particularly noticeable in the area to the north of Ottenser Hauptstrasse and **Ottenser Spritzenplatz**, where one of Hamburg's best open-air markets takes place

Punk by the Stuhlmann-Brunnen, Platz der Republik.

twice a week. Film and photo studios, casting firms, advertising agencies, publishers, editorial offices of magazines and design studios have moved into the numerous old factories and commercial premises along Friedensallee and in the area around Planckstrasse, Völckersstrasse and Gaußstrasse. The "creative" professionals working in these firms also like to live in the area.

And when you've found an apartment here, you naturally like to spend an evening in a local pub or restaurant. Not, of course, **Bundschuh** at the corner of Rothestrasse and Arnoldstrasse with its 1970s atmosphere (though it has got the best fried potatoes anywhere in Ottensen and excellent beer as well). And not in one of the many Turkish, Greek or Italian restaurants in the locality. No, those who've made it to Ottensen have drawn their own kind of places to the area. The new arrivals go to **Café Katelbach** (at the corner of Eulenstrasse and Grosse Brunnenstrasse), **Eisenstein** or **Leopold** (restaurants in Friedensallee) or **Bolero-Bar** in Bahrenfelder Strasse.

Yuppie-generated expansion is particularly evident in Friedensallee. Hamburg's Filmhaus with its **Filmhauskneipe** and the **Monsuntheater** (where song and dance or plays are performed) have long been established here but now there is the **Medienhaus** as well. This media temple has not only various small firms and three exquisite apartments on its premises but also **Leopold**, a restaurant devoted to German cuisine. The owners of **Eisenstein,** only separated by a courtyard from the Medienhaus, had a good nose for this *zeitgeist* ambience when they took over part of an old ship's propeller factory. Now guests enjoy their meals (including what are probably Hamburg's best pizzas) under a 10-metre (32-ft) high ceiling next to the old factory chimney.

To the north of Friedensallee, the **Theater in der Basilika** is in an old factory in Borselstrasse. Despite the

A good area for local bars.

GASTSTÄTTE *Am Rain*

Schultheiss Bier

MEYER&CO
Bestattungen

ecclesiastical sound of its name, it is a totally secular, modern and experimental small theatre presenting plays by authors such as Christopher Durang or Dario Fo.

Industrial arts: Right in the middle of this area of "misused" factories, less than two minutes' walk north of Friedensallee is *the* factory, Hamburg's famous **Fabrik**. Like the legendary Onkel Pö's in Eppendorf (now sadly closed), the Fabrik is one of Hamburg's musical institutions. At the corner of Bahrenfelder Strasse and Barnerstrasse, this music factory is easily recognised by its striking red crane, standing out like a dinosaur of some bygone industrial age. Many of the big names of jazz, pop, rock and folk music have appeared here: Miles Davis, Abdullah Ibrahim and Roger Chapman, to name but three.

Somewhat to the east of the Fabrik, Barnerstrasse crosses Gaussstrasse. At the corner of Gaussstrasse and Nernstweg **Werkstatt 3** and **Werkhof** have

set up in an old shampoo factory. The latter is a cooperative effort by various "alternative" skilled craft workshops; the former a community culture centre offering courses, readings and concerts.

If you go from the Fabrik south down Bahrenfelder Strasse and back towards the heart of Ottensen, towards Spritzenplatz and Hauptstrasse, you reach a residential area, south of Ottenser Hauptstrasse, which is dominated by houses typifying the art nouveau and late 19th-century styles of architecture.

However, apart from Motte, the local community cente, where a good deal of committed work among young people, foreigners and the socially deprived is carried out, and a condiments factory you can smell a mile off, there isn't much of interest in this area – except, that is, for a small, half-hidden wine bar in Karl-Theodor-Strasse, **Traube**. Accept the fact that you won't be able to park anywhere near it and probably won't get a seat inside either, but this is a place definitely worth visiting.

Fabrik: famous music scene.

ALONG THE ELBE

If you want to get to know Hamburg, go to the elegant residential districts along the Elbchaussee. That was what author Johann Ludwig Ewald recommended. Only a few years later, Stendhal praised "one of the most beautiful views anywhere in the world". Even today, Hamburg's westerly suburbs – Othmarschen, Nienstedten and Blankenese – are regarded as "typical Hamburg", especially where they are at their most splendid along the Elbchaussee.

The Elbe heads out of Hamburg in a northwesterly direction towards the sea about 100 km (60 miles) away, after having travelled through many European countries. The residential areas on its banks to the west of Hamburg are Germany's "best residential address", Hamburg's Beverly Hills, if you like.

This river gives these suburbs their typical ambience, bringing them to life. When heavy rain clouds hang low over the horizon in autumn, the river flows like liquid lead. When winter gales arrive, the water level rises threateningly. Then in summer the atmosphere is sometimes almost Mediterranean with reddening evening skies and the fragrance of flowers.

The river is always busy. Some 14,000 ships a year are piloted from Cuxhaven, at the mouth of the Elbe, to Hamburg. Huge freighters, rusty tankers, container ships and barges are a common sight. But even old sailing ships and modern yachts can still be seen making their way through the dangerous sandbanks to Hamburg.

Hamburg's finest avenue: The economic significance of the Elbe was recognised centuries ago. Fishermen, ferrymen and pilots settled on both banks of the river, building their houses and villages. But from the 18th century onwards numerous Hamburg families began to move to the heights above the Elbe. Enthusing about the views across the river, rich shipping owners, merchants and bankers – the Baurs, Brandts, Godeffroys, Roosens and Schliekers – set up their summer residences along the bumpy, dusty **Elbchaussee**. The quiet parks and dignified houses built in simple Classicist style were in harmony with the north German landscape and somewhat reserved style of Hamburg society. The Elbe became part of a philosophy of life. Twenty of the city's top 40 families live on Elbchaussee.

Not only the upper crust has lost its heart to the Elbe suburbs. There are perfectly normal people living in the 589 houses along Elbchaussee, a road stretching for some 8 km (5 miles) along the river. But none of them are exactly poor. Blankenese and Nienstedten are, on average, the most expensive housing areas in Hamburg with rents of DM 25 per sq. metre (10 sq. feet). An unrestricted view of the Elbe may well cost three times as much. Naturally the "wet" side of the Elbchaussee is preferred for the view it offers, and property prices here are as high as lakeside lots on the Alster. The road was 200 years old in 1988.

The drawing power of the Elbe attracts many who do not live along its expensive banks. Thousands of downtown Hamburgers like to stroll through the Elbe suburbs on summer evenings and weekends. Elbchaussee itself has been transformed into a seemingly endless convoy of cars. More than 30,000 pass along it daily, polluting the priceless air. But pedestrians taking the riverside path, probably Hamburg's most popular walk, fortunately notice little of the traffic on what the poet Detlev von Liliencron once described as the world's most beautiful road.

The Elbe-side walk begins at **Neumühlen** landing stage right next to **Övelgönne Museum harbour**. The oldest ships in this museum are *Catharina*, a 101-year-old fishing cutter and *Elbe 3*, a 102-year-old lightship. Occasionally this historic fleet sets sail

Preceding pages: watching the Elbe flow. **Left,** mansion in Hamburg's Beverly Hills.

on the Elbe – much to the delight of the crowds. However, the romantic atmosphere is severely affected by a huge concrete monstrosity, a ventilation shaft for the tunnel under the Elbe which was completed in 1975.

Fisherman's village: The old village of fishermen and pilots which was **Övelgönne** had its origins in the 16th century. Now it is made up of a single row of cottages in which mainly artists and intellectuals live. Over the years, locals have beaten back the sand to create small gardens and wrought-iron verandas, but nowadays the path cuts through these gardens. The oldest cottages are 18th-century (Nos. 65/66, 70/71, 72/75 and 88/89). At **Övelgönne Seekiste**, a private museum (No. 83) has a collection of shipping exhibits.

Several restaurants along Övelgönne beach are a big attraction on summer days. The closest one can get to lively action on the Elbe is in **Strandperle**, a small beach pub where Hamburgers and tourists come to enjoy a beer with a port panorama. If all the tables are full, you just take your drink and sit on the sand. Courting couples and Elbe addicts aren't bothered by the foul smells coming up from the river. On some days it stinks of oil and chemicals, on others of rotting fish.

Övelgönne is at the foot of the heights above the Elbe, immediately below Elbchaussee. Malicious tongues maintain that those who can't afford a villa along Elbchaussee go for a property down in Övelgönne. Steep lanes with names like Himmelsleiter ("heavenly ladder") link the two. These socio-topographical differences were amusingly described by the Övelgönne poet and painter Hans Leip (1893–1983) in his novel *Jans Himp und die kleine Brise*. Leip himself is famous for a song which went round the world in World War II, *Lili Marleen.*

Villas and haute cuisine: The picturesque cottages of Övelgönne do indeed look somewhat shabby compared to the huge villas along Elbchaussee. **Land-** **Elbe beach.**

haus **Weber** (Elbchaussee 153) and shipping magnate Brandt's **Säulenhaus** (Elbchaussee 186) are two masterpieces of early 19th-century architecture. But this bit of Elbchaussee is not only of architectural interest. Gourmets flock to thatch-covered **Landhaus Scherrer** (Elbchaussee 130), famous for its fish dishes, and the post-modern building housing the excellent French restaurant **Le Canard** (Elbchaussee 139), provides outstanding views over the river.

Baron-Voght-Strasse leads to the **Klein Flottbek equestrian centre** where the German show-jumping championships take place each year. Fences such as *Pulvermanns Grab* are much feared by the show-jumping community. One of the many traditions of this prestige event is that, as at Ascot in Britain, women add to the atmosphere of the occasion by sporting a colourful collection of hats.

Baron-Voght-Strasse joins the Elbchaussee near Teufelsbrück landing

Övelgönne Museum Harbour.

stage. Nearby, on the "dry" side of the road, is **Elbschlösschen** (Elbchaussee 372), originally country residence of the Altona merchant Johann Heinrich Baur. It borders on **Elbschloss brewery** (No. 374), which was established in 1874, and **Landhaus Lindenhof** (No. 388), a late 18th-century residence originally belonging to the merchant Berend Roosen.

Elbchaussee starts to climb up the heights near the small **Nienstedter Kirche**. This church, built in 1750–51, is one of the road's outstanding landmarks. Many of Hamburg's upper crust marry here. After the ceremony, wealthy "newly weds" can celebrate their marriage in **Restaurant Jacob** opposite. The latter is world famous because of its patio – as painted by Max Liebermann in 1902, a painting on view at Hamburg's Kunsthalle and illustrated in the art chapter (*pages 88–95*).

Nienstedten: Just behind the church is the heart of the old village of Nienstedten. However, there are now very

few of the old thatched cottages left. But the **cemetery**, in contrast, is not short of a few famous names: Chancellor von Bülow, shipping magnate Essberger, poet Hans Henny Jahnn and Baron Caspar von Voght.

Hirschpark was named after a deer enclosure created on the orders of Cesar VI Godeffroy. Cesar VI was probably the most talented of the Godeffroy family. He was known as the "King of the South Seas" because his firm had 50 trading stations there.

After an incident in 1960 when a building worker killed a deer that had attacked him, the deer park was closed. But Hamburgers couldn't come to terms with a deer-less Hirschpark and protested. An action committee was established to bring about the re-opening of the park – successfully as it turned out, although the red deer were replaced by less aggressive fallow deer.

The Hirschpark's most prominent landmark is its unique avenue of limes. These 200-year-old trees have already served as a backdrop for several films. Another local feature well known beyond Hamburg is the thatched-covered **Witthüs**, where the organ builder and poet Hans Henny Jahnn lived shortly before his death in 1959. Tea and cakes make it a popular stopping-off place for people out for a stroll.

The resort town of **Blankenese** begins where Hirschpark ends. No other district of Hamburg can match it for flair. The word actually means "white tongue of land" but nowadays this district is certainly not colourless. Although **Dockhuden** and **Falkenstein** are part of Blankenese, the district is epitomised by the small so-called **Treppenviertel** ("stepped quarter") – a colourful mixture of old fishermen's cottages, Classicist-style country residences, art nouveau "palaces" and bungalows.

The history of Blankenese has been shaped by storm floods, the struggle for survival, poverty and deprivation. The first recorded mention of the village was in 1302 when there was a ferry across the Elbe here. When the village came under Danish rule in 1640, its 200 inhabitants mainly lived from fishing. In the 19th century, when merchant shipping became increasingly important, Blankenese sailors sailed the Seven Seas in their small but highly manoeuvrable schooners, transporting oranges from Seville and coffee from Brazil. In its heyday, about 140 years ago, the Blankenese fleet employed some 1,500 men. But then steamships took over and Blankenese's sailors missed the boat.

Streets in Blankenese remind one of the district's maritime past; they were often named after traditional captain's families. In **Sagebiels Fährhaus** on Blankeneser Hauptstrasse this eventful past is still very much in evidence – in the form of old Blankenese sea dogs. Some of them are members of the exclusive Albatross Society, only open to captains who have (literally) sailed round Cape Horn.

Steps down to the Elbe.

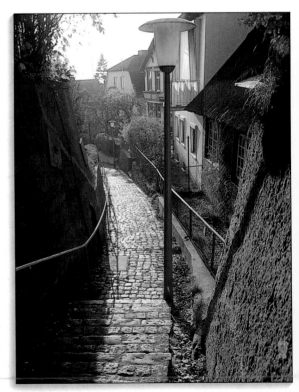

But these busy times are over. Instead there is a touch of holiday atmosphere among the steep lanes of Blankenese's Treppenviertel. When the weather is good, all the wicker chairs on the beach in front of the **Strandhotel**, an art nouveau building erected in 1902, are taken. Blankenese sailing club is a hive of activity and sailing boats weave their way between the big freighters or launches that bring boat-loads of tourists to Blankenese.

"Lugarno, for example… Portofino, Vancouver, Yarmouth on the Isle of Wight, Herrsching on Ammersee… Rio or Lake Constance… each one has its advantages. But where else can you see ocean-going ships sailing past your legs?" Hans Liep was quite enthusiastic about this "village with overseas traffic", as publicity brochures describe Blankenese. It is indeed a major tourist attraction. The view of Blankenese from the water reveals why. The houses clinging to the slopes of **Süllberg**, **Kiekeberg** and **Mühlenberg** seem to

Blankenese seen from the river.

have forced their way into the narrow valleys. The First Commandment in Blankenese is also an expression of brotherly love: new buildings shall not take away their neighbours' view of the beautiful Elbe.

There is also a good view of the river from **Süllberg**, the highest pinnacle in the area (75 metres/246 ft). A mere two centuries ago, the hill was avoided because it was said to be inhabited by a witch. But a certain Peter Hansen refused to be frightened off and opened a milk bar for day-trippers there in 1837. A viewing tower and restaurant followed which are still in operation today.

The maze of steps and narrow lanes of Blankenese opens up again and again to reveal new perspectives and attractive views. But you need to be fit to tackle this quarter. The most demanding path linking the beach and Blankeneser Hauptstrasse has no less than 163 steps and is 260 metres (853 ft) long. The oldest fishermen's cottages are hidden away amongst luxuriant vegetation on a

GOING TO THE RACES

Hamburg begins with an H, like horses. And because the city is situated between the farming regions of Schleswig-Holstein and Lower Saxony, it's not surprising that it has a tradition of horse-breeding. Horse-breeding, horse dealing and horse racing have always been closely intertwined and Hamburg over the years has become an ideal place for gambling: on the one hand, there is plenty of money in the hands of dealers and punters; on the other hand, there is plenty of horseflesh.

Gambling is actually a necessity for the sport. Without bets, there would be neither horse racing nor harness racing and horse-breeding would have the status of merely a loss-making hobby.

With an eye to the English equestrian tradition, horse racing in Hamburg chose an English word for its various annual championships: the Derby. The city's significance in the world of equestrian sports is underlined by the fact that four out of five German championships are staged here: the flat-racing Derby and the show-jumping, dressage and horse-and-carriage championships. Only the harness-racing Derby has been lost to Berlin.

Since 1869 the German flat-racing Derby has taken place in the Horn district of Hamburg on the first Sunday in July (1945 was the only year it was cancelled). It is the climax of a week's races when bets totalling over DM11 million are placed – with the trend still going upwards. The owners, breeders, trainers and jockeys take some DM3 million home with them.

Of course, the biggest prize money can be won in the Derby itself, nearly three quarters of a million in all. It is a race for three-year-old fillies and colts, although most of the starters are colts.

The flat-racing Derby Week is organised by Hamburger Renn-Club whose 350 members are hand-picked Hamburg celebrities. It's their job to find the sponsors whose money is added to the proceeds from bets and starting fees to make up the total prize money. Decades ago, the club handed over the 40-hectare (98-acre) track in Horn to the City of Hamburg which has placed a leisure park, youth hostel and kindergarten in the grounds. After all, racing only takes place for one week of the year. But for those seven days some 250 people are needed to run the proceedings.

The flat-racers profit from the know-how of Hamburg's other mecca of equestrian sports, the Volkspark harness-racing track in the district of Bahrenfeld, northwest of Altona. Harness racing is an all-the-year-round sport in Hamburg. There are races on 100–120 days of the year, usually Thursday evenings (from 6.30 pm) and Sunday afternoons (from 2 pm).

The organisers, Hamburger Trabrenngesellschaft, maintain the track and keep up the buildings – a glassed-in main stand with catering facilities and the numerous stables. This is the very heart of Hamburg's harness racing – where the trainers, professional jockeys and the mostly overlooked and worst-paid members of the racing fraternity, the stable lads, carry out their daily work.

Up to 1,400 races a year, some under floodlights, are held in Bahrenfeld. The horses run counter-clockwise over distances of between 1 mile and just under 2 miles. Harness racing in Hamburg attracts prize money of between DM1,500 and 75,000. The total pot for the first five places adds up to about DM7.3 million a year, an average of DM5,426 per race. Of course, this is peanuts compared to the prize money at Derby Week but betting is what brings in the money at harness racing. Nearly half a million people come to races at Bahrenfeld – the Derby Week only attracts 150,000 – and bets totalling some DM40 million are placed. The betting trend is upwards here too.

There is one highlight of the Hamburg equestrian sporting calender where betting plays no part: the four-day German show-jumping, dressage and horse-and-carriage Derby staged in Flottbek every spring. But even without betting there's plenty of money at stake over the legendary show-jumping course here. Each year there are prizes worth more than DM400,000 to be won – DM50,000 alone for the winner of the show-jumping Derby. The legendary German rider Fritz Thiedemann still holds the record for the most number of wins: five in all.

steep, aptly-named lane, **Rutsch** which means "slide" (Nos. 1 and 2), **Elbterrasse** (Nos. 4–6 and 5–7) and **Krumdals Weg** (Nos. 14 and 18). These are "twee and dreehüs" houses with a common hall between the flats.

Refuge for artists: The poet Richard Dehmel (1863–1920) lived in the first house of the street named after him. A collection of his furniture and other mementos can be viewed on request. Gerhart Hauptmann, Paul Claudel and Hans Leip were among Dehmel's frequent guests. The artist Eduard Bargheer loved Blankenese because of the wonderful light there. Now the creatively eccentric artist Horst Janssen lives on Blankeneser Mühlenweg.

In comparison with the narrow confines of the Treppenviertel there is plenty of room up in the "village". The local **market** takes place next to the church on Tuesdays, Fridays and Saturdays. Malicious tongues like to talk of furcoated ladies walking from stall to stall comparing the price of potatoes. The "village" has numerous parks and in one of them, **Gosslers Park**, the local administrative offices are housed in a temple-like palace with 34 Doric columns. **Baurs Park** was laid out by the Altona merchant Georg Friedrich Baur in 1802. It became known as the "cannon park" because Baur had each of his homeward-bound ships welcomed by a salvo from his cannons.

However, Blankenese's most beautiful building is merchant Peter Godeffroy's **White House** (Elbchaussee 547), designed by Christian Frederick Hansen. Godeffroy owed the splendid interior of this 1790 building to chance: a ship carrying Roman rarities bound for the King of Prussia was shipwrecked in a storm and Blankenese people took possession of anything that floated ashore. Hansen bought the loot at an auction. Since, however, the house is privately owned (by the shipping magnate Liselotte von Rantzau), it is not open to the public.

Falkenstein with its huge houses and extensive gardens is in the west of Blankenese. In **Sven-Simon-Park** at Falkensteiner Ufer you can visit Elke Dröscher's **Doll Museum** with its 300 dolls and 60 dolls' houses.

When ice floes block shipping on the Elbe, a visit to **Schinckels park** is recommended. The ice on the meadow attracts scores of children who thunder across it on their extremely flat and heavy sledges, steered by 3-yard sticks. The ice doesn't melt until almost Easter, a festival marked by traditional bonfires. In earlier times the various parts of Blankenese would vie to build the biggest bonfire. Lots of Christmas trees are still saved for the spectacular Easter bonfires down on the beach.

Schulauer Fährhaus with its bottled ship museum and Willkommhöft is actually outside Hamburg, in the neighbouring town of Wedel. The unique Willkommhöft does, however, have a strong association with the port of Hamburg. Every incoming and outgoing ship is greeted by its own national anthem.

Elbe skipper.

WALDDÖRFER VILLAGES

Turn-of-the-century villas, country houses and cottages; petit-bourgeois estates, fields and meadows, woods and ten farms; no manufacturing industry; a few businesses and only a little commerce: these are the characteristics of the Walddörfer.

Though hardly "wooded villages" and still a part of the city of Hamburg, **Lemsahl-Mellingstedt**, **Duvenstedt**, **Wohldorf-Ohlstedt**, **Bergstedt** and **Volksdorf** are home to just 35,000 inhabitants in an area covering 51 sq. km (19 sq. miles). Here, north-east of the city centre, you find nothing of the scintillating cultural melting plot that is Ottensen; nothing of the idyllic decay that is Schanzenviertel; and nothing of the intellectual, hedonist flair represented by Eppendorf. Here, distinguished, hanseatic peace and quiet reigns supreme.

About half of Hamburg's wooded area is in the Walddörfer. Nowadays, only a few names of roads or landscapes point to the economic significance these woods once had. In medieval times they served as common land for local farmers who drove their grazing pigs onto the wooded meadows. Later, they became the lucrative basis of Hamburg's timber industry. These days, the woods are a popular local recreation area.

The history of the Walddörfer is the story of the decline of medieval nobility and the simultaneous ascendancy of the mercantile middle class. In Hamburg's possession since the 14th century, all the Walddörfer had been previously pawned or sold by lords of the manor.

Waterway: In medieval times the most important link was the river Alster. In the 14th century Hamburg bought the entire river from the counts of Holstein in order to secure the supply of water for the city's mills from the source of the river to where it flowed into the Elbe. The Alster was used to transport every-thing of importance for this region: lime from Segeberg and timber, peat, tiles, grain and gin from Wulksfelde. The boats used were flat-bottomed barges. Once unloaded, they were towed back upstream, mostly by women.

The first means of mass transportation linking the Walddörfer with Hamburg was an electric narrow-gauge railway which ran from Altrahlstedt, where it linked up with the Hamburg-Lübeck route, to Volksdorf and Wohldorf. This privately-run railway operated from 1904 until its closure in 1934 but it lost much of its usefulness after the opening, in 1918, of the Walddörfer line, part of the Hamburger Hochbahn network. This direct link to the city centre proved the breakthrough for the large-scale residential settlement of the Walddörfer.

Lemsahl-Mellingstedt: These two villages have only been part of Hamburg since 1937. With a written history going back to 1271, Mellingstedt is the older, but only Lemsahl has been able to keep its village-like character. The village green is surrounded by farm buildings, though they are, in fact, little more than 100 years old.

There is, however, evidence of early settlements in the area – the remains of a early-medieval road discovered at the end of the 19th century in **Wittmoor** and of a Bronze Age burial field at **Bilenbarg** between Lemsahl and Wittmoor. The medieval road enabled early settlers to cross the marsh safely. The **Alstertal Museum** (Wellingsbütteler Weg 79g) has some 2nd- and 9th-century remains of this road.

The Saxon tribes who originally populated the area made use of a large bend in the river Alster to build the Mellingburg, a stronghold to which they fled when the Slavs threatened. Nowadays, this is a particularly beautiful section of the **Alsterwanderweg** (Alster footpath). Weary walkers can always call in for refreshment at the **Mellingburger Schleuse** restaurant. **Treudelberg estate** is also on this bend of the river and its manor house, built around 1860 in Biedermeier style, stands at the end of an elegant and tree-lined drive.

Duvenstedt: Though Duvenstedt, like Lemsahl-Mellingstedt, is a 1937 new-comer, its links with Hamburg go back to medieval times, when the Hamburg cathedral chapter bought the tithe rights from the local lords of the manor in 1261.

The old village with eight farms was located at the junction of Duvenstedter Damm and Poppenbütteler Chaussee. Shortly after the turn of the century, the village structure began to crumble as the process of suburbanisation slowly set in. Most of the villas were built around this time. The only visible re-mains of the old village can be seen in the area between Duvenstedter Damm and Specksaalredder.

Duvenstedter brook, marsh and swampland left behind by the last Ice Age, belongs to Lemsahl-Mellingstedt and Duvenstedt. The brook was a catch-ment area for the water from melting glaciers which had spread from Scandi-navia as far south as this area during the last Ice Age. Despite medieval man's early use of the brook – as common land for the surrounding villages – many rare plants have survived in this habitat.

Now officially classified as a nature-protected area, the brook is purposely being allowed to return to its original wilderness state – before man's inter-ference. Red deer are being raised in a specially protected enclosure, and paths have been laid out to encourage long nature walks.

Wohldorf-Ohlstedt: This region was originally two villages: Wohldorf be-came part of Hamburg in 1440, Ohlstedt in 1463. The village of **Ohlstedt** was probably founded in the early Saxon period before Christianity reached the area north of the Elbe. In 1463 Hamburg council bought it from Hartwich von Hummelsbüttel, one of the last repre-sentatives of a once powerful family with their ancestral home in Stegen.

Map of the Walddörfer.

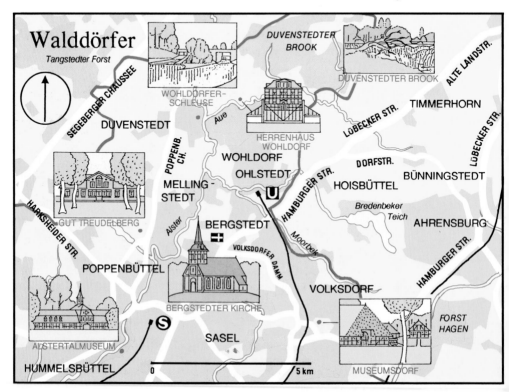

Nowadays, Ohlstedt is a suburb of villas. Little remains of the village structure that was still intact at the beginning of this century. The **Kate** in Alte Dorfstrasse is Ohlstedt's oldest house, built about 1850. The old circular layout of the village around a green is still visible (Ohlstedter Platz) but the farm houses have either been torn down or modernised.

In the mid-1920s Ohlstedt got its own typical Walddörfer station, a red-brick building designed in the style of country houses in the area. Ohlstedt's **village hall** and **school** were both designed by Hamburg's master architect, Fritz Schumacher.

On Ellerbrookswisch and Ohlstedter Stieg is the so-called **Norwegian estate**. At first glance, one could mistake these bungalows for modern ecologically designed housing. They were actually built in 1943 when the bombing raids on Hamburg made thousands homeless. These wooden houses were brought all the way from Norway for a few privileged representatives of the Nazi regime.

At **Schleusenredder** there is a two-storey half-timbered house on a historical spot. In 1529 a house was built there for the lock-keeper. Nowadays, this is a popular place for a day out and the restaurants that still exist remind one of the fact that the lock-keepers were also the local licensees. The **Wohldorfer locks** have now been equipped with rollers to transport small leisure craft and the towpath has now been turned into the **Alsterwanderweg**, a pretty path for walkers or cyclists.

Wohldorf manor house, on Herrenhausallee, was where the lords of the manor, usually two Hamburg councillors, resided. The baroque half-timbered construction was built on an island in a small lake caused by the damming of the river Ammersbek, a tributary of the Alster.

This island was also the site of Wohltorpe Castle, destroyed in 1347. The present-day manor house, built in

Wohldorfer Mühle restaurant.

1712, replaced an earlier building known as the "Spieker" (pleasure house). Built in 1625, this house served a dual purpose: as administrative seat (up to 1830) and summer residence for many generations of Hamburg senators. In 1969 the manor house and Wohldorf estate were acquired on lease by the Hamburg businessman Alfred C. Toepfer. The house was renovated and opened as a centre for conferences and the like; meanwhile the estate continued to be farmed.

Right in front of the manor house is the millpond, or **Mühlenteich**. The actual mill is to be found at Mühlenredder 35. The present building was constructed in 1863–64 but there have been mills on the site since 1471. The two half-timbered buildings between the mill and the Manor House now house restaurants. One of them, "Zum Bäcker", used to contain a couple of cells where the lord of the manor put any unruly subjects.

To the north of the manor house is

Wohldorf estate, originally created in 1437. In 1933 a concentration camp was temporarily set up here. To the east of the manor house the Ammersbek was dammed to form another pool, **Kupferteich**, as early as 1622. The reference to copper in its name points to the economic use to which water power was put by the **copper beaters** who, from 1687 onwards, worked raw copper into sheets at this site.

After a brief interlude as a paper mill and then as a weaving mill, the whole complex was shut down in 1899 and some parts of it demolished. What remains is the Alte Kupferhof (Herrenhausallee 95), a house built around 1750, where the former owners used to live; the Küpfermühle, where the copper beaters were housed (Herrenhausallee 64); and the ruins of workers' dwellings built in 1880.

Bergstedt: The original village was probably established between 100 and 400 AD as a Saxon settlement. In medieval times it was an important religious

Farmhouse in the Volksdorf Museum village.

centre and the present-day parish has one of the oldest **churches** anywhere in Hamburg. It was originally built around 1150 and extended in 1293. Its present exterior dates back to 1745. The colourfully painted wooden ceiling (1685) and the carved wooden baptismal angel (1768) are particularly worth seeing.

The original circular form of the village around the pond at **Bergstedter Markt** is still evident. Of the five farm houses that once existed, parts of the Kramerhof (1770) and Siemerhof (1870) have survived. The old mill (Alte Mühle), located at the point where the Saselbek flows into the Alster, is a 19th-century building but there has been a mill located on this spot since the 13th century.

Volksdorf: The village has belonged to Hamburg since 1437 but the first historical mention of a settlement dates from 1296.

With more than 16,000 inhabitants, Volksdorf is the largest of Hamburg's five Walddörfer. Its development from a hamlet of seven farms was dramatic. In 1920 only 206 people lived here. Just nine years later there were 3,470. It was in those years that Hamburg's city planners gave Volksdorf its now typical garden suburb character.

In Volksdorf the **underground station** is as big as in many medium-sized towns – a key to that rapid development. Architecturally speaking, it is a typical Walddörfer station: red brick, white "Georgian" windows, tiled roof. Redbrick buildings are particularly common throughout these north-eastern suburbs. **Im Alten Dorfe** was the main street of a linear village.

A small section of the original village has survived to form the heart of Volksdorf's **Museum village** (Im Alten Dorf 48). This open-air museum graphically portrays what rural life was like in the Walddörfer, even though not all the exhibits and buildings are from the locality.

The late 17th-century Spiekerhus, Instenhaus and Dorfkrug are all reno-vated buildings from the original village. Harderhof was rebuilt after a fire. Other buildings worth visiting are Grützmühle, which was brought from Hummelsbüttel; a 1657 barn (Durchfahrtsscheune) from the Lauenburg region; the smithy (Schmiede), which is actually a reconstruction of an old Wohldorf smithy; and a reconstructed gateway house (Durchfahrtshaus) which was originally located elsewhere in the same street.

A late 1920s, neo-Classical building known as the **Ohlendorffsche Villa** is also located here. It now houses the local authority offices. Behind the villa, a park of the same name stretches southwards as far as Eulenkrugstrasse.

Nowadays, the heart of Volksdorf is composed of shops, a swimming baths and a 1970s business centre named after the resistance group "Die Weisse Rose" (the White Rose). A statue commemorates the struggle of this group, led by brother and sister Hans and Sophie Scholl, against the Nazis.

Further evidence of Volksdorf's rural past are to be found outside the open-air museum; a cottage and smithy at Lerchenberg; a farm labourers' dwelling built around 1850 on the other side of the underground in Kattjahren; and a mid 19th-century farm labourers' house at the corner of Eulenkrugstrasse and Im Hain. A good example of turn-of-the-century middle-class country-style housing is the Landhaus Klöpper on the far side of Farmsener Landstrasse (Klosterwisch 8). It now houses a children's home.

The local **grammar school** (Walddörfergymnasium Im Allhorn) is the unmistakable work of Hamburg's master architect Fritz Schumacher. This school was built in 1929–31 despite the determined opposition of local residents. The architecture and reformist educational theories of the Weimar Republic – close proximity of man and his natural surroundings – are united in this building to a degree unmatched elsewhere in Hamburg.

OHLSDORF AND ALSTERTAL

Hamburg's **Ohlsdorf cemetery**, northeast of the Alster on the way to Walddörfer, is twice as big as the Principality of Monaco, Europe's largest and one of its prettiest. But Ohlsdorf is not just a place for the dead.

The cemetery: Right from the start Ohlsdorf cemetery – the second largest in the world after Chicago – was designed with space in mind. As Hamburg grew into a metropolis in the late 19th century, the city's powers-that-be showed the necessary foresight to buy up land for a cemetery which would offer room for every (dead) Hamburger, irrespective of denomination. The plan was for Ohlsdorf to replace all the church cemeteries which had served Hamburg's needs up till then.

Now the cemetery is as much a place for Sunday afternoon strollers as for cremated souls. Whole families come cycling through on weekends. Grandpa and grandchildren can be seen feeding the tame squirrels and ducks, or wandering along Ohlsdorf's 17 km (10 miles) of roads and paths. There are even two bus routes (170 and 270) through what rates as Hamburg's biggest and most beautiful park.

The architects: This parkland landscape, modelled on English gardens, was the work of Johann Wilhelm Cordes (1840–1917). His plans and photos won a Grand Prix at the Paris World Exhibition in 1900.

Cordes' parkland landscape features are still visible in Ohlsdorf. He maintained all the typical characteristics of the existing landscape while planting trees on the edges of the cemetery to create a natural "green belt" around this oasis of peace. He also had domestic and exotic trees planted in various parts of the cemetery.

The section designed by Cordes (the first half spreading out from the main entrance) was opened on 1 July 1877.

Preceding pages: gravestones in Ohlsdorf. **Below, Map of Ohlsdorf.**

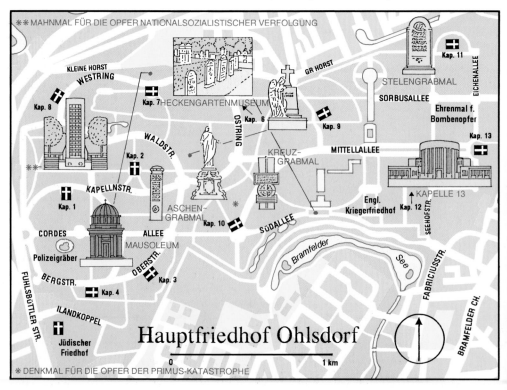

** MAHNMAL FÜR DIE OPFER NATIONALSOZIALISTISCHER VERFOLGUNG

KLEINE HORST
WESTRING
Kap. 8
Kap. 7
HECKENGARTENMUSEUM
GR HORST
STELENGRABMAL
SORBUSALLEE
Ehrenmal f. Bombenopfer
Kap. 11
Kap. 13
Kap. 6
OSTRING
Kap. 9
Kap. 2
WALDSTR.
KREUZ-GRABMAL
MITTELALLEE
KAPELLE 13
Engl. Kriegerfriedhof
Kap. 12
**
KAPELLNSTR.
Kap. 1
ASCHEN-GRABMAL
Kap. 10
SÜDALLEE
CORDES
Polizeigräber
ALLEE
MAUSOLEUM
OBERSTR.
Bramfelder
See
BERGSTR.
Kap. 3
Kap. 4
ILANDKOPPEL
FUHLSBÜTTLER STR.
Jüdischer Friedhof
EICHENALLEE
SEEHOFSTR.
FABRICIUSSTR.
BRAMFELDER CH.

Hauptfriedhof Ohlsdorf

0   1 km

* DENKMAL FÜR DIE OPFER DER PRIMUS-KATASTROPHE

244

The buildings he created reveal a preference for late-baroque architecture with a definite weakness for rose decorations and sandstone steps.

The rest of the cemetery bears the hand of Fritz Schumacher and Otto Linne, who took over Cordes's job in 1920 after his death. New, geometrical lines were drawn in the parkland landscape under their direction but Linne maintained the original idea and planted new tree-lined roads and park-like groups of trees. But he was not interested in reproducing a natural landscape for his visitors.

Strolling through Ohlsdorf cemetery you can come across the names of many famous people: Hamburg's postwar peace poet Wolfgang Borchert (AG 5,6), the popular actor Hans Albers (Y 23, 245/254), the shipping magnate Albert Ballin (015) and the actor Gustaf Gründgens (06,5), all have resting places here. The list of famous occupants could be continued almost *ad infinitum*.

Professional mourners and bearers.

Ohlsdorf not only has numerous artistically designed gravestones but also a number of striking buildings. One of them is the **old crematorium** designed by Ernst-Paul Dorn. The oldest crematorium in western Germany, it is actually located outside the cemetery grounds on Alsterdorfer Strasse.

The **new crematorium** was designed by Fritz Schumacher and built in 1930–33. It is not only a milestone in Schumacher's architectural development but it also marked the end of his long career as Hamburg's chief architect. In 1933 he was summarily thrown out of office by the Nazis.

Monuments: Right opposite this crematorium is the **Memorial for the Victims of Fascism** (Kirschenallee near Chapel 13) and the **Memorial for the Victims of Bombing** designed by Gerhard Marcks (at the Bramfelder Chaussee entrance). Many prisoners of war and foreign nationals brought to Hamburg by the Nazis as forced labour, lie buried near Sorbusallee.

The neighbouring **Jewish cemetery** (Illandkoppel) is also well worth a visit. It is open daily except from 8 am–4 pm on Saturdays, but intending visitors must not enter with their heads uncovered. There is an enchanted, wild atmosphere about the place.

Nature seems to be taking hold of this part of Ohlsdorf again. Jews are forbidden, for religious reasons, from caring for their graves, which is why they have been allowed to run wild. This is Hamburg's most extensive Jewish cemetery, since all the city-centre burial grounds were full by 1883.

The **cemetery synagogue** (1883–84) is a beautiful building designed by August Pieper with the memorial to **Gabriel Riesser** another attraction. This great Jewish democrat, well known beyond the bounds of Hamburg, was one of the earliest propagators of equal rights for Jews. To the east of the synagogue stands the **Memorial for the Victims of the Holocaust** with the inscription which reads: "Unstilled the tears for those of our people who were struck down."

The village: Ohlsdorf cemetery has influenced and changed the whole district of the same name. **Ohlsdorf** itself was first mentioned as far back as 1303 and it remained a quiet farming village right up to the last few decades of the 19th century. Nowadays the suburb, which is part of the administrative district of Fuhlsbüttel, has some 18,000 inhabitants and also includes **Klein-Borstel**, a residential area to the east of the railway station of the same name.

Opposite Ohlsdorf station there are the very popular swimming baths, **Im Grunen Grunde** (but usually simply referred to as "Ohlsdorf"), the first baths in Hamburg where males and females were not strictly segregated.

Another less popular place to visit is referred to as "Santa Fu" in Hamburg: **Fuhlsbüttel prison**. When it was built, Ohlsdorf was still on the outskirts of Hamburg. The idea was for offenders to reflect on their criminal ways in supposedly "idyllic" green surroundings.

But there is also a dark side to the history of Santa Fu. The Nazis established a concentration camp here (1933–36) and later turned it into a Gestapo prison. Finally from 1943 to 1945, Fuhlsbüttel became one of the external camps linked to Neuengamme concentration camp. In the former entrance building (Suhrenkamp 98) a memorial to those who did not survive their time in Fuhlsbüttel is open on Sundays from 10 am to noon and at other times by appointment.

Unfortunately anyone looking for Ohlsdorf's or Klein-Borstel's rural past will be disappointed. Only one farm is left (Wellingsbütteler Landstrasse 59) and even here you can find a late 19th-century villa.

Klein-Borstel: One of Hamburg's prettiest and most popular walks passes through Klein-Borstel: the so-called **Alsterwanderweg**. This towpath route leads along the banks of the Alster from the city centre as far as Wohldorf-

Grave in Ohlsdorf designed by Ernst Barlach.

Ohlstedt on the outskirts. But you'd need a whole day to walk this distance. The most attractive part of the walk is from Klein-Borstel to Poppenbüttel and Mellingburger Schleuse. The meadows on both banks of the Alster attract crowds of cyclists, walkers, picnicking families and sun-worshippers on warm summer days.

You can also explore the Alster by boat, with canoes, rowing boats or the like, for hire at various places (e.g. Ratsmühlendamm). There is no better way of discovering the romantic side of Hamburg than from this non-canalised stretch of the river. Along the banks there are *haute bourgeois* villas (many with their own little landing stages) and coffee gardens where coffee and apple cake can make any day out that bit more appetising.

Alstertal: The area to the east of **Hamburg airport** in Fuhlsbüttel is not just one of the city's "green lungs". Four districts (Wellingsbüttel, Poppenbüttel, Sasel and Hummelsbüttel) make up

Alstertal, a total of 2,971 hectares (11 sq. miles) with some 63,000 inhabitants. It is a good-to-superior residential area with lots of beautiful houses and old villas dating from the days when rich Hamburgers had their country residences built in rural surroundings beyond the city walls.

Once a manorial village on the Alster, **Wellingsbüttel** was considered in the 17th and 18th centuries to be under the Holy Roman Emperor's direct rule. In 1806 the King of Denmark bought the manor and Wellingsbüttel therefore became an integral part of Holstein. From 1817 to 1938 it belonged to citizens of Hamburg and was then acquired by the city itself.

Two listed buildings are particularly attractive: the Wellingsbüttel **manor house** (built around 1750 and redesigned in 1889–90) and the half-timbered **Torhaus** (1757, designed by Georg Gregenhofer). In the manor house (which is reached via Friedrich-Kirsten-Strasse) the original layout of

Gatehouse in Wellings-büttel.

the rooms has survived on the ground floor. The middle room has an attractive rococo plasterwork ceiling. Since 1963 the Hansa-Kolleg has had its home here, a further education establishment which enables young people who have already been at work to go back to school and do further exams.

The Torhaus (Wellingsbütteler Weg 79g) houses one of the Alstertal's cultural attractions, the **Alstertal Museum**. It contains exhibits from prehistoric and early historical times, since there have been human settlements in the Wellingsbüttel area for some 14,000 years. Quite a few important prehistoric finds have been made hereabouts. The museum also has exhibits illustrating the history of shipping on the Alster from medieval times. It is open 11 am– 1 pm and 3–5 pm at weekends.

Anyone looking for relics from the so-called "good old days" of rural Wellingsbüttel will be disappointed. There is only a single cottage left on Wellingsbütteler Weg. But despite this, it is still worth strolling through Wellingsbüttel's streets where there are quite a few beautiful late 19th-century villas with large magnificent gardens. **Hoheneichen** railway station is a good place to start such a tour.

Sasel: Expansive areas of detached housing are the predominant feature of Sasel. The first mention of this former Holstein village was back in 1296 but the real development of the area did not begin until the 1920s. A Hamburg housing association bought the whole area and began the slow and back-breaking work of turning it into what it is today.

Most of the work was done by the members of the association themselves with each plot of land developed by its future inhabitants. While the work was going on most of them lived in huts on site, until the small detached houses were finished. Before World War II, Sasel was one of the largest areas of urban development on the outskirts of Hamburg. When it became part of the

18th-century Wellingsbüttel manor house.

city in 1937, there were already 5,835 people living in the vicinity.

Mellingburg with the above-mentioned Schleuse (lock) on the Alsterwanderweg that still regulates the water level of the Alster, is also part of Sasel. In former times it was part of the Alster-Trave canal and acted as a dam to enable boats to travel upstream on the upper reaches of the river.

At **Saseler Markt** you can still see the old manor house which was built in the late 19th century. Another building belonging to the manor, lovingly referred to as the "cowshed", housed a school for many years. Remains of the old village hall can still be seen; it now houses the local public library. Meteorologists have also found a home in Sasel. The German Meteorological Service had an observatory and instruments office in Frahmredder.

Poppenbüttel: Another part of Alstertal is the residential area of Poppenbüttel, which celebrated its 650th anniversary in 1986. From 1136 to 1803 Poppenbüttel belonged to Hamburg cathedral chapter and in 1937 it officially became part of Hamburg.

There are two explanations of its funny-sounding name. "Poppen" was either an old family name or referred to a group of religious figures which used to stand at an Alster crossing-place and were known in the local dialect as "Poppen" (dolls). The ending, *büttel*, is common in the area and was derived from the old Lower Saxon word *betele*, the term for a dwelling.

In the 1930s Poppenbüttel became a popular destination for day-trippers escaping from the pressures of the city. The large restaurants and cafés of those days have gone but **Kupferteich**, a relic of early industrial times, and **Poppenbütteler Schleuse** have remained popular.

Poppenbüttel, too, has a "relic" of Nazi times. Near the station, Jewish women from one of the external camps were forced to build prefabricated houses for bombed-out Hamburgers in the 1940s. The walls were concrete slabs and a flat gable roof was placed on top. Now these houses have been turned into a historical monument (open from 5–7 pm on Tuesdays and 10 am–noon on Sundays).

Hummelsbüttel: The quartet of Alstertal districts is completed by Hummelsbüttel. As late as 1950 it was still a real village, quite some way from the main road or rail links. However, in the 1960s a rapid process of development began with the result that Hummelsbüttel's tallest multi-storey buildings are now located right at the heart of the old village. The last remaining relics of rural times can be seen in **Hummelsbütteler Landstrasse** and a cottage (Grützmühlenweg 13) built around 1800. A well preserved row of boundary stones refers back to the time when Hummelsbüttel was on the border between Hamburg and Pinneberg.

The area of housing on Alte Landstrasse, Wesselblek, Alster and Am Gehöckel was originally settled in Ice Age and Bronze Age times. Two large fields of urns were unearthed here and more Ice Age finds were made in the Heublick, Am Hehsel and Alte Landstrasse areas.

Up to the end of the 19th century there was a mill and bakery in the street whose name refers back to that era: Grützmühlenweg, "groat's-mill-way". The old mill's machinery can now be seen at the Museum Village in Volksdorf.

Walkers and naturalists will enjoy a stroll through the neighbouring **Raakmoor**, which stretches westwards along the length of Glashütter Landstrasse. Here you can still see cotton grass in flower and, with a bit of luck and patience, some rare species of birds. In summer this landscape is ideal for horse riding and in cold winters it is excellent for tobogganing or ice skating.

This part of Hummelsbüttel also has the last remaining working farms from what used to be a flourishing agricultural settlement.

VIERLANDE AND ALTES LAND

Hamburg a farming village? This may be hard to believe but it's actually true. Germany's largest fruit, vegetable and flower garden is on the river Elbe – and part of the city-state of Hamburg. There are more apple, pear and cherry trees in Altes Land and more vegetables and flowers in Vierlande than anywhere else in Germany. As early as the Middle Ages this fertile soil in the glacial valley of the Elbe, watered by the river and many small tributaries, was farmed quite intensively with the produce then sold at Hamburg markets.

The medieval structure of settlement is still visible today. Mile after mile of farmhouses wind their way along the dykes built to keep back the water. Behind them the long narrow strips of fertile land are divided up by ditches. But structural changes have naturally affected the Elbe marshes over the centuries. Modern agricultural technology is now changing the landscape. More and more ditches are being filled in to make room for the large agricultural machinery needed to run modern farms economically. What is more, increasingly large areas of land are disappearing under greenhouse complexes to prolong the growing season.

The starting point for any trip through **Vierlande**, a 130-hectare (321-acre) region southeast of the city centre, between the Elbe and Bille rivers, is normally Bergedorf. Buses depart from the suburban railway station (S-Bahn) for the Vierlande villages, but in summer a three-hour boat trip on an Alster steamer from Jungfernstieg to Bergedorf harbour is an ideal way of getting some impression of the traditional landscape. The notable Vierlande villages of **Curslack**, **Altengamme**, **Neuengamme** and **Kirchwerder** present an unusually concentrated picture of traditional architecture.

Curslack is the place to visit for an insight into what life was like for the Elbe marshland farmers in past centuries. The open-air museum, **Rieck-Haus** (Curslacker Deich 284), is a Vierlande farmhouse originally built in 1530. It was rebuilt several times in subsequent years, the last "modernisation" being in 1663. The facade on the dyke side of the farmhouse with its beams and decoration is one of the most beautiful and best-kept traditional gabled buildings in Vierlande. The interior has the traditional division into three parts: first, the barn and stables; second, the communal cooking, eating and sleeping quarters; and third, the living and sleeping quarters for the farmer's family.

Obviously this farm was a prosperous one. There are Delft tiles on the walls, paintings on the ceiling and marquetry decorating the furniture. Even the sliding doors to the bed alcoves are artistically decorated with stars and flowers.

A lot of what seems strange to us nowadays actually had a very practical purpose centuries ago. The elaborate table legs with a bulge in the middle were designed thus to prevent mice climbing onto the table. The cords hanging down in the alcoves were certainly not there for mere decoration, people plagued by gout and rheumatism needed every help they could get to climb out of bed. There is a strip of wood inside the clothes chest, just below the rim. This was where the farmer's family would put some pennies away for a rainy day.

The traditional Vierlande costumes also had a very practical purpose. They were decorated with several dozen silver buttons which could be sold if the family fell upon hard times.

A stroll along the **Curslacker dyke** takes you past several other historical buildings. Worth seeing is **St Johannis-Kirche** (No. 142) built around 1600 as a half-timbered hall and then extended to become a church about 200 years later. The separate wooden bell tower is a typical feature of Vierlande churches with a shingle-roofed cupola that is one of the best examples of late baroque architecture in the area.

Altengamme is famous for its **St Nikolai-Kirche** with its splendid interior. Two outstanding features are the inlay work on the pews and the painted ceiling. The imaginative hatstands in the men's pews are a Vierlande speciality. The houses around the church reflect the revival of Vierlande architecture which began in Altengamme around the turn of the century. One classic example of this is the vicarage built in 1902, which has a splendidly decorated facade.

Neuengamme has a variety of architectural styles. At the centre of the village (Achter de Wisch 23) stands the oldest residential building in Vierlande, a 16th-century house. Three richly decorated farmhouses along Neuengammer Hausdeich were built in the heyday of Vierlande during the 16th and 17th centuries (No. 254 in 1653, No. 343 in 1626 and No. 413 in 1559).

Elsewhere in the village there is evidence of a dark chapter in Hamburg's history at the site of **Neuengamme concentration camp** south of Neuengammer Hausdeich in Jean-Doldier-Weg. A total of 106,000 people were deported from all over Europe to be interned by the Nazis at Neuengamme. More than half of them did not survive. After the war a prison was erected on the site – a move that can be seen either as the ultimate expression of bad taste or as an example of the democratic administration of justice. Whatever the standpoint, this prison will soon be a thing of the past.

Kirchwerder became important because of the customs and ferry houses at **Zollenspieker**, for many years the only official ferry across the Elbe linking Hamburg and the Lüneburg area. Customs dues have not been levied here since 1806 but Zollenspieker still serves as a ferry station.

Towards the end of the 19th century the ferry house was turned into a café

Typical wooden church in Vierlande.

and restaurant to attract day-trippers. Unfortunately the renovation work rather spoilt the appearance of the original 1621 building. But sitting in the restaurant high above the river or enjoying coffee under the lime trees in the garden watching the ships slowly pass along the Elbe is still a very pleasant experience.

The real heart of Kirchwerder is actually quite a long way away from Zollenspieker. **St Severin-Kirche** and the **cemetery** are particularly worth a visit. The oldest parts of the church are 13th-century and the cemetery has more historical gravestones than any other place in Vierlande.

In the other part of this area, **Marschlande**, fewer traditional buildings have survived. The urban influence is most noticeable in Moorfleet where motorways and industry have taken hold of what was once a simple rural village. The heart of Moorfleet around the baroque half-timbered church of St Nikolai has not changed so much and

Half-timbered facade near Kirchwerder Hausdeich.

several older buildings can still be seen.

Motorways and large residential estates have changed life in neighbouring Allermöhe. Now visitors are less attracted by the old heart of the village with its Dreieinigkeits church (built between 1611 and 1614) than by the new residential development south of Nettelnburg railway station. Considered an successful example of modern housing development, Neu-Allermöhe is characterised by lots of green areas, numerous small canals and smallish housing units.

Despite the many changes, all the Marschlande communities have hidden treasures well worth unearthing. In **Reitbrook** an attractive cluster of buildings has survived near the dyke: the Odemannsche Fährhof built in 1605, the Kornmühle (corn mill) built in 1870 and the Müllerhaus (miller's house) where Alfred Lichtwark, who founded Hamburg's Kunsthalle (art gallery), was born in 1852.

In **Billwerder** two buildings remind

visitors of the time when prosperous Hamburgers had their summer residences in what was then an idyllic landscape: the baroque **Glockenhaus** (Billwerder Billdeich 72) with its attractive 17th-century frescoes and a unique collection of exhibits illustrating the history of painting and the **Predigerwitwenhaus** (Billwerder Billdeich 96). A remarkable feature of **Ochsenwerder** is the **St Pankratius-Kirche** (1673–74) with its splendid interior and Johann Leonhard Prey's copper-plated west tower.

Altes Land: This area south of the Elbe stretching over 170 sq. km (65 sq. miles) from Finkenwerder in the east to Stade in the west, attracts its visitors predominantly in May. At the time, millions of fruit trees transform the whole area into a sea of white and pink blossom. After all, Altes Land is Europe's largest homogeneous fruit-growing region. But at other times of the year Altes Land also has its attractions – for example in autumn when the farmers bring in the harvest and sell fresh fruit juice or home-made fruit brandy from roadside stands.

The Este and Lühe dykes, ideal for walks, wind their way through Altes Land, between proud farmhouses with artistic half-timbering and varying tile designs. Some farmhouses still have their splendidly decorated 17th- and 18th-century wooden gates. The most beautiful examples of these decorated farmhouses are to be seen in **Neuenfelde** where the first of these driveway gates is also said to have been built. Another curious feature are the "bride's doors" on the gable side of the houses. These narrow, decoratively carved and painted doors could only be opened from the inside. Generally they were only ever opened on two occasions: weddings and funerals.

For the people of Hamburg Altes Land begins in **Cranz** on the river Este, where the Elbe ferry from Blankenese docks, or in **Grünendeich** on the river Lühe where the Elbe trip from St Pauli

Half-timbered houses in Altes Land.

Landungsbrücken terminates. Of course, there are other ways of getting to Hamburg's fruit garden but there is no more pleasurable means than by boat.

To the east of Cranz is Neuenfelde, which like Cranz and Francop is part of Hamburg. However, the majority of the area known as Altes Land is actually in Lower Saxony. In **Neuenfelde** the 200-year-old farmhouse (Nincoper Strasse 45) is well worth a visit. With its "bride's door", splendid decorative gate and magnificent gables it has all the characteristic features of farmhouses in the area.

The small redbrick church, **St Pankratius**, is a typical example of a north German baroque country church. The organ was built by the organ builder Arp Schnitger who lived in Neuenfelde from 1684 onwards and was buried in the church in 1719. The Neuenfelder population is particularly proud of the Sietas shipyard, not only the oldest but now the only yard on the Lower Elbe.

The "pearl of Altes Land" is what they call **Jork**. Though only a small village, it was actually the place where the German poet Gotthold Ephraim Lessing married his wife Eva König in 1776. The wedding did not, however, take place in the baroque church but in the house of a Hamburg businessman known as Schüback, who was originally from a local family. Jork is also famous for excellent local cuisine. At the **Herbstprinzen** in Osterjork and **Estehof** in Estebrügge you can enjoy local specialities and local atmosphere.

The oldest half-timbered house in the area, a fruit barn built in 1587, is in **Guderhandviertel**. The proud-looking stone-and-brick tower of **Hollener Kirche** is probably 12th century.

Right at the heart of this collection of villages is **Steinkirchen** which owes its name to the simple fact that it had a stone church as early as the 14th century. The present church, a proud-looking redbrick building with a wooden tower, is famous for its splendid baroque interior.

Hot-house flowers.

BERGEDORF

When a Bergedorfer says "I'm going into town," he doesn't mean Hamburg. The town centre he's referring to is the old heart of Bergedorf between Mohnhof and Lohbrügger Markt.

History: For centuries now, the people of Bergedorf, to the southeast of the city, have preferred to lead a life of their own. Back in the Middle Ages, knights, merchants and travellers sought protection on the heights above the river Elbe and in the lowlands along the river Bille. Even now, Bergedorf is far from happy if Big Brother in Hamburg interferes with its local politics. The proud people of Bergedorf – who are mainly industrious farmers, market gardeners, skilled craftsmen and businessmen – are used to responsibility and risk. Their resilience is hardly surprising if you consider Bergedorf's eventful history.

The first recorded mention of Bergedorf was in 1162. From 1201–27 it was under Danish rule. In 1275 the Duke of Saxony granted Bergedorf its municipal charter but for over 400 years (1420–1867) it was governed by the states of Hamburg and Lübeck working together. In 1867 the former bought it from the latter for the princely sum of 200,000 thalers. In 1938 the final chapter in Bergedorf's colourful history was opened when it was incorporated into Hamburg.

Bergedorf is Hamburg's second-largest district in terms of size (154.76 sq. km/59 sq. miles) but with only 96,918 inhabitants it is also the smallest district in terms of population. It is also the home of many particularly large families and was ex-Chancellor Helmut Schmidt's constituency. He represented the people of Bergedorf for four legislative periods at the federal parliament in Bonn.

Nowadays, there are three ways of getting to Bergedorf from Hamburg; the suburban rail link (S-Bahn), the old main road (B5) and new motorway (A25), and the ferry up the Elbe and Bille. The waterborne journey from Jungfernstieg in the centre of Hamburg, through canals to the Elbe and then upstream to the small harbour in the centre of Bergedorf, takes a total of three hours.

Bergedorf's Mauritius: The name of Bergedorf is sure to stir up some interest among philatelists since Bergedorf stamps from the 1861–67 period have quietly become a kind of north German Penny Black. At international auctions they are fetching top prices.

Astronomers will probably be surprised to hear that their colleagues in Bergedorf discovered the second-brightest star in the universe in 1989 – a quasar HS 1700+6416. Actually, **Bergedorf Observatory** (Am Gojenberg) is one of the leading centres of German astronomy – and it is open to the public.

Bergedorf is also a centre of forestry with Lohbrügge, at the northern end of the district, the home of the federal German forestry office. Experts from Lohbrügge are just as at home in domestic woods as they are in tropical rain forests. Successful graduates of what is also a training institute can earn themselves a diploma in forestry.

Songs, news and protests: Bergedorf's vocal talents have achieved national and international fame. An above-average number of locals sing in some 35 choirs and choral societies, all descendents of the **Bergedorfer Liedertafel** founded in 1838, one of the oldest choral societies in Germany.

Another superlative Bergedorf has earned comes in letters, not notes. It is the only district in Hamburg with its own surviving local newspaper. Founded in 1874, the *Bergedorfer Zeitung* also publishes local editions for Reinbek, Geesthacht, Schwarzenbek, Lauenburg and Boizenburg (Ex-GDR). Bergedorf's claim to literary fame is as the birthplace of Low German author Herta Borchert. Her more famous son,

**Left,
Bergedorf's
13th-century
castle, built
by the
Danish
governor.**

Wolfgang, was one of Germany's leading postwar pacifist writers.

Bergedorf also has a rather special and enlightened service for women: after nightfall, three pink-coloured "women's night cars" will give any woman from Bergedorf or the surrounding area a house-to-house ride for just 3 marks. Other committed citizens have made a name for themselves with protests against the transportation of nuclear waste, housing shortages and the destruction of green areas.

Even though a large part of the old centre of Bergedorf was sacrificed to build modern roads, there is more than enough to see for the historically – or artistically – minded. **Bergedorf Castle** was built as a moated fortification by the Danish Prince Albrecht of Orlamünde in 1212. His aim was to protect the old trading route from Hamburg to Lübeck. In later times it was the seat of the two cities' administrative officials and now the **Bergedorf and Vierlande Museum**, with agricultural exhibits and an art history section. The medieval north wing and entrance were rebuilt around the turn of the century in the simple north German red-brick Gothic style, a characteristic feature being the stepped gables.

Between the castle and the western end of the Altstadt is the Lutheran **St Peter and Paul's**, a half-timbered church with a 16th-century tower, richly decorated interior and rustic gospel paintings. There are still some half-timbered houses in Bergedorf's main shopping street.

Stadt Hamburg (Sachsentor 2) is the oldest inn in Hamburg. In the 1950s it was renovated and moved slightly to the east; now it belongs to the Block House chain of steakhouses, common all over northern Germany. The wrought-iron sign over the door is 18th century.

The **Kornwassermühle** (water mill) at Alte Holstenstrasse 86 was also the product of Albrecht of Orlamünde's efforts. It was renovated in 1839. Near the mill there is a 8-metre (26-ft) high crane which loaded cargoes on to Hamburg-bound boats around the turn of the century. The **Alte Bahnhof** (old station) at Neuer Weg was designed by Alexis de Chateauneuf and built in 1842 for the first railway line between Hamburg and Bergedorf. The station (pictured on the following page) is actually the second-oldest railway station in Germany and has recently been converted into a museum in time for its 150th anniversary.

Anyone who still has some time and energy left for more architecture could complete the circuit round the heart of Bergedorf by taking a look at the beautiful and expensive late 19th- and early 20th-century villas situated between Chrysanderstrasse, Reinbeker Weg and Daniel-Hinsch-Strasse.

Most famous man: Bergedorf's most famous resident, though himself a Berliner by birth, is the industrialist Dr. Kurt A. Körber. Among the many projects he has sponsored is the **Haus am Park,** built in 1977 as a senior citizens'

Maritime pub on the Bille.

home, advice and encounter centre, theatre and concert hall. Körber established Hauniwerke in 1947, now the world's leading manufacturer of tobacco machines. As well as serving as patron to many worthy causes, Körber also founded the Bergedorf Discussion Circle in 1961. This internationally renowned event takes place three times a year. Experts from East, West and the Third World are invited to discuss issues of importance for a free industrialised society.

Only five minutes' walk away from the Haus am Park along Wentorfer Strasse is the 35-metre (114-ft) high tower of **Bergedorf town hall**. It was built around the magnificent core of the Messtorff villa with its splendid hall of mirrors, mahogany room and marble staircase. The Bergedorfers are just as proud of their town hall as they are of three other buildings designed by the famous Hamburg architect Fritz Schumacher in the 1920s: Luisen-Gymnasium (grammar school) at

Bergedorfer Gehölz, the Hansa-Gymnasium on Hermann-Distel-Strasse and the District Court (Amtsgericht) on Ernst-Mantius-Strasse.

Little Amsterdam: If you want living proof of the fact that modern housing need not necessarily result in anonymous concrete jungles, pay a visit to **Neu-Allermöhe** (accessible via S-Bahn station Nettelnburg). You might well think you've landed in Amsterdam. Along little canals where boats are moored and swans swim to and fro, there are three- or four-storeyed apartment houses, terraced housing, town houses and even some "eco" (ecologically-conscious) houses which have grass growing on their roofs.

Several common architectural features crop up here: reddish-brown bricks, white window-frames, bay windows and winter gardens. Half of the houses are owner-occupied, the other half are council housing. In all, 10,000 people live in this new part of Bergedorf which has been provided with almost every-

One of Bergedorf's half-timbered houses.

thing the locals need: day nurseries, children's play house, primary school, community centre, shopping centre, pubs, restaurants, surgeries and a bank. In keeping with this rather self-conscious new district, all the streets are named after famous German women.

It has been a successful project: right next to Neu-Allermöhe in the direction of Hamburg there are plans for a large-scale "Allermöhe II" with 5-6,000 housing units. The present inhabitants of the area hope that architects and politicians will again avoid the town-planning mistakes of many of their predecessors.

Fight for the land: Bergedorf is surrounded by different sorts of culture. There are 13,000 hectares (50 sq. miles) of grain, rape, strawberries, tomatoes, lettuce, cucumbers, primulas, roses, asters or daffodils in the neighbouring Vierlande. Some 200 hectares (494 acres) are grassland, and many areas are covered by greenhouses, with some 1,050 horticultural and 150 agricultural establishments in the area.

This fruitful soil is in the glacial valley of the river Elbe between the Bergedorf slopes and the present-day course of the river. Two tributaries, the Dove and Gose Elbe, cut through this low-lying region, adding to the fertility.

As late as the 12th century, this area was nothing more than a couple of islands surrounded by bog. Later the land was divided up into 16-hectare (40-acre) lots stretching from the main dyke to the rear dyke for tenant farmers to work. The results of their efforts over the centuries are in evidence at every local market.

But man's attempts to win land by reclaiming it from the river have suffered repeated setbacks over the years. Storm tides have repeatedly broken the dykes and flooded the low-lying marshy land. With very little in the way of natural barriers between here and the North Sea, Bergedorf is vulnerable. When Hamburg's catastrophic storm tide brought killer floods on 17 February 1962, at least 50 dykes burst and 100,000 people were cut off. Altogether 318 died.

Ever since, money has been spent to improve the defenses. Hamburg's 29 km (18 miles) of dykes will be raised from six to seven metres and widened from 50 to 80 centimetres by 1994.

Environmental problems: Bergedorf nowadays has also had to come alive to the problems of a polluted environment. Right next to Moorfleet is the industrial area of Billbrook. To the west of Bergedorf is the highly industrialised Billstedt, an incineration plant, one of north Germany's largest chemical plants (Norddeutsche Affinerie), Tiefstack power plant, several small chemical and metal-working firms and the infamous chemicals firm of Boehringer (now compulsorily closed down because of its environmental pollution). Air and soil pollution have become a greater threat to life in Bergedorf than floods and burst dykes. Now the locals are fighting for and not against nature.

Left, Germany's second oldest railway station at Bergedorf. Right, the romantic Bille valley.

TRAVEL TIPS

GETTING THERE

BY AIR

In recent years, Hamburg Airport, locally known as Fuhlsbüttel, has developed into a hub of air traffic in Northern Europe and now plans are afoot for extensions to the present airport or even construction of a new one. Hamburg has direct air links to all the major European cities and several non-stop transatlantic routes. For airport information tel: 50750.

From the airport you can get to the city centre by taxi or the regular Jasper coach service which goes to the main railway station. The 110 bus also provides a link to the suburban rail station of Ohlsdorf.

BY LAND

The best way into the city from the south is by car on the A7 *autobahn* via Hannover or from the southwest on the A1 *autobahn* via Bremen. The A1 bypasses the city to the south-east and goes on to Lübeck, intersecting, to the east of the city, with the A24 *autobahn* which goes to Berlin.

The A7 heads north through Hamburg for Kiel and Denmark, passing through the new Elbe tunnel and the city – Altona and the Elbe suburbs. Shortly before leaving Hamburg, another *autobahn* branches off the A7 heading for Itzehoe and the North Sea coast. From Bremen, the Elbe tunnel is clearly signposted on the A1.

Hamburg has three mainline inter-city rail stations (Hauptbahnhof, Dammtor and Altona) with excellent links to all major German cities and most European capitals. Bundesbahn information is on tel: 19419.

BY SEA

From Hamburg there is a direct ferry link to Harwich on the east coast of England. The 21-hour journey is operated by Scandinavian Seaways, departing every other day. In the UK tel: 0255 241234; in Hamburg tel: 389030.

TRAVEL ESSENTIALS

VISAS & PASSPORTS

A valid passport is the only requirement to enter the Federal Republic (including all parts of new Germany). Members of the European Community (EC) only need identity cards. Holders of Australian, Canadian, Japanese, New Zealand, South African and United States passports automatically get three-month permits on crossing the border, but visas are required for longer stays. Visitors from outside the EC are not allowed to take up any employment.

MONEY MATTERS

The German Deutschmark (D-Mark) is a decimal currency made up of 100 pfennigs. The coins come in denominations of 1, 2, 5, 10 and 50 pfennigs, and 1, 2, and 5 DM. The notes are in denominations of 5, 10, 20, 50, 100, 200, 500 and 1,000 DM. Money may be changed at any bank and local money changers (*Wechselstuben*) usually found in train stations, airports and in tourist areas. (*For banking hours, see below*). It is advisable to carry traveller's cheques instead of cash, as the former can be replaced if lost or stolen; remember to keep the cheque numbers separately noted.

Although the Germans aren't very fond of credit cards, you can pay your bills in hotels, restaurants or big department stores with American Express, Diner's Club, Visa or MasterCard. You may have problems, however, in smaller towns or villages. Eurocheques can be cashed practically everywhere.

CHANGING MONEY

Principal money changing locations:
Hauptbahnhof (Halle), tel: 30800475, daily 7.30am–10pm.
Hauptbahnhof (Südsteg), tel: 30800480, Monday–Saturday 7.30am–3pm and 3.45pm–8pm, Sunday 10am–1pm and 1.45pm–6pm.
Bahnhof Altona, tel: 3903770, Monday–Saturday 7.30am–3pm and 3.45pm–8pm, Sunday 10am–1pm and 1.45pm–6pm.
Flughafen Fuhlsbüttel, tel: 598883, daily 6.30am–10.30pm.

WHAT TO WEAR

Whatever the season, pack both a raincoat and your sunglasses because the weather can be very unpredictable indeed. Even if you come in the hottest summer months (July and August) you are advised to bring one warm sweater or cardigan. And for your trip to the North Sea and the Baltic you should bring a jacket or a raincoat.

Alternatively, you can "go native" and buy a *Friesennerz* (a yellow rubber raincoat) and a pair of rubber boots quite cheaply. Most Germans are very fashion-conscious, especially in big urban areas such as Berlin, Hamburg or Munich. Long evening dresses and tuxedos are still worn when attending the opera, although this is beginning to change.

CUSTOMS

There are no restrictions on the amounts of local or foreign currency you can bring into the Federal Republic. You are also allowed to bring any personal belongings and equipment as well as reasonable quantities of food for your own consumption. In addition, visitors may bring in limited quantities of tobacco, alcohol, etc., duty-free. European (EC) citizens can import 300 cigarettes or 150 cigars or 75 large cigars or 400 gm tobacco; 1½ litres of wine; 750 gm of coffee (beans) or 300 gm instant coffee; 150 gm of tea or 60 gm of instant tea; 75 gm of perfume; and ³/₈ litres of toilet water.

These limits apply to goods bought in ordinary shops. If bought in duty-free shops, there are slightly lower limits. European nationals other than those from the EC have a slightly smaller allowance.

VAT

VAT (*Mehrwertsteuer*) in Germany comes in two rates: 14 percent and 7 percent. Fourteen percent VAT (MWST) is added to all goods except food, books and newspapers which are taxed at 7 percent. All services such as the hairdressers add 14 percent VAT. Restaurant menu prices include 14 percent VAT. The tax can be deducted if you buy expensive articles, provided you fill in a sales form when buying the article. Present both the form and article at customs when you return home, have it stamped and send it back to the shop where you bought the article, which will then reimburse you.

GETTING ACQUAINTED

POLITICS

Of the many city-states that were dotted around the map of Germany in the Middle Ages, only Hamburg and Bremen have survived. Since 1949 they have enjoyed the status of Federal States within the Federal Republic of Germany. Hamburg was founded in the 7th and 8th centuries but did not receive its town charter until the 12th and 13th centuries. It was not officially recognised as an Imperial Free City until 1768.

Traditionally, Hamburg's government has been known as the Senate, its parliament as the Bürgerschaft. Apart from the 1953–57 period when Christian Democrats headed a coalition government, Hamburg has been ruled by Social Democrats since 1946. The Liberals (FDP) have been involved in several coalitions, including the present one.

AREA & POPULATION

Hamburg covers an area of 755.3 sq. km (291 sq. miles), of which 8 percent is water. It is certainly a green city – 42 percent of its area is covered by farmland, woods, parks and gardens. 1.6 million people live in Hamburg, 10 percent of them foreigners. The first census in 1811 recorded a total of 106,983 inhabitants of what is now the city centre and of the two suburbs of St Georg and Hamburger Berg (later rechristened St Pauli). The million mark was passed before World War I. In the mid-1960s Hamburg's population reached the record total of 1.85 million before falling in the two decades that followed. Since 1988 this trend has been reversed.

Some 950,000 Hamburgers belong to the Lutheran church and 170,000 are Roman Catholics. There are also some 20 more churches or religious denominations represented in the city.

ECONOMY

Trade and the port continue to dominate Hamburg's economy. In recent decades the city's manufacturing industry has gone through radical structural changes and electrical engineering, mechanical engineering and chemicals are now more important than the traditional shipbuilding industry. The petroleum and aerospace industries are also extremely important nowadays, and the service sector has developed.

Besides the traditional strengths of trade, banking and insurance, media has become an important sector in Hamburg.

The unemployment rate is around 10 percent and thus above the national average. Hamburg offers a total of 730,000 jobs with over 43 percent of them taken by women and 7 percent by foreigners. Hamburg's gross earnings of over DM95,000 per head of population puts the city in second position behind Frankfurt am Main (around DM102,000).

Hamburg's universities and colleges are also an important economic and cultural factor with over 60,000 students studying in the city. The University of Hamburg, founded in 1919, now has more than 40,000 students and is the fifth-largest in Germany after Munich, Berlin, Cologne and Münster.

WEIGHTS & MEASURES

Germany uses the metric system. Some useful metric equivalents:

1 gram = 0.03563 oz
1 kilogram = 2.2046 lbs
1 metric tonne (1,000 kilos) = 0.9842 ton
1 litre = 1.7598 pints
1 centimetre = 0.3937 inch
1 metre = 3.281 ft
1 kilometre = 0.62137 mile
1 sq. cm = 0.155 sq. inch
1 sq. metre = 10.764 sq. ft
1 hectare (10,000 sq. metres) = 2.4711 acres
1 cu. cm = 0.061 cu. inch
1 cu. metre = 35.315 cu. ft

TEMPERATURES

In Germany, temperature is measured on the Celsius or Centigrade (C) scale.

Celsius	Fahrenheit
100	212
90	194
80	176
70	158
60	140
50	122
40	104
30	86
20	68
15	59
10	50
+5	41
0	32
−5	23
−10	14
−15	+5

ELECTRICITY

Germany's electrical supply works on the 220-volt system. Two-pin plugs are in use nationwide.

BUSINESS HOURS

Most shops are open from 9.30am to 6–6.30pm. Small shops such as bakeries, fruit and vegetable shops and butcher's shops open as early as 7am, close for 2½ hours about noon, re-open at around 3pm and remain open until 6.30pm in the evening. Shops located in the railway stations and airports usually have late shopping hours (some are open till midnight). Business hours are usually 8am–5.30pm. Government offices are open to the public in the mornings from 8am–12 noon.

Banking hours are Monday to Friday from 9am–noon and 1.30pm–3.30pm. In most towns, banks are open until 5.30pm on Thursdays. There are slight variations in the different federal states.

PUBLIC HOLIDAYS

Public holidays draw a line right through the Federal Republic. On the one side are the Catholic states and on the other the Protestant. Below, the dates in parentheses are national public holidays:
New Year's Day: 1 January.
The Magi: 6 January.
Good Friday: changes from year to year; refer to German calendar.
Easter Monday: changes from year to year; refer to German calendar.
May Day: 1 May.
Christi Himmelfahrt (Ascension Day): changes from year to year; refer to German calendar.
Whit Monday: changes from year to year; refer to German calendar.
Fronleichnam (Corpus Christi Day): in Catholic states. Changes from year to year; refer to German calendar.
Mariä Himmelfahrt: in some Catholic states. Changes from year to year; refer to German calendar.
Day of German Unity: 3 October.
All Saints' Day: 1 November in Catholic states.
The Day of Prayer and Repentance: changes from year to year; refer to German calendar.
Christmas Day: 25 December.
Boxing Day: 26 December.

FESTIVITIES & FAIRS

If you look hard enough, you can always find an excuse to celebrate; in Hamburg there is always something going on at any time of the year. Principal occasions include the **Hafengeburtstag** (Port Anniversary) on 10 May. Then, three times a year in spring, summer and autumn, there's the huge funfair at Heiligengeistfeld, Hamburg's **Dom** – a spectacle featuring all the latest hits from the world of pleasure technology. In August/September there's the **Alstervergnügen** around the Inner Alster when clowns, pantomime groups and bands compete with sausage stalls, champagne stands and Indian, Italian, Chinese or Thai chefs for the crowds' favour. There are usually so many people it's hard to decide where to go next – especially as you're (literally) swimming with the crowd.

For years now, the **Stuttgarter Weindorf** (wine village) in June or July has been a popular attraction at Rathausmarkt, contradicting the prejudiced view of North Germans as people who drink nothing but beer. When the weather's good, two other events are particularly attractive in the summer: the **Schleswig-Holstein Music Festival**, initiated and organised by Justus Frantz (some of the concerts are held in Hamburg) and the **Hamburger Sommer** (May to September) with its No-Budget Short-Film Festival, the European Low-Budget Film Festival, open-air concerts in the Stadtpark, the International Summer Theatre at Kampnagelfabrik, the Midsummer Jazz Festival, the Rathaus Concerts and the open-air cinema at Rathausplatz.

In addition to all this, Hamburg has developed into a fair and congress venue. Besides numerous specialist congresses taking place regularly, the Hamburg Exhibition Centre also stages exhibitions and fairs such as **Reisen** (Travel), **InternorGa** (catering), **Du und Deine Welt** (international family exhibition), **Hanseboot** (boat show) and **Art Hamburg** (international art fair).

WEATHER & CLIMATE

When you start talking about the weather in Hamburg, you're on a difficult subject in statistical terms; apparently it rains less in Hamburg than in Munich. Actually Hamburg's total rainfall is considerably less than in the Bavarian capital – the only problem is that Hamburg's is spread around through the year. "Schmuddelwetter" (muddled weather) is how the locals refer to it and they don't seem to get too worked up about it anyway. After all, it gives them a chance to demonstrate how anglophile they all are and get out their umbrellas. It's certainly a good idea to bring rain protection with you.

Although summer is not normally particularly hot (with a mean temperature of just over 17°C/62°F), autumn often brings a beautiful Indian summer. Even Hamburg's winters are, statistically speaking, far from bitter. Moreover, the fact that there's usually a pleasant breeze normally blows away the exhaust fumes.

The only thing about Hamburg's weather which really irritates are the weeks in winter when it doesn't rain and there's no snow but you still don't see the sun for days on end. Then, even the most hardened local patriots start to dream about more southerly climes.

COMMUNICATIONS

MEDIA

The press in the Federal Republic is diverse. The range extends from conservative newspapers like the *Frankfurter Allgemeine Zeitung*, socialist newspapers like the *TAZ* (*Tageszeitung*) highbrow papers like the *Süddeutsche Zeitung*, to the popular press, the most infamous being the *Bildzeitung*. The former GDR newspaper *Neues Deutschland* is now published with a new, rather serious image, whereas the *Junge Welt* has a more critical and defiant approach. For information on cinema, theatre, exhibitions and concerts, consult any local paper. Foreign newspapers and magazines are available in every town. There are also international bookshops, especially at railway stations, airports and city centres.

Detailed information about what's going on in Hamburg is available in the three city-listings magazines – *oxmox*, *Prinz* and *Szene Hamburg* – available at every newspaper stand or kiosk.

Radio and television broadcasting in Germany is under public control. There are two national TV stations, ARD and ZDF, with ARD having local stations in each state. DFF (formerly the East German channel) now broadcasts ARD programmes. For those who speak or understand German the main news programmes on TV are *Heute* at 7pm (ZDF), and *Tagesschau* at 8pm (ARD).

ARD also maintains nine radio stations: NDR, RB, SFB, WDR, HR, SWF, SDR, SR and BR. The third channel of these stations broadcasts the current traffic reports (on FM). Younger listeners may appreciate the more relaxed Radio 110 in Berlin.

POSTAL SERVICES

The post offices (*Postamt*) are usually open from 8am to 6pm, with smaller ones closing at noon for lunch. You can have your mail sent care of an individual main post office provided it is marked *poste restante*; it will be left at the counter identified by the words *Postlagernde Sendungen*. The postal rates for letters and postcards within the old German states of what used to be West Germany are DM1 for letters up to 20 gm and 60 pfennigs for postcards. The same rates apply for mail to Andorra, Austria, Belgium, Denmark, France, Great Britain, Italy, Liechtenstein, Luxembourg, Monaco, the Netherlands, San Marino, Switzerland and Vatican City. Standard letters (up to 20 gm) to all other countries cost DM1.30 plus 20 pfennigs for air mail; postcards must have an 80-pfennig stamp.

For the five new German states the following rates continue to be applicable:

Abroad:

letters up to 20 gm	70 pfg
postcards	50 pfg

Inland:

letters up to 20 gm	50 pfg
postcards	30 pfg

The inland rates quoted above are also applicable for letters and postcards to Albania, Bulgaria, China, Yugoslavia, North Korea, Cuba, Laos, Mongolia, Austria, Poland, Roumania, Soviet Union, Czechoslovakia, Hungary and Vietnam.

Local post boxes (*Briefkasten*) are emptied at least twice a day (morning and evening); those designated with a red point are emptied more frequently. On Saturdays, there is only one service. For sending telegrams you have either to dial 1131 on a private telephone or go to the post office. The charges are 80 pfennigs per word within Germany and Europe; for overseas telegrams inquire at the post office.

TELEPHONE

In public pay phones insert 30 pfennigs for local calls. For long-distance calls you can also dial direct from most of the yellow public phone boxes but remember to take enough coins with you (10-pfennig pieces and 1- and 5-mark pieces), or you can go to a post office where an operator makes the connection. Every place of any size in Germany has its own dialling code, which is listed under the local network heading. Should you have a language problem, dial 00118 (international directory enquiries). The former East German directory enquiry service is not yet standardised and differs from town to town. Phone calls from foreign countries to Germany must still be preceded by (49) for the West and (37) for the East.

EMERGENCIES

EMERGENCY SERVICES

Police. Tel: 110.
Fire Brigade. Tel: 112.
Poison Information Centre. Tel: 63853345/46.
Emergency medical service. Tel: 228022.

Emergency dental service. Tel: 11500. Saturday, Sunday and public holidays 10am–noon and 4pm–6pm, Wednesday and Friday, 4pm–6pm or tel: 4683260.
Emergency veterinary service. Tel: 434379.
Nighttime chemist service; each chemist shop has details of the nearest outlet open in the evenings and at night; this information is also available by phoning the emergency medical service.

LOST & FOUND

Fandbüro der Hansestadt Hamburg and der Hamburger Hochbahn, Bäckerbreitergang 73. Tel: 351851.
Fandbüro der Bandesbahn, Stresemannstrasse 114. Tel: 39182685.
Fandbüro der Bandespost, Hühnerposten 12. Tel: 23951195.

GETTING AROUND

PUBLIC TRANSPORT

Hamburg has an excellent public transport system with underground (U-Bahn), suburban rail (S-Bahn) and bus services. There are now 750,000 cars and lorries officially registered in Hamburg and hundreds of thousands of commuters from the surrounding region also try to get to work by road. So Hamburg's roads are not much different from any other big city – congested. There are a great many separate bike paths so there's no reason to stick to the car.

Hamburg Tourist Board offers a nicely-priced means of getting around with its Hamburg Card, available for DM9.50 in all the Tourist Board's offices. It is valid for a whole day and enables the user to travel on all the public transport services in the Greater Hamburg region and visit 11 museums free. There are also reductions of 25–40 percent for trips with the "Hummelbahn", Alster steamers and harbour launches.

Useful telephone numbers are:
Hamburger Verkehrsverband-Information (HVV), tel: 322911, daily 7am–8pm, for all suburban rail, ferry and bus services.
Zentraler Omnibusbahnhof (ZOB), Adenauerallee 78. Tel: 247575, for bus services.
ADAC-Informationsdienst. Tel: 11600, 1169. Information for the motorist.

UNDERGROUND

The U1 (blue) line runs from Ohlstedt in the northeast (Walddörfer) via Hauptbahnhof, stations west of the Alster and Ohlsdorf (Cemetery) to Garstedt.

The U2 (red) line runs from Niendorf in the northwest via Hauptbahnhof to Barmbek and Wandsbek.

The U3 (yellow) runs from Barmbek westwards around the Alster, via St Pauli and Landungsbrücken to Hauptbahnhof and eastwards to Mümmelmannsberg, where Hamburg borders on Schleswig-Holstein.

SUBURBAN RAIL

The suburban rail network (S-Bahn) runs well beyond Hamburg's borders – as far as Elmshorn (S5) in the northwest, Wedel (S1) in the west and Neugraben (S3 and S31) in the southwest (via Harburg and Wilhelmsburg). In the northeast the trains run as far as Ahrensburg (S4) and in the southeast as far as Bergedorf and Aumühle (S21). There is a surcharge for 1st class seats on suburban rail lines.

AKN

Another suburban rail link, identified with an "A", reaches as far as Barmstedt, Quickborn and Kaltenkirchen to the north and northwest of Hamburg.

FARES

Hamburg has a passenger transport executive uniting all the underground, suburban rail, harbour ferry and bus services and commonly referred to as HVV (Hamburger Verkehrs-Verbund). An adult ticket for the whole region costs DM5.20 and for the central region DM3.20. Short journeys costs DM2.10. Children aged between 4 and 12 pay DM1.10. Surcharges have to be paid for 1st-class seats in the S-Bahn as well as for express or night buses. There are reduced fares for families and groups. Detailed information can be obtained from all HVV Offices; the city-centre addresses are:

Hauptbahnhof, Eingang Kirchenallee. Open: Monday–Friday 7am–9pm, Saturday 8.30am–3pm, Sunday 11am–7pm.

HHA-Kundenzentrum, Steinstrasse 27. Open: Monday, Tuesday, Wednesday, Friday 9–4.45pm, Thursday 8am–6pm.

Haltestelle Jungfernstieg, Eingang Neuer Wall. Open: Monday–Friday 6am–7pm, Saturday 8am–2.30pm.

Bahnhof Dammtor. Open: Monday and Friday 6am–7pm, Tuesday–Thursday 10.30am–7pm.

BUSES

Apart from the buses which cover the most populous areas of Hamburg, there are also numerous routes to outlying districts. If you take the S3 to Wilhelmsburg, for example, you can get on a 156 bus and travel through the Port (also possible with the 152 and 151 which crosses Kohlbrandbrücke). The latter runs from Altona Station through the Elbe tunnel to Finkenwerder and Cranz. Other buses which pass through the Port are the 451, 252 and 153.

HARBOUR FERRIES

HVV not only has its land-based routes but also a number of ferries. From Landungsbrücken, for example, you can take the ferry to Altenwerder or further on to Finkenwerder. Information on all the ferry routes is available from HVV Offices.

TAXIS

Autoruf. Tel: 441011.
Behindertentaxi. Tel: 4105458 (pre-booking).
das Taxi. Tel: 611122.
Funktaxi Hamburg. Tel: 686868.
Funktaxi-Ruf Hamburg. Tel: 7743553.
Hansa Funktaxi. Tel: 211211.
Taxi-Ruf Hamburg. Tel: 611061.

CYCLE HIRE

Tourismus-Zentrale in Bieberhaus, Hachmannplatz, tel: 30051245, May–September, advance booking necessary.
Fahrrad-Richter, Barmbeker Strasse 16. Tel: 275095.

WHERE TO STAY

HOTELS

Many of the city's noblest hotels are now just history (e.g. the St Petersburg on the site of the present-day Alsterarkaden), demolished, redeveloped or simply destroyed in World War II. Only two of the traditional luxury hotels have survived. For many years, Hotel Atlantic was the No. 1. This was where the rich stayed when they had booked their cruise from Hamburg. Now the undisputed No. 1 is Vier Jahreszeiten, for many years a family hotel but now owned by the Japanese. But it's not just the leading hotel in Hamburg, Germany or Europe; worldwide, Vier Jahreszeiten holds second place behind the Oriental in Bangkok. Naturally the prices are in line with this rating so most visitors to Hamburg have to make do with admiring the white building on the Inner Alster from outside.

Besides these top addresses, Hamburg also has numerous very good and good hotels. However, they are frequently fully booked, in itself a fine recommendation. Ninety percent occupancy is common, particularly thanks to Hamburg's reputation as a congress and trade fair venue. Another reason, however, is the fact that the City of Hamburg has taken over many of the cheaper guest houses and hotels as accommodation for those seeking political asylum or immigrants from the East. So if you don't go for a package deal, it's a good idea to book early. Information on hotels is available from:

Tourismus-Zentrale Hamburg, Burchardplatz 14. 2000 Hamburg 1. Tel: 040/300510.
Tourist-Information-Büro, Hauptbahnhof, Hauptausgang Kirchenallee (am Bahnsteig 1).
Tel: 040/326917.
Private rooms can be booked via **Agentur Zimmer Frei**, Heimweg 3. Tel: 040/412070/79.

The approximate prices given with the hotels listed below are for double rooms. Price ranges are as follows: Expensive DM250+, Moderate DM150–250 and Inexpensive less than DM150. This list is a selection of some of Hamburg's more interesting venues.

EXPENSIVE

Atlantic, An der Alster 72–79. Tel: 28880.
Aussenalster, Schmilinskystrasse 11–13. Tel: 241557.
Elysée, Rothenbaumchaussee 10. Tel: 414120.
Garden, Magdalenenstrasse 60. Tel: 449958.
Hanseatic, Sierichstrasse 150. Tel: 485772.
Intercontinental, Fontenay 10. Tel: 414150.
Marriott, ABC-Strasse 52. Tel: 35050.
Prem, An der Alster 9. Tel: 241726.
Ramada Renaissance, Grosse Bleichen. Tel: 349180.
Reichshof, Kirchenallee 34. Tel: 248330.
Strandhotel, Strandweg 13. Tel: 861344.
Vier Jahreszeiten, Neuer Jungfernstieg 14. Tel: 34940.

MODERATE

Abtei, Abteistrasse 14. Tel: 442905.
Baseler Hof, Esplanade 11. Tel: 359060.
Bellevue, An der Alster 14. Tel: 248011.
Graf Moltke, Steindamm 1. Tel: 2801154.
Hafen Hamburg, Seewartenstrasse 9. Tel: 311130.
St Georg, Kirchenallee 23. Tel: 241141.
York, Hofweg 19. Tel: 2202653.

INEXPENSIVE

Alameda, Collonaden 45. Tel: 344000.
Alsterkrone, Schwanenwik 14. Tel: 225218.
Am Dammtor, Schlüterstrasse 2. Tel: 450570.
Arndt, Steindamm 23. Tel: 243333.
Bei der Esplanade, Collonaden 45. Tel: 342961.

Benecke, Lange Reihe 54–56. Tel: 245860.
Bergunde, Eppendorfer Baum 5. Tel: 482214.
Blume, Hofweg 73. Tel: 2201839.
Elite, Binderstrasse 24. Tel: 454627.
Pension Sarah Petersen, Lange Reihe 50. Tel: 249826.
Pfeiffer, Hallerstrasse 2. Tel: 447830.
Preuss, Moorweidenstrasse 34. Tel: 445716.
Schwanenwik, Schwanenwik 29. Tel: 2200918.
Sphinx, Colonnaden 43. Tel: 351377.
Sternschanze, Schanzenstrasse 101. Tel: 433389.

YOUTH HOSTELS

Jugendherberge auf dem Stintfang (located on a small hill above the Port), Alfred-Wegener-Weg 5. Tel: 31348.
Jugendgästehaus Horner Rennbahn (somewhat out of the city centre but with good public transport links), Rennbahnstrasse 100. Tel: 6511671.
Jugendpark Langenhorn (only for groups or families), Jugendparkweg 60. Tel: 5313050.

CAMPING SITES

Camping Anders, Kieler Strasse 650. Tel: 5704498.
Campingplatz Schuldt, Kronsaalsweg 86. Tel: 5404994.
Campingplatz Buchholz, Kieler Strasse 374. Tel: 5404532.

FOOD DIGEST

RESTAURANTS

Connoisseurs claim that Hamburg has a broader and more diversified range of restaurants than any other city in Germany. You don't need to worry about quantity taking over from quality – there are menus here to suit every taste, from local dishes to exotic meals and from simple cooking to haute cuisine.

HAUTE CUISINE

Some of the "best 444 restaurants in Germany" are in Hamburg. So they deserve a special mention here along with a few other luxury restaurants – listed in their order of (published) merit.
Landhaus Scherrer, Elbchaussee 130. Tel: 8801325. Monday–Saturday noon–2.30pm and 6pm–10.30pm.

Le Canard, Elbchaussee 139. Tel: 8805057. Monday–Saturday noon–1.30pm and 7pm–9.30pm.

Landhaus Dill, Elbchaussee 404. Tel: 828443. Tuesday–Sunday noon–3pm and 6pm–11pm.

La Mer, in Hotel Prem, An der Alster 9. Tel: 245454. Daily 12.30pm–3pm and 6.30pm–midnight.

Petit Delice, Grosse Bleichen 21 (Galleria). Tel: 343470. Monday–Saturday noon–3pm and 6pm–10pm.

Anna e Sebastiano, Lehmweg 30. Tel: 4222595. Tuesday–Saturday noon–3pm and 7pm–10pm.

L'Auberge Française, Rutschbahn 34. Tel: 4102532. Monday–Friday noon–2pm and from 6.30pm.

Cölln's Austernkeller (caviar and lobster restaurant), Brodschrage 1-5. Tel: 326059. Monday–Friday 10am–midnight and Saturday from 6pm.

La Fayette, Zimmerstrasse 30. Tel: 225630. Monday–Friday noon–2.30pm and 6.30pm–10.30pm , Saturday from 7pm.

Fischereihafen-Restaurant, Grosse Elbstrasse 143. Tel: 381816. Daily 11.30am–10.30pm.

Haerlin/Vier Jahreszeiten, Neuer Jungfernstieg 9-14. Tel: 3494641, Monday–Saturday 11am–3pm and 6pm–10pm.

Il Ristorante, Grosse Bleichen 16. Tel: 343335. Daily noon–midnight.

Ventana, Grindelhof 77. Tel: 456588. Monday–Friday noon–3pm and 6pm–midnight, Saturday 6pm–midnight.

Amadeus/Die Insel, Alsterufer 35. Tel: 4106955. Monday–Sunday 8pm–2am.

Atlantic-Grill/Atlantic-Hotel, An der Alster 72. Tel: 2888-0. Monday–Sunday noon–3pm and 6pm–11.30pm.

Bistro Canard, Martinistrasse 11. Tel: 4604830. Monday–Saturday noon–2.30pm and 6.30pm–10.30pm.

Fontenay-Grill/Inter-Continental, Fontenay 10. Tel: 443430. Daily noon–3pm and 6pm–midnight, Saturday from 6pm.

STEAK HOUSES

Block House, Kirchenallee 50, and a dozen more in various parts of Hamburg. Tel: 243350. Monday–Sunday 11am–1am. Fair prices, good food.

Cottage, Lokstedter Steindamm 7. Tel: 5533669. Monday–Sunday 11am–midnight. Recommended.

Denver, Neuer Wall 34. Tel: 366575 or Dockenhudenerstrasse 34. Tel: 869858. Monday–Sunday 11am–midnight. Not just for the rich.

Farmer-Steakhouse, Jahnring 21. Tel: 516668. Monday–Sunday noon–midnight.

John Johnson, Steindamm 43. Tel: 2802614. Monday–Thursday and Sunday 11am–1am, Friday and Saturday 11am–10.30am. Lots of variety.

Steakhouse Arizona, Barmbeker Strasse 150. Tel: 484866. Monday–Sunday noon–midnight. Reasonable prices.

Steakhouse California, Isestrasse 1. Tel: 4200504. Monday–Sunday noon–midnight. Lots of variety.

CHINESE

Hong-Kong, Gärtnerstrasse 103. Tel: 400417. Sunday–Friday noon–3pm and 6pm–11pm.

Hsie Lin Men, Nobistor 14. Tel: 3195510. Monday–Sunday noon–3pm and 6pm–1am.

Man Wah, Spielbudenplatz 18. Tel: 3192511. Monday–Friday noon–3am, Saturday and Sunday noon–midnight.

Peking, Lincolnstrasse 10. Tel: 310833. Monday–Sunday noon–2am.

Peking-Entenhaus, Rentzelstrasse 48. Tel: 458096. Monday–Friday 6pm–midnight, Saturday and Sunday noon–3pm and 6pm–midnight.

FRENCH

Benedikt, Dorotheenstrasse 182. Tel: 4603464. Monday–Friday noon–3pm and from 6pm, Saturday from 6pm.

Bistro Canard, Martinistrasse 11. Tel: 4604830. Monday–Saturday noon–3pm and 6.30pm–11.30pm.

Brasserie Maxim, Gänsemarkt 50. Tel: 344160. Monday–Sunday 11am–midnight.

Café des Artistes (in Mövenpick), Grosse Bleichen 36. Tel: 3410032. Monday–Saturday noon–3pm and 6.30pm–11.30pm – food till 10pm.

Casse Croute, Büschstrasse 2. Tel: 343373. Monday–Sunday noon–3pm and 6.30pm–midnight.

Chez Jacques, Gertigstrasse 42. Tel: 2792938. Monday–Saturday noon–2.30pm and 6pm–11.30pm.

Cristo's, Sierichstrasse 46. Tel: 2793699. Monday–Saturday noon–2.30pm and 6pm–midnight.

Dominique, Karl-Muck-Platz 11. Tel: 344511. Monday–Friday noon–3pm and 6pm–11pm, Saturday from 6pm.

L'Auberge Française, Rutschbahn 34. Tel: 4102532. Monday–Friday noon–2.30pm and 6.30pm–11.30pm.

Le Paquebot, Gerhart-Hauptmann-Platz 70. Tel: 326519. Monday–Saturday 11am–4pm and 6pm–midnight, Sunday from 6pm–midnight.

Le Provençal, Lattenkamp 8. Tel: 513828. Tuesday–Sunday 7pm–11pm.

Le Relais de France, Poppenbütteler Chaussee 3. Tel: 6070750. Monday–Saturday 6.30pm–10pm. Bistro open from noon–2pm and 6.30pm–10pm.

Le Restaurant du Parc, Grasweg 70. Tel: 2705049. Monday–Friday noon–2.30pm and 6pm–11pm, Saturday 6pm–11pm.

Martial, Langenfelder Damm 10. Tel: 404152. Tuesday–Saturday noon–2.30pm and from 7pm, Sunday from 7pm.

Rexrodt, Papenhuderstrasse 35. Tel: 2297198. Monday–Sunday 7.30pm–11.30pm.

GREEK

Calypso, Hofweg 50. Tel: 221916. Monday–Friday noon–3pm and 6pm–12.30am, Saturday 6pm–12.30am, Sunday noon–3pm and 6pm–12.30am.

Irodion, Winterhuder Marktplatz 12. Tel: 461201. Monday–Friday noon–3pm and 5pm–midnight, Saturday and Sunday noon–midnight.
Lukullion, Walddörferstrasse 70. Tel: 6521378. Monday–Sunday noon–3pm and 5pm–midnight.
Poseidon, Karolinenstrasse 1. Tel: 432152. Monday–Sunday 11am–2.30pm and 5pm–2am.
Satki, Eppendorfer Weg 210. Tel: 4202599. Monday–Sunday 6pm–midnight.

INDIAN

Calcutta-Stuben, Papenhuder Strasse 30. Tel: 223904. Monday–Sunday, 6pm–11pm.
Indra, An der Alster 23. Tel: 246095. Monday–Sunday 11.30am–2.30pm and 5pm–12.30am
Jaipur, Lerchenfeld 14. Tel: 2209475. Monday–Sunday 5pm–midnight.
Maharani, Dorotheenstrasse 180. Tel: 4807868. Monday–Saturday 6pm–midnight, Sunday noon–10.30pm.
Satidal, Schrammsweg 10. Tel: 4803153. Monday–Sunday 6pm–midnight.
Satliba, Osterstrasse 10. Tel: 4919262. Tuesday–Sunday 7pm–midnight.
Shalimar, Dillstrasse 16. Tel: 442484. Monday–Saturday 6pm–midnight, Sunday 6pm–11pm.
Taj Mahal, Schulterblatt 88. Tel: 433661. Tuesday–Sunday 5pm–midnight.

ITALIAN

Al Campanile, Spadenteich 1-3. Tel: 246738. Monday–Friday noon–3pm and 6pm–2am, Saturday 6pm–2am.
Bologna, Hudtwalckerstrasse 37. Tel: 4601796. Monday–Friday noon–3pm and 6pm–midnight, Saturday 6pm–midnight.
Borsalino, Barmbekerstrasse 165. Tel: 476030. Sunday–Saturday noon–3pm and 6pm–midnight.
Cuneo, Davidstrasse 11. Tel: 312580. Monday–Saturday 6.30pm–2am.
Difronte, Kampstrasse 27. Tel: 4396454. Monday–Friday 5pm–1am.
Etna, Dorotheenstrasse 33. Tel: 2704837. Monday–Friday noon–3pm and 6pm–midnight, Saturday 6pm–midnight.
Fra Diavolo, Hudtwalckerstrasse 16. Tel: 475735. Monday–Friday noon–2.30pm and 6.30pm–midnight, Sunday 6.30pm–midnight.
Il Gfrombiano, Eppendorfer Landstrasse 145. Tel: 4802159. Monday–Saturday noon–2.30pm and 7pm–11.30pm.
Made in Italy, Hofweg 25. Tel: 222701. Monday–Friday noon–3pm and 6pm–midnight, Saturday and Sunday 6pm–midnight.
Picco Bello, Schenkendorfstrasse 30. Tel: 222536.
Roma, Hofweg 7. Tel: 2202554. Monday–Friday noon–3pm and 6.30pm–10.30pm, Saturday from 6.30pm.
Satle u. Pepe, Sierichstrasse 94. Tel: 273880.

Senzanome, Mühlenkamp 54. Tel: 276717. Monday–Sunday noon–2.30pm and 6.30pm–midnight.
Toni's Örtchen, Lehmweg 6. Tel: 4207698. Tuesday–Sunday from 7pm.
Trattoria Toscana, Holländische Reihe 25. Tel: 396086. Monday–Friday noon–3pm and 6pm midnight, Saturday 6pm–midnight.
Tre Fontane, Mandsburger Damm 45. Tel: 223193. Wednesday–Monday noon–3pm and 7pm–11pm.

JAPANESE

Daitokai, Milchstrasse 1. Tel: 4101061. Monday–Saturday noon–3pm and 6pm–11pm.
Fuji, Richardstrasse 18. Tel: 296668. Monday–Friday noon–2pm and 6pm–11pm, Saturday 6pm–11pm.
Japan-Stübchen, Hoheluft-Chaussee 49. Tel: 4202661. Monday–Sunday 6pm–1am.
Matsumi, Colonnaden 96. Tel: 343125. Monday–Saturday noon–2pm and 6pm–10.30pm.
Wa-Yo, Hofweg 75. Tel: 2271140. Tuesday–Sunday 6pm–11pm
Yamato, Ernst-Merck-Strasse 4. Tel: 247904. Wednesday–Monday 6pm–midnight.

YUGOSLAVIAN

Bei Marija, Klosterwall 4 a. Tel: 324895. Monday–Friday 11am–11pm, Saturday 11am–3pm and 6pm–11pm.
Beograd, Schiffbeker Weg 96. Tel: 7314788. Tuesday–Sunday noon–3pm and 6pm–midnight.
Rila, Finkenau 1. Tel: 2206027. Tuesday–Sunday 5pm–1am.

PORTUGUESE

A Portugalia, Kleiner Schäferkamp 28. Tel: 417555. Tuesday–Saturday 5pm–1am, Sunday noon–midnight.
Benfica, Vorsetzen 53. Tel: 3193826. Monday–Sunday noon–midnight.
Galego, Vorsetzen 70. Tel: 371171. Monday–Sunday 10am–midnight.
Porto, Ditmar-Koel-Strasse 15. Tel: 3194813. Daily, 11.30am–midnight.
Portugal, Loogestieg 3. Tel: 478767. Monday–Friday 4pm–midnight, Saturday and Sunday noon–midnight.
Satgres, Vorsetzen 42. Tel: 371201. Monday–Sunday noon–midnight.

SPANISH

La Sepia, Schulterblatt 36. Tel: 432484. Monday–Sunday noon–3am.
Madrid, Grindelberg 69. Tel: 4228103. Tuesday–Thursday 6pm–midnight, food till 11pm.
Marbella, Dorotheenstrasse 104. Tel: 275757. Tuesday–Sunday 6pm–midnight.

Olympiada Hellas, Reimarusstrasse 13. Tel: 313626. Tuesday–Sunday noon–midnight.

SYRIAN

A'Shamra, Rentzelstrasse 50. Tel: 454975. Tuesday–Sunday from 6pm.

THAI

Arang, Kleine Reichenstrasse 16–18. Tel: 327906. Monday–Saturday noon–3pm and 6pm–11pm.

Baan Thai, Gänsemarkt 50. Tel: 340441. Monday–Sunday noon–midnight.

Dong Nai, Stellinger Weg 47. Tel: 493618. Tuesday–Saturday 6pm–11pm, Sunday noon–11pm.

Kim-Chi, Schanzenstrasse 27. Tel: 434165. Monday–Friday 6pm–midnight, Saturday and Sunday 5pm–midnight.

Phuket, Fuhlsbütteler Strasse 306. Tel: 6321167. Monday–Friday 5pm–midnight, Saturday and Sunday noon–midnight.

Satla Thai, Brandsende 6. Tel: 335009. Monday–Sunday noon–3pm and 6pm–midnight.

Sukhotai, Dornbusch 4. Tel: 336489. Monday–Saturday noon–3pm and 6pm–11.30pm.

TURKISH

Anadolu, Johnsallee 64. Tel: 451455. Monday–Sunday from noon.

Arkadasch, Grindelhof 17. Tel: 448471. Monday–Sunday 11.30am–midnight.

Atnali, Rutschbahn 11. Tel: 4103810, Monday–Sunday from noon.

Serafim, Papenhuderstrasse 22. Tel: 2295234. Monday–Sunday noon–1am.

Yakamoz, Schrammsweg 28. Tel: 4602234. Monday–Sunday noon–1am.

VEGETARIAN CUISINE

Café Koppel, Koppel 66. Tel: 249115. Daily 11am–8pm.

Charfromon, Wandsbeker Königstrasse 63. Tuesday–Saturday noon–2am, Sunday 11am–midnight (sometimes has live music).

Die Grüne Kochmütze, wholemeal cuisine, Steinstrasse 19. Tel: 335526. Monday–Friday 8am–5pm , first Saturday of the month 10am–5pm.

Golden Temple, Eppendorfer Baum 34. Tel: 483801. Monday–Saturday 10am–noon or 10pm, Sunday noon–3pm or 3pm–8pm.

Hexenkeller, An der Verbindungsbahn 6. Tel: 451324. Tuesday–Sunday 4pm–midnight.

Horizont, Wholemeal Restaurant & Café, Harkortstieg 4. Tel: 3893336. Monday–Sunday 6pm–midnight, Sunday 11am–3pm Brunch. A bit expensive.

Natur-Gourmet, Papenhuder Strasse 37. Tel: 2278308. Monday–Friday noon–4pm.

Sushi-Bar, Vegetarian Snack-Bar, Bahrenfelder Strasse

208. Tel: 3909212. Tuesday–Sunday noon–midnight.

Villa Massimo, Marktstrasse 55. Tel: 4302464. Monday–Sunday 6pm–2am, food till midnight.

Winterhuder Kaffeehaus, Winterhuder Markt 16. Tel: 478200. Daily 10am–midnight.

Zorba the Buddha, Karolinenstrasse 7-9. Tel: 4394762. Daily 11am–midnight.

TYPICAL HAMBURG COOKING

Alt Hamburger Aalspeicher, Deichstrasse 43. Tel: 362990. Monday–Sunday 11am–midnight.

Brahmsstuben, Ludolfstrasse 43. Tel: 478717. Thursday–Tuesday 7pm–11.30pm.

But'n Dammdoor, Mittelweg 27. Tel: 444512. Monday–Friday 11am–1am, Sunday 5pm–1am.

Deichgraf, Deichstrasse 23. Tel: 364208. Monday–Friday 11am–11pm, Saturday 6pm–11pm.

Fischerhaus, Fischmarkt 14. Tel: 314053. Monday–Sunday 10am–11pm.

Historischer Gasthof Anno 1750, Ost-West-Strasse 47. Tel: 330070. Monday–Friday noon–midnight, Saturday 5pm–midnight.

Krause, Steindamm 101. Tel: 2802222. Monday–Friday 11.30am–8.30pm.

Old Commercial Room, Englische Planke 10. Tel: 366319/366368. Monday–Sunday 11am–1am.

Zum Alten Rathaus, Börsenbrücke 6-10. Tel: 367570. Monday–Friday noon–midnight, Saturday 6pm–midnight.

Zur Schlachterbörse, Kampstrasse 42. Tel: 436543. Monday–Friday 10am–1am.

CAFES BY REGION

ALTONA

Brooklyn, Grosse Brunnenstrasse 105. Tel: 3901040. Sunday 11am–4pm. Reasonable prices.

Café Katelbach, Grosse Brunnenstrasse 60. Tel: 3905511. Monday–Saturday noon–3pm, Sunday 10am–3pm. Good, inexpensive, recommendable.

Café Treibeis, Gaußstrasse, im Werkhof. Tel: 393357. Saturday 11am–2pm, Sunday noon–2pm. Inexpensive and varied menu.

Eisenstein, Friedensallee 9. Tel: 3904606. Monday–Saturday 11am–3pm, Sunday 10am–3pm. Brunch.

Loretta, Thadenstrasse 78. Tel: 435787. Sunday 11am–3pm. Tried and tested breakfast buffet.

EIMSBUTTEL

Café Strauss, Wiesenstrasse 46. Tel: 493131. Monday–Friday 11am–2pm, Saturday and Sunday 10am–3pm. Huge selection, good prices.

Meisenfrei, Eppendorfer Weg 75. Tel: 4919121. Monday–Friday 11am–3pm, Saturday and Sunday 10am–3pm. Moderately priced and good.

Schotthorst, Eppendorfer Weg 58. Tel: 4918121. Saturday and Sunday 10am–4pm. Large selection for any wallet.

Sweet Virginia, Bismarckstrasse 10. Tel: 406195. Monday–Friday from 9.30am, Saturday and Sunday from 10am. Low prices, but exclusive atmosphere.

EPPENDORF

Café Lindtner, Eppendorfer Landstrasse 88. Tel: 475571. Monday–Saturday 8.30am–noon, Sunday 10am–noon. Good daily buffet, affordable restaurant, rich in tradition.

Factory, Hoheluft-Chaussee 95. Tel: 4203711. Monday–Friday 10am–2pm, Saturday and Sunday 9am–2pm. Broad selection of the finest quality.

Herzog, Eppendorfer Landstrasse 31. Tel: 464159. Monday–Saturday from 10am, Sunday 11am–3pm. Large selection at yuppie-style prices.

Kaktus, Heinickestrasse 3. Tel: 483508. Monday–Friday noon–2pm, open from Saturday 8pm to Sunday morning 8am – moderate.

Legendär, Lehmweg 44. Tel: 473207. Monday–Friday 10am–1pm, Saturday and Sunday 10am–3pm. Broad range of choices.

CITY

Andersen, Jungfernstieg 36. Tel: 353015. Monday–Saturday 7.30am–7pm, Sunday 9am–7pm. The quality is excellent.

Café Oertel, Esplanade 29. Tel: 340275. Monday–Friday 6.30am–6.30pm, Saturday 6.30am–4pm. Recommendable and inexpensive.

Café Schöne Aussichten in the old botanical gardens. Tel: 340113. Monday–Friday 11am–6pm, Saturday–Sunday 11am–3pm. For professional breakfast diners.

Loft (in der Galleria), Grosse Bleichen 21. Tel: 354337. Monday–Saturday 10am–4pm. Not cheap, but popular.

Marriott, ABC-Strasse 52. Tel: 3505-0. Monday–Sunday 6.30am–11am, Sunday noon–3pm. Brunch.

SCHANZENVIERTEL/ST PAULI

Café im Buch, Beim grünen Jäger 21. Tel: 4302636. Monday–Friday noon–3pm, Saturday and Sunday 10am–3pm. Superb.

Café Klatsch, Glashüttenstrasse 17. Tel: 4390443. Monday–Sun 10am–7.30pm. For all tastes.

September, Feldstrasse 60. Tel: 437611. Monday–Saturday from 10am, Sunday 10am–2pm. The former "Journal" has a lot to offer, even brunch on Sunday. Extremely cozy and affordable.

ST GEORG

Café Gnosa, Lange Reihe 93. Tel: 243034. Tuesday–Sunday 11am–4pm. Always very busy.

Café No. 1, Lange Reihe 9–11. Tel: 246925. Monday–Sunday from 9am. Not expensive.

Max & Consorten, Spadenteich 7. Tel: 245617. Monday–Sunday 10am–2pm, Sunday from 10am large buffet. Relaxed 1960s atmosphere.

UHLENHORST

Café Schwanenwik im Literaturhaus, Schwanenwik 38. Tel: 2201309. Monday–Friday 10am–noon, Saturday and Sunday 10am–3pm. Large selection.

AROUND THE UNIVERSITY

Café Backwahn, Grindelallee 148. Tel: 4106141. Monday–Sunday 10am–6.30pm. Affordable and delicious.

Café Neumann, Grindelhof 11. Tel: 447738. Monday–Friday 7am–6.30pm, Saturday 7am–1pm. Self-service, therefore inexpensive.

Café Sommergarten, Mittelweg 26. Tel: 4105473. Monday–Sunday 8am–6pm. Anything you want, everything affordable.

Funk-Eck, Rothenbaumchaussee 137. Tel: 444174. Monday–Friday 7.30am–8pm, Saturday and Sunday 8am–8pm. Big selection starting at DM6.

Objektiv, Grindelhof 39. Tel: 447779. Monday–Sunday 9am–6pm. Including country-style fare – not expensive.

Schantil, Heinrich-Barth-Strasse 17. Tel: 446176. Monday–Sunday 10am–4pm. Something for every wallet.

Stradiwadi, Rentzelstrasse 17. Tel: 453575. Monday–Friday from 9am, Saturday and Sunday from 10am. Relaxed atmosphere, affordable.

Unique, Rentzelstrasse 6. Tel: 448204. Monday–Saturday from 11am, Sunday 11am–3pm. Broad selection, a breakfast paradise on Sunday.

AROUND THE PORT

Berni Fick, Fischmarkt 5. Tel: 313261. 24-hour drinking den.

Bierhaus am Fischmarkt, Grosse Elbstrasse 128. Tel: 3895888. Monday–Friday 10am–2am, Saturday till 5am and Sunday till 6pm. A real harbour pub.

Gröninger, Ost-West-Strasse 47. Tel: 331384. Monday–Saturday noon–midnight. Beer from their brewery in the cellar.

Haifischbar, Grosse Elbstrasse 128. Tel: 3809342. open daily from 9am for drinking games.

Strandcafé, Övelgönne 1. Tel: 3903443. Daily 10am–2am either inside or outside on the terrace.

Strandperle, Am Schulberg. Tel: 8801112. Sunday–Friday 11am–8pm, Saturday 11am–10pm. A meeting place for locals and tourists, right on the Elbe.

THINGS TO DO

HAMBURG BY WATER

The "classic" boat trip is the harbour tour with one of the HADAG ships, which also offer special trips down the Elbe to Stade or Glückstadt or up the river to Lauenburg near what used to be the East German border. But you can also travel through the Kiel Canal to the Baltic or along old trading routes to Bad Bevensen (Elbe-Seiten-Kanal).

There are various cruises on the Outer Alster and trips along Hamburg's canals (and Speicherstadt) which start from the Inner Alster. But why not hire a boat yourself and row along delightful waterways to the Stadtpark?

BOAT TRIPS

Big Harbour Tour: Brücke 2, St Pauli Landungs-brücken, adults DM12, children under 14 DM6; parents with several children DM30.
Kiel through the Kiel Canal: Brücke 3, St Pauli Landungsbrücken, adults DM54, children DM34.
Vierlande trips: from Jungfernstieg, daily except Tuesdays, 10.15am, adults DM34, children DM17 (return fares).
Alster cruises: from Jungfernstieg every half hour (April–October) for five or more landing stages DM5. Alster round trips: from Jungfernstieg, adults DM10, children DM5.
Dusk trip: from Jungfernstieg, in summer, 8pm daily, adults DM17, children DM8.50.
Canal trips: from Jungfernstieg, daily dep. at 10.15am, 1.45pm and 4.15pm, adults DM20, children DM10.
Canal trips: from Jungfernstieg, daily dep. at 9.15am, 12.45pm, 2.45pm and 5.15pm, adults DM17, children DM8.50.
Bridge trips (over 100 bridges): from Jungfernstieg, Tuesday 10.15am, adults DM23, children DM11.50.

HAMBURG FOR CHILDREN

The "Grosse Hafenrundfahrt" (or big harbour tour) starts from Brücke 2 (*see above*) almost every hour; if lots of people want to go, the boats leave more often. *He lücht* (he lies) is the name Hamburgers give to the "experts" who supply information about the harbour during these trips. The Barkassen-Hafentour also leaves hourly from various landing stages and lasts about an hour too. It'll take you right through the port into some of the most interesting parts of this maritime world. For information on various tours, tel: 37680021/24.

Particularly recommended is a visit to the Speicherstadt. This warehouse complex is not only huge but also unique – there's nothing like it anywhere in the world.

At St Pauli-Landungsbrücken you can also visit a museum sailing ship called *Rickmer Rickmers*, an old three-master barque which is open to visitors every day from 9am till 6pm (Tel: 353119). Another fairly old ship is mooored at Überseebrücke – a freighter called *Cap San Diego* (Tel: 3905546, open Friday, Saturday and Sunday 10am–4pm), which was due to be scrapped till Hamburg saved it and turned it into a museum.

It's only a short walk from here to Övelgönne where you can visit a real Museum Harbour, which is always open and always full of old sailing boats, coastal ships, cutters and fishing boats. If you've got a bit more time and fancy a boat trip along the Elbe, you can travel as far as Wedel and take a look at Willkommhöft in the Schulauer Fährhaus. This place is famous the world over since it booms out a welcome to every ship that sails in and out of the Port of Hamburg. In the Fährhaus itself is the **Buddelschiffmuseum** with several hundred ships in bottles from all over the world and lots of other maritime exhibits. Open daily 10am–6pm (ring 04103/83094 for details).

The Alster in Hamburg's city centre is actually the biggest lake in any European city. Actually it's a dammed river which flows through Hamburg from the north. Between these two rivers, the Elbe and the Alster, and a third one called the Bille, Hamburg has a big network of canals (or "Fleet" as they are called here) and bridges. The city has more bridges than Venice, Amsterdam or London.

Boat trips for the Alster and the Bridge's Trip depart from Jungfernstieg; get details by ringing 341141/341145. From April–October boats depart daily every half hour from 10am to 6pm. Fares vary from DM6–12. If you fancy a row or sail on the Alster, there are at least half a dozen boat-hire places around the lake.

Most of Hamburg's cultural attractions have special programmes for children.
Zoological Museum, Martin-Luther-King-Platz 3. Tel: 41233880. Open Tuesday–Friday 10am–7pm and every 2nd and 4th Saturday in the month from 10am till 5pm. Loads of information about different kinds of animals and man's relationship to them and lots about threatened species.
Electrum, The Electricity Museum, Klinikweg 23 (near Hamburger Strasse Underground). Tel: 6363641. Open Tuesday–Sunday 9am–5pm. Plenty of sparks flying!
Falkenstein Dolls' Museum, Grotiusweg 79, in Sven-Simon-Park. Tel: 810582. Open Tuesday–Sunday 11am–5pm.

German Games Museum (Spielemuseum), Glockengiesserwall 3. Tel: 324272. Open Friday 2–8pm, Saturday/Sunday 10am–8pm, Friday games evenings from 8pm (on Wednesday and Thursday only open by special arrangement; admission DM2.50 for kids and DM5 for adults). Collection of ancient and modern games.

Museum für Hamburgische Geschichte, Holstenwall 24. Tel: 34912-2360. Open daily 10am–5pm (except Mondays). This is Hamburg's most interesting history museum. Includes a model railway exhibition.

Hamburg also has theatres with special plays for children. Details of what's on are available in the daily papers or by ringing the theatre:

Kellertheater Hamburg, Karl-Muck-Platz 1. Tel: 324312 and 337124. Monday–Friday 10am–6pm and Saturday 10am–1pm.

Theater an der Marschnerstrasse, Marschnerstrasse 46. Tel: 292665. Comedies, children's ballet and unusual Hamburg dance groups.

Theater für Kinder, Max-Brauer-Allee 76. Tel: 382538/383759. Plays start Monday–Friday at 4.30pm, Saturday 2.30pm and 5pm.

EXPLORING WITH CHILDREN

Hamburg's most famous church is simply known as **Michel** (St Michaelis). It's in Krayenkamp (tel: 371727) and also has a viewing platform at the top of the tower. Michel is Hamburg's most famous landmark and the best example of baroque church architecture anywhere in North Germany. Open on weekdays 9am–5.30pm, Sunday noon–5.30pm. Visitors can get up the tower on weekdays (9am–5pm) and Sunday (11.30am–5pm) – there is a lift.

Hamburg's **Rathaus** claims to be bigger than Buckingham Palace. Tel: 3681-0. Guided tours: Monday–Thursday 10am–3pm, Friday, Saturday and Sunday 10am–1pm (on the half hour). Walk on to **Planten un Blomen**, a park on the old walls that used to surround Hamburg, with a roller- and ice-skating rink and a great playground. There's also a new Japanese Garden and the Old Botanical Garden, a huge greenhouse complex with exotic plants (get to it from Stephansplatz or the Congress Centrum). For details tel: 41232327. Open daily 9am–4.45pm. The new and bigger **Botanical Garden** is in Klein-Flottbek, Ohnhorststrasse 18, near Klein Flottbek station (tel: 82220, open daily from 9am till an hour before sunset).

Not far from the park is Hamburg's unmissable **TV Tower**, over 200 metres (656 ft) tall (Lagerstrasse 2–8, tel: 438024). Take the lift to visit the revolving restaurant up near the top. (Open all year from 9am–11pm.) The lift costs DM2.50 for the under-12s, everyone else has to pay DM4.

The **Planetarium** (in the Stadtpark, near Borgweg Underground, tel: 516621) has good talks and tours. There are films too (with a different programme each month): Sunday 11am, 2.30pm and 4pm, Wednesday 4pm and 6pm, Friday 6pm. You can see stars each day at 11am and 2.30pm and 4pm. Good view from the tower.

Hagenbeck Tierpark (tel: 5400010) is one of the most interesting zoos in Europe with over 2,000 animals and a big programme especially for children each summer. The zoo is open daily from 8am. There's a "Troparium" and a "Dolphinarium", with animal feeding times for seals and penguins at 10.15am and 3.30pm every day. From spring to autumn there are also shows with dolphins and sealions: Monday–Friday in summer at 11am, 12.30pm, 2.45pm and 4.15pm; spring and autumn Monday–Friday 11.30am, 1.30pm and 3.30pm; Saturday and Sunday 11am, 12.30pm, 2.45pm and 4.15pm.

In St Pauli you shouldn't miss the **Panoptikum** (Spielbudenplatz 3, St Pauli U-bahn station next to the famous Davidswache Police Station, tel: 310317), which has one of the biggest collections of wax figures in Europe. Open daily 11am–9pm, Saturday till midnight, Sunday from 10am. The under 16s pay DM3 and adults pay DM5.

In St Georg the traditional **Hansa-Theater** (Steindamm 17, tel: 241414) has music-hall shows with acrobatics and magic (4pm and 8pm, Sunday 3pm and 7pm; tickets cost DM15–35).

Just beyond Landungsbrücken is the biggest and one of the oldest **fish markets** in Northern Europe, which starts at 5am in summer months and is all over by 9.30am, Sundays only. The market runs along the side of the river (Grosse Elbstrasse), and its merchandise is by no means restricted to fish; once you get near it, you can't fail to hear the crowds.

Organised **sightseeing tours** to all these places depart daily from Kirchenallee by the main railway station at 10am, noon, 2pm and 4pm; trips last between 1½ and 2½ hours.

CITY WALKS

Although Hamburg is an urban metropolis, it offers numerous attractive walks. Large areas of water, parks and elegant residential districts can make you forget you're in Germany's second-largest city.

Outer Alster: Starting at Kennedy-Brücke (which separates the Inner from the Outer Alster), you can stroll round the Alster in about three hours, past magnificent villas from Alte Rabenstrasse to Krugkoppelbrücke, and stopping off in one of the numerous cafés en route. From Fernsichtbrücke, next to Krugkoppelbrücke, you can see as far as the towers of the city centre. Alster steamers, swans, yachtsmen and rowing dingies criss-cross the lake.

On the eastern banks, in Uhlenhorst, there are roads with suitable names: Bellevue and Schöne Aussicht. It is on the latter that you'll be surprised to find a Shiite mosque. From Schöne Aussicht you can walk on to Schwanenwik and then An der Alster, taking advantage of the lakeside path to avoid the traffic. Passing one of Hamburg's two finest hotels, the Atlantic, you are soon back where you started. By crossing Kennedy-Brücke and the road itself, you reach Esplanade. There are wonderful views of the lake, the city centre and the so-called Art Island from the 13th floor of Finnlandhaus, where there is an excellent Finnish restaurant. If you're lucky, you might even experience one of those wonderful "blue hours" on the Alster, just after sunset.

Övelgönne: A walk through Övelgönne begins in Altona at the impressive Rathaus. From there you cross to a park known as Altonaer Balkon and go down Kaistrasse and Neumühlen to the refrigerated warehouse at Neumühlen-Kai. Once you've had a good look at the small boats decorating the Museum Harbour, move on to picturesque Övelgönne with its terraces of what used to be fishermen's and sailors' cottages. About half way, the so-called "Himmelsleiter" leads up to Hamburg's noblest road, Elbchaussee. A bit further on and you get to "Strandperle", a popular pub in summer when many guests simply take their drinks down onto the Elbe sand.

Port city: Start from the Rathaus and walk along Rathausstrasse, Speersort and Burchardstrasse to the famous Chilehaus, a block of offices designed to look like a ship's bows. From here it's only a stone's throw to the Elbe via Pumpen and Messberg. If you walk on via Dovenfleet and Zippelhaus in a westerly direction, you'll not only pass some attractive trading houses but also see the redbrick facades of Speicherstadt on the other side of Zollkanal; cross one of several bridges to have a look round this, the world's largest homogeneous warehouse complex.

CULTURE PLUS

MUSEUMS

See also Hamburg for Children, above.

Alstertal-Museum, Wellingsbütteler Weg 75 a. Tel: 5366679. Saturday, Sunday 11am–1pm and 3pm–5pm. This museum at the gateway to the former Wellingsbüttel is dedicated to the early history of the Alster valley. The history of the village of Wellingsbüttel and folklore artifacts.

Altonaer Museum, Museumstrasse 23. Tel: 3807514. Tuesday–Sunday 10am–6pm. Has exhibits on the history of Altona, models of northern German ships and houses, figure-heads, pottery and a collection of regional landscape paintings.

Assids Indio-Museum Mana Kumaka, Kramerkoppel 24. Tel: 6560657. By appointment. Museum for the colonial history of the South American Caribbean Indians.

Botanische Schausammlung und Schaugewächshäuser, Marseiller Strasse 7. Tel: 41232337. Monday–Thursday 9am–4pm, Friday 9am–3pm. This original "laboratory for mercantilism" contains a collection focusing on useful plants.

Botanischer Garten, Hesten 10. Tel: 8222470. Summer daily 9am–8pm, winter 9am–4pm. Chinese and Japanese gardens including more than 10,000 plants from all over the world.

Buddelschiff-Museum, Schulauer Fährhaus, Wedel. Tel: 83094. Daily 10am–6pm, November–February, closed Mondays.

Deutsches Maler-und Lackierer-Museum, Billwerder Billdeich 72. Tel: 343887. Saturday and Sunday 10am–1pm, November–March, Wednesday 10am–1pm. History of the trade (painting and decorating) and its guild, located in an 18th-century villa.

Ernst-Barlach-Haus, Baron-Voght-Strasse 50 a. Tel: 826085. Tuesday–Sunday 11am–5pm. More than 100 sculptures and over 300 drawings and prints by Ernst Barlach.

Freilichtmuseum Kiekeberg, Am Kiekeberg 1, 2107 Rosengarten-Ehestorf. Tel: 7907662. March–October, Tuesday–Friday 9am–5pm, Saturday–Sunday 10am–6pm. November–February, Tuesday–Sunday 10am–4pm. Rural culture and presentations of handicrafts, animals and an exhibit on agrarian technology.

Garten der Schmetterlinge, Am Schlossteich, 2055 Friedrichsruh. Tel: 04104/2306. March–October. Open: 9am–5pm. Free-flying butterflies kept in glass houses in the Bismarck Palace gardens.

Gedenkstätte Ernst Thälmann, Tarpenbekstrasse 66. Tel: 474184. Tuesday–Friday 10am–5pm, Saturday and Sunday 10am–1pm. Former residence of the Hamburg labour leader; with library and archive.

Geologisch-Paläontologisches Museum, Bundesstrasse 55. Tel: 41234999. Monday–Friday 9am–6pm, Saturday 9am–noon. University museum for geology and the evolution of man.

Hamburger Kunsthalle, Glockengiesserwall. Tel: 24862612. Tuesday–Sunday 10am–6pm. Paintings from the Gothic period to the present, sculptures from the 19th century to the present, graphic arts, medallions, and coins.

Hamburger Museum für Archäologie und die Geschichte Hamburgs (Helms-Museum), Museumsplatz 2. Tel: 77170609. Tuesday–Sunday 10am–5pm. Pre- and early-history of Hamburg.

Heimatmuseum Wandsbek, Böhmestrasse 20. Tel: 684786. Tuesday 4pm–6pm and by appointment. History of Wandsbek, from village to city district. A room is dedicated to Matthias Claudius.

Hillers Car Museum (Automuseum), Kurt-Schumacher-Allee 42, next to the Main Station. Tel: 246577. Open daily 10am–5pm. Cars from 1895 onwards; motor bikes.

Hamburgisches Museum für Völkerkunde, Binderstrasse 14, (Hallerstrasse Underground). Tel: 441950. Open daily 10am–5pm. This Ethnology Museum has many fascinating exhibits showing how different peoples live all over the world.

Jenisch-Haus in Jenisch-Park, Baron-Voght-Strasse 50. Tel: 828790. April–October, Tuesday–Saturday 2pm–5pm, Sunday 11am–5pm; November–March, Tuesday–Saturday 1pm–4pm, Sunday 11am–4pm. Museum for interior design of bourgeois homes in suburbs near the Elbe.

Johannes-Brahms-Gedenkräume, Peterstrasse 39. Tel: 344688. Tuesday and Friday noon–1pm, Thursday 4pm–6pm, first Saturday of the month 10am–2pm. The composer's printed music, photographs, letters and music-stand.

Kunsthaus, Ferdinandstor 1. Tel: 335803. Tuesday–Sunday 10am–6pm, Wednesday 10am–8pm. Forum for Hamburg artists, with alternating exhibitions.

Kunstverein, An der Kunsthalle. Tel: 327845. Tuesday–Sunday 10am–6pm, Wednesday 10am–8pm. Alternating exhibitions of contemporary art.

KZ-Gedenkstätte Neuengamme, Jean-Dolidier-Weg 39. Tel: 7231031. Tuesday–Sunday 10am–5pm. Multimedia show on the history of a concentration camp where more than half of the 106,000 prisoners lost their lives.

Museum Altes Land, Westerjork 49, 2155 Jork. Tel: 04162/1333. Tuesday–Sunday 10am–4pm. Museum of agriculture with special emphasis on regional living conditions and water.

Museum der Arbeit, Maurienstrasse 19. Tel: 29842364. By appointment for groups. On the social history of labour. Includes a collection of machines. The museum also organises tours of the city.

Museum für Bergedorf und die Vierlande, Schloss Bergedorf, Bergedorf. Tel: 72522894. Tuesday–Thursday and Sundays 10am–5pm. History of the Elbe marshes, Bergedorf Castle, and the city of Bergedorf.

Museum für Hamburgische Geschichte, Holstenwall 24. Tel: 35042360; Tuesday–Sunday 10am–6pm. History of the city up to the present. Includes an impressive model of the harbour in the 19th century and a gigantic model train set on a scale of 1:32.

Museum für Kunst und Gewerbe, Steintorplatz 1. Tel: 24862630; Tuesday–Sunday 10am–6pm. Art from Antiquity and the Middle Ages, the Middle and Far East; collections of photographs and graphic arts as well as a Jugendstil (art nouveau) section.

Museum für Völkerkunde, Rothenbaumchaussee 64. Tel: 44195524. Tuesday–Sunday 10am–6pm. European and transoceanic cultures represented. Large exhibition of ethnic masks.

Museumsdorf Volksdorf, Im alten Dorfe 46-48. Tel: 6035225. Daily 9am–5pm, houses may be visited daily at 3pm, closed Mondays. The only open-air museum in Hamburg, featuring a 200-year-old northern German community house.

Museumshafen Övelgönne, Övelgönne 42, Anleger Neumühlen. Tel: 397383. Accessible at all times. Restored sailing vessels for light transport and coastal shipping.

Museumsschiff Cap San Diego, Überseebrücke. Tel: 365481. Daily 10am–6pm. Cargo ship built in 1962.

Övelgönner Seekiste, Övelgönne 61. Tel: 8809327. Saturday and Sunday 2pm–6pm and by appointment. Private collection of maritime rarities in a fisherman's house from 1863.

Planetarium, Hindenburgstrasse (im Stadtpark). Tel: 516621. Monday, Tuesday, Thursday, Sunday 10am–3pm, Wednesday and Friday 10am–7pm; tours: Wednesday 4pm and 6pm, Friday 6pm, Sunday 11am, 2.30pm, and 4pm. Theatre-in-the-round, research on outer space, and the history of astronomy; many special lectures.

Postmuseum, Stephansplatz 5. Tel: 3572395. Tuesday, Wednesday, Friday 10am–3pm, Thursday 10am–6pm. Telephone and telegraph equipment including a model of the optical telegraph between Cuxhaven and Hamburg from 1837, the fastest ship dispatch service of its time.

Puppenmuseum, Grotiusweg 79. Tel: 810582. Tuesday–Sunday 11am–5pm. Dolls and everything concerning dolls from the 18th to the 20th century.

Rickmer Rickmers, Landungsbrücken, Brücke 1. Tel: 35693119;. Daily 10am–6pm. A windjammer sailing ship that was built in Bremerhaven in 1896. From the middle of the 1920s it sailed under the name *Sagres* and was used by the Portuguese navy as a training vessel. It was given to Hamburg in 1983. There is also a restaurant on board.

Rieck-Haus, Curslacker Deich 284 (Curslack). Tel: 7231223. April–September, Tuesday–Sunday 10am–5pm; October–March, Tuesday–Sunday 10am–4pm (closed from 15 November–15 December). Open-air museum in the grounds of a Vierlande farm dating from the 16th to 19th centuries.

Stadtteilarchiv Ottensen, Am Born 6. Tel: 3903666. Thursday 4pm–7pm. Documents and photographs on the history of the former workers' quarter housed in an old factory.

Tabakhistorische Sammlung Reemtsma, Parkstrasse 51. Tel: 822054. By appointment. Exhibitions on tobacco and the history of smoking in the former residence of Philipp F. Reemtsma.

CHURCHES

Since the Reformation, the Roman Catholic Church has increasingly lost its hold on Hamburg. Nowadays, the Lutheran Church is dominant with its six deaneries. Although Hamburg does not have a cathedral, it has five "Hauptkirchen" (main churches):

St Jacobi, Jakobikirchhof 22.

St Katharinen, Katharinenkirchhof.

St Michaelis, Englische Planke.

St Nikolai, Harvestehuder Weg 118.

St Petri, Bergstrasse Ecke Mönckebergstrasse.

The main Roman Catholic church is:

St Marien, Danziger Strasse 60.

Because Hamburg is a port city, there are also several seamen's missions:

Danish Church, Ditmar-Koel-Strasse 2.

English Church, St Thomas à Becket, Zeughausmarkt.

Finnish Church, Ditmar-Koel-Strasse 6.

Norwegian Church, Ditmar-Koel-Strasse 2.
Swedish G. Adolf Church, Ditmar-Koel-Strasse 6.

THEATRES & ENTERTAINMENT

There's always a lot going on in Hamburg's theatres. Hansa-Theater has music-hall entertainment, Winterhuder Fährhaus popular comedies, Thalia Theater has *Black Rider* and Operettenhaus *Cats*. John Neumeier is often on stage his ballet stars and Freddy Quinn could be appearing in St Pauli Theater. At Kampnagelfabrik there might be a foreign theatre group. Theatre, opera, music and ballet fans are spoiled for choice. If you're lucky, you might even get to the "world's smallest stage" with its two-person cast. Their "stage" will be magically pulled out of a small case and the resultant performance will be breathtaking – perhaps a 7-minute version of the *Flying Dutchman*. If you can understand the Alpine tales or the stories about Old Russia they relate, you'll have one of the most memorable evenings you've ever spent at the theatre.

Venues:
Altonaer Theater, Museumstrasse 17.
Tel: 391545/46.
Deutsches Schauspielhaus und Malersaal, Kirchenallee 39. Tel: 248710.
English Theatre, Lerchenfeld 14. Tel: 225543.
Ernst-Deutsch-Theater, Ulmenau 25. Tel: 2270140.
Hamburger Kammerspiele, Hartungstrasse 9.
Tel: 4140140.
Hamburger Puppentheater, Moorkamp 5.
Tel: 418647.
Hamburgische Staatsoper, Grosse Theaterstrasse 34. Tel: 351555. Box office, tel: 351721.
Hansa-Theater, Steindamm 17. Tel: 241414.
Kampnagelfabrik, Jarrestrasse 20-26. Tel: 2791066.
Kellertheater, Karl-Muck-Platz 1. Tel: 845652.
Klecks-Theater, Alter Steinweg 43. Tel: 343436.
Komödie Winterhuder Fährhaus, Hudtwalckerstrasse 13. Tel: 474081.
Markthalle, Klosterwall 9-21. Tel: 339491.
Monsun Theater, Friedensallee. Tel: 3903148.
Musikhalle, Karl-Muck-Platz. Tel: 34691.
Neue Flora Theater, Stresemannstrasse 159 a.
Tel: 431650. Advance ticket sales, tel: 27075-270.
Ohnsorg-Theater, Grosse Bleichen 25. Tel: 3508030.
Operettenhaus Hamburg, Spielbudenplatz 1.
Tel: 311170. Advance ticket sales, tel: 27075-270.
Piccolo Theater, Juliusstrasse 13. Tel: 435348.
St Pauli Theater, Spielbudenplatz 29. Tel: 314344.
Thalia Theater, Raboisen 67. Tel: 328140.
Theater für Kinder, Max-Brauer-Allee 76.
Tel: 382538.
Theater im Zimmer, Alsterchaussee 30. Tel: 446539.
Theater in der Basilika, Borselstrasse 16.
Tel: 3904611.
Theater-Kneipe-Variete Schmidt, Spielbudenplatz 24. Tel: 314804.
Theater Scena Polska, Bleicherstrasse 50.
Tel: 4392790.

BOX OFFICES

Alsterhaus, Jungfernstieg 16-20. Tel: 352664.
Karstadt, Mönckebergstrasse 16. Tel: 326233.
Box office E. Schumacher, Colonnaden 37.
Tel: 343044.
Box office Kartenhaus, Gertigstrasse 4. Tel: 2701169.
Box office Last Minute at the corner of Grosse Bleichen and Poststrasse. Tel: 353565.

SPORTS

In Hamburg sport is nearly always wet; water sports are the most popular. The Outer Alster is an ideal arena – unless it's frozen over. Sailing, rowing and canoeing are popular pastimes on the lake. On Hamburg's many canals courting couples or whole families enjoy pleasantly relaxing days out in rowing and paddle boats. In the 19th century the city had 15 rowing clubs; now there are 23. Of course there are numerous yachting clubs, too, with a regular programme of regattas.

ROWING CLUBS

Hamburger und Germania Ruder-Club, Alsterufer 21. Tel: 440659.
Ruder-Club Favorite Hammonia, Alsterufer 9.
Tel: 448400.
Ruder-Club Allemannia von 1866, An der Alster 47a. Tel: 246600.
Rudergesellschaft Hansa, Schöne Aussicht 39.
Tel: 223758.

YACHTING CLUBS

Norddeutscher Regatta Verein, Schöne Aussicht 37. Tel: 2290815.
Hamburger Segel-Club, An der Alster 47 a.
Tel: 2802400.
Segel-Club Oevelgönne von 1901, Antwerpenstrasse 19. Tel: 7101504.
Mühlenberger Segelclub, Mühlenberg 59.
Tel: 8663108.
Blankeneser Segel-Club, Jollenhafen Blankenese.
Tel: 862373.

BOAT HIRE

Bobby Reich, Fernsicht 2. Tel: 487824.
Bodo's Bootssteg, Alte Rabenstrasse. Tel: 440654.
Bootshaus Poppenbüttel, Marienhof 4. Tel: 6066677.
Bootshaus Silwar, Eppendorfer Landstrasse 148 b. Tel: 476207.
Kapff-Dornheim, Isekei 1. Tel: 474369.
Hamburger Yachtschule, Schöne Aussicht 20 a. Tel: 2200030.
Nehls, Alsterufer 2. Tel: 457108.
Pieper H., An der Alster. Tel: 247578.
Alfred Seebeck, An der Alster (opposite Hotel Atlantic). Tel: 247652.

OTHER SPORT FACILITIES

If you prefer to keep the ground under your feet, Hamburg still has plenty to offer. Golf fans can go along to **Golf-Club Ahrensburg**, Am Haidschlag 39-45 in 2070 Ahrensburg. Tel: 04102/1309.
Grossflottbeker Tennis, Hockey and Golf Clubs, Otto-Ernst-Strasse 22-23. Tel: 827208.
Tennisverein Club an der Alster, Hallerstrasse 89. Tel: 443266.

Equestrian enthusiasts will pay a visit to **Hamburger-Renn-Club**, Rennbahnstrasse 96. Tel: 6518229; **Flottbeker Reithalle**, Hemmingstedter Weg 2. Tel: 828182; **Hamburger Trabrenngesellschaft**, Luruper Chaussee 30. Tel: 894004.

And if you like to watch other professional sportsmen, try one of Hamburg's two First Division soccer clubs. Hamburger Sportverein, HSV, plays its home games in the **Volksparkstadion** while FC St Pauli welcomes its guests in the unique atmosphere at **Millerntorstadion**.

NIGHTLIFE

Hamburg's nightlife is more colourful than ever. The range of bars, clubs, pubs and cafés prove that this "gateway to the world" has opened much wider in recent years. Wherever you go, it's party time as the in crowd dash from one "trendy" place to another. Even Hamburg's famous red-light area around the Reeperbahn is filled with new (night)life. There's something to suit every taste, whatever the style – from pop to rock, jazz to folk, disco to soul. But trends come and go, and with them the clubs. Now they're all the rage, but in a couple of months they may be totally out.

DISCOS & MUSIC CLUBS

After Shave, Spielbudenplatz 7. Tel: 3193215. A well-known spot for rock and jazz-rock.
Birdland, Gärtnerstrasse 122. Tel: 405277. Tends toward jazz, folk and mainstream music.
Blockhütte, Grosse Freiheit 64. Tel: 310801.
Charabon, Wandsbeker Königsstrasse 63. Tel: 686510.
Docks, Spielbudenplatz 19. Tel: 3194378. Spex and rave parties not on the level of hip hop. Always way ahead of the trends with new ideas.
Downtown, Gertigstrasse 57. Tel: 2798484. Following in the footsteps of the infamous Café Kaputt. Live music, mixed crowd. A pub for chatting.
Endlich Unendlich, Spielbudenplatz 5. Tel: 247465. Friday 11pm–3am, Saturday 11pm–whenever. Ask about what is on in the late-night dance club.
Fabrik, Barnerstrasse 36. Tel: 391070. One of the favourites of the spontaneous crowd. From rock to jazz, experimental programmes as well as early morning music sessions.
Grosse Freiheit 36, Grosse Freiheit 36. Tel: 3193649. *The* great place for free rockers!
Intermezzo, Ulmenstrasse 17-19. Tel: 470147. Parties for disco fans.
Kick & Co., Klausstrasse 1. Tel: 3905536. Special kicks, hard'n'heavy.
Kir, Max-Brauer-Allee 241. Tel: 438518. No pop or other trendy styles. For party corpses who have come back to life after 36-hour dance parties.
Knust, Brandstwiete, Friday and Saturday 8pm. Slow dance locale.
Logo, Grindelallee 5. Tel: 4105658. An indestructible, action-packed rock club.
Madhouse, Valentinskamp 46. Tel: 344193. Popular dance spot – loud, kinky and intense.
Markthalle, Klosterwall 9-21. Tel: 339491. Everything, including cabaret and avant-garde.
Molotow Music Club, Spielbudenplatz 5. Mostly dance music, but also punk and heavy metal.
Onkel Pö's Carnegie Hall, Weg beim Jäger 95. Tel: 5536489. Second time around for the great, old innovator.
Prinzenbar, Kastanienallee 22. A well-kept secret. New trends and choices for dancing.
Scalatti, Grosse Brunnenstrasse 61. Tel: 3906089.
Skyy, Spielbudenplatz 166. Tel: 3191711. The big disco addition to the red light district; its own group "The Chimes" gives it a special image.
Stairway, Neuer Pferdemarkt 13. Tel: 432062.
Trinity, Eimsbütteler Chaussee 5. Tel: 4398094. Synergy parties, after-show parties.
Unit, Talstrasse/Ecke Reeperbahn. Urban dance action, new hip hop, vogueing parties, mental rap rock, among other things.
Villon, St Georgs Kirchhof 7. Tel: 249293. First rate folk, cabaret and classic songs.
Westwerk, Admiralitätsstrasse 74. Tel: 363903.

BARS

Bar du Nord, Dorotheenstrasse 33. Tel: 2794354. From 8.30pm.

G.S. (Grand Slam), Bundesstrasse 18. Tel: 418666. From 7pm.

Havanna, Fischmarkt 4–6. From 7pm.

Hemingway, Markusstrasse 4. Tel: 352448. From 8pm.

Meyer Lansky's, Pinnasberg 60. Tel: 3191009. From 8pm.

Old Fashion Bar, Eppendorfer Weg 211. Tel: 4220227. Monday–Saturday from 7pm.

Sterzinger's American Diner, Thielbek 3–5. Tel: 340780. From 8.30pm.

NIGHTLIFE IN THE NEW RED LIGHT DISTRICT

439, Vereinsstrasse 38. Tel: 4391550. Monday–Sunday 9pm–4am. Dingy late-60s style pub with music no less than 200 decibels – not for kids.

Bar Centrale, Clemens-Schultz-Strasse 66. Tel: 3192657. Sunday–Thursday 8pm–4am, Friday and Saturday 8pm–6am. One of the first night spots in the new red light district. Still recommended for meeting people.

Chaplin, Schulterblatt 83. Tel: 4301728. Sunday–Thursday 6pm–1.30am, Friday and Saturday from 7pm. Cocktails at affordable prices in an unobtrusively colourful atmosphere.

Gaststätte Sparr, Hamburger Berg 4. Monday–Sunday from 9pm.

Gun Club, Hopfenstrasse 30. Monday–Sunday from 9pm. Sometimes vintage rock – an endless number of footstompers – sometimes heavy metal; not for sensitive types or those with weak nerves.

Havanna Bar, Fischmarkt 4-6. Tel: 313636. Sunday–Thursday 8pm–2.30am, Friday and Saturday 8pm–4am. A newcomer with lots of room, not too stylish, very much in keeping with the trend. You can stop off here when nothing else is happening or if you want to be around intelligent and creative drinkers.

Holiday Bar, Hans-Albers-Platz 1. Monday–Saturday from 10pm. Somewhat dignified with pleasant flair.

La Paloma, Gerhardstrasse 2. Tel: 314512. Monday–Sunday 24-hour action. Jörg Immendorf's mini port for the midnight pint.

Lehmitz, Reeperbahn 22. Tel: 314641. Monday–Sunday 24-hour, round-the-clock pub for drinking games with cheap tequila and hot music.

Luxor, Max-Brauer-Allee 251. Tel: 4300124. Monday–Sunday 7.30pm–4am. The former favourite of the heavy-drinking set has improved, but there are still a few bad surprises lurking about like unexpectedly "interesting" people.

Mary Lou's, Hans-Albers-Platz 3. Tel: 314628. Monday–Sunday from 9pm. Meeting point.

Mitternacht, Gerhardstrasse 16. Tel: 310613. Monday–Sunday 11pm–4am. The trend-setter. Somewhat gloomy, but original.

Molotow, Spielbudenplatz 5. Monday–Sunday from 10pm. Serious punks and heavy music, with atmosphere, action and low prices.

Prinzenbar, Kastanienallee 29. Tel: 3192462. Friday and Saturday from 10pm. Wonderfully old-fashioned place for trends in party, soul, and newcomer music.

Tempelhof, Hamburger Berg 12. Tel: 314628. Monday–Sunday from 9pm. Directly under "Camelot" (for women only). It wavers between in and old-fashioned. Sometimes a party house, sometimes not.

Unit, Talstrasse 3-5. Tel: 313164. Thursday–Sunday from 10pm. The address for special acts, with "Tekno house club" dancing.

SHOPPING

Naturally Hamburg has got its Armani, Jil Sander, Hermes, Lagerfeld, Dior and Lacroix or whatever they happen to be called. But you can find shops like those in lots of other cities as well. If you want a really original souvenir of Hamburg which won't fade with time, you have to go to St Pauli. That's where you can get what generations of sailors before you have had – a tattoo from "Germany's oldest tattooists": Götz, formerly Hoffmann, Hamburger Berg 8, tel: 313033, or from Tattoo Lutz und Lena Schumacher, Silbersackstrasse 11. Tel: 315548.

If you prefer less obtrusive souvenirs that won't hurt (except possibly your purse), Hamburg has plenty to offer. Start with the city-centre shopping arcades; Hanseviertel (Poststrasse) offers fashion, shoes, dolls, antiques, lobsters and oysters – in a word, almost everything that's expensive and has style. Two smaller arcades are opposite in Grosse Bleichen: Galleria and Kaufmannshaus.

Another typical feature of Hamburg is Harrys Hamburger Hafen Basar in Bernhard-Nocht-Strasse 63, a labyrinth of curiosities. Another source of astonishment in St Pauli is the selection of cowboy boots on sale at Hundertmark, Spielbudenplatz 9.

If you tried to explain to your friends at home what *Labskaus* was, you'd have problems. Even the experts can't agree on what goes into this typical Hamburg dish – with or without herrings or beetroot? *Labskaus* in tins is available from the traditional Old Commercial Room (Englische Planke 10).

High and Mighty (Ballindamm 2) is said to attract customers from far and wide – hardly surprising since this store specialises in over-sized clothes for "tall and strong men". Another typical

Hamburg shop is Schmeding Bernhard (Vorsetzen 2) where you can get almost everything to do with ships and the sea.

If you want to follow the example of the many Anglophiles in Hamburg, go to Ladage & Oelke (Neuer Wall 75). Now nearly 150 years old, this shop is an institution, selling British "lifestyle" off the peg. On the other hand, Pappnase & Co (Grindelallee 92) has everything you could need for theatrics or juggling.

The Speicher am Fischmarkt (Grosse Elbstrasse 92) has a colourful assortment of all kinds of household goods and furniture, with beautiful Kelim carpets on sale. If your interest is art and architecture, there's no better bookshop than Sautter & Lackmann (Admiralitätstrasse 71); Dr. Goetze (Bleichenhof, Bleichenbrücke 9) is the shop in Hamburg for maps and travel literature. If older books are your line, here are a few addresses of secondhand bookshops in Hamburg:
Antiquariat Pabel, Krayenkamp 10 b and Englische Planke 6.
Bücherkabinett A.u.C. Simon, Poststrasse 14.
Henner Wachholz, Mittelweg 43.
Max Wiedebusch, Dammtorstrasse 20.

MARKETS

Munich has got its Viktualienmarkt and Hamburg has its Fischmarkt – in St Pauli. Actually there are hardly any stalls selling fish but the name has stuck. This market is an experience not to be missed – every Sunday morning between 5am and 9.30am (from 7am in winter months). If you go really early, you'll miss the crowds that are always there from about eight onwards. But if you don't make it till 9.30, you've still got a good chance of a bargain because that's when things are going cheap.

Other attractive markets are held in Isestrasse (Tuesday and Thursday mornings) and Goldbekufer (Tuesday, Thursday and Saturday mornings).

LANGUAGE

WORDS & PHRASES

Good morning	Guten Morgen
Good afternoon	Guten Tag
Good evening	Guten Abend
Good night	Gute Nacht
Goodbye	Auf Wiedersehen
I don't understand	Ich verstehe Sie nicht
Do you speak English?	Sprechen Sie Englisch?
Could you please speak slower?	Könnten Sie bitte etwas langsamer sprechen?
What's that in English?	Was heisst das auf Englisch?
Yes/No	Ja/Nein
Please/Thank you	Bitte/Danke
Never mind	Bitte; keine Ursache
Turn to the right! (left)	Biegen Sie nach rechts (links) ab!
Go straight on!	Gehen Sie geradeaus weiter!
Above/below	oben/unten
Where is the next hotel?	Wo ist das nächste Hotel?
Do you have a single room?	Haben Sie ein Einzelzimmer?
Do you have a double room?	Haben Sie ein Doppelzimmer?
Do you have a room with a private bath?	Haben Sie ein Zimmer mit Bad?
How much is it?	Wieviel kostet das?
How much is a room with full board?	Wieviel kostet ein Zimmer mit Vollpension?
Please show me another room!	Bitte zeigen Sie mir ein anderes Zimmer!
We'll (I'll) be staying for one night.	Wir bleiben (Ich bleibe) eine Nacht.
When is breakfast?	Wann gibt es Frühstück?
Where is the toilet?	Wo ist die Toilette?
Where is the bathroom?	Wo ist das Badezimmer?
Is there a bus to the centre?	Gibt es einen Bus ins Stadtzentrum?
Is there a guided sightseeing tour?	Werden kommentierte Besichtigungstouren durchgeführt?
church	Kirche
memorial	Denkmal
castle	Schloss
old part of town	Altstadtviertel
Where can I buy souvenirs?	Wo kann ich Souvenirs kaufen?
Do you know a nightclub/disco?	Kennen Sie einen Nachtklub/eine Disko?
Where is the nearest cinema?	Wo ist das nächste Kino?
What film does it show?	Was für ein Film läuft dort?
Where is the post office?	Wo ist das Postamt?
Where is the nearest bank?	Wo ist die nächste Bank?
Where can I change money?	Wo kann ich Geld wechseln?
Where is the pharmacy?	Wo ist die Apotheke?
What time do they close?	Wann schliessen sie?
open/closed	geöffnet/geschlossen

close/far	nah/weit	jam	Marmelade
cheap/expensive	billig/teuer	egg	Ei
free (of charge)	kostenlos	milk	Milch
price	Preis	coffee	Kaffee
change	Wechselgeld	tea	Tee
Have you got any change?	Können Sie wechseln?	sugar	Zucker
		butter	Butter
telephone booth	Telefonzelle	Can we have	Können wir bitte
Is this the way to the station?	Ist das der Weg zum Bahnhof?	the bill, please?	bezahlen?
Where is platform one?	Wo ist Gleis eins?	to pay	bezahlen
Where is the airport?	Wo ist der Flughafen?	tip	Trinkgeld
Can you call me a taxi?	Können Sie mir ein Taxi rufen?	to complain	sich beschweren
Can you take me to the airport?	Können Sie mich zum Flughafen fahren?	Monday	Montag
Where do I get a ticket?	Wo kann ich eine Fahrkarte kaufen?	Tuesday	Dienstag
		Wednesday	Mittwoch
departure/arrival	Abfahrt/Ankunft	Thursday	Donnerstag
When is the next	Wann geht der nächste	Friday	Freitag
flight/train to...?	Flug/Zug nach...?	Saturday	Samstag, Sonnabend
to change (flights/trains)	umsteigen	Sunday	Sonntag
exit	Ausgang/Ausfahrt	January	Januar
entrance	Eingang/Einfahrt	February	Februar
travel agency	Reisebüro	March	März
picnic area	Rastplatz	April	April
gas (petrol) station	Tankstelle	May	Mai
bridge	Brücke	June	Juni
crossroads	Kreuzung	July	Juli
no parking	Parken verboten	August	August
no stopping	Halten verboten	September	September
one-way street	Einbahnstrasse	October	Oktober
hospital	Krankenhaus	November	November
ferry	Fähre	December	Dezember
fee	Gebühr	0	Null
height	Höhe	1	eins
width	Breite	2	zwei
length	Länge	3	drei
Have you anything	Haben Sie etwas	4	vier
to declare?	zu verzollen?	5	fünf
customs	Zoll	6	sechs
		7	sieben
Do you know a	Kennen Sie ein	8	acht
good restaurant?	gutes Restaurant?	9	neun
Can you recommend	Können Sie etwas	10	zehn
anything?	empfehlen?	11	elf
Could we order	Können wir bitte	12	zwölf
a meal, please?	bestellen?	13	dreizehn
menu	Speisekarte	14	vierzehn
lunch	Mittagessen	15	fünfzehn
evening meal	Abendessen	16	sechzehn
knife/fork/spoon	Messer/Gabel/Löffel	17	siebzehn
napkin	Serviette	18	achtzehn
beer/wine	Bier/Wein	19	neunzehn
bread/cheese	Brot/Käse	20	zwanzig
meat	Fleisch	30	dreissig
sausage	Würstchen	40	vierzig
honey	Honig	50	fünfzig
noodles	Nudeln	60	sechzig
potatoes	Kartoffeln	70	siebzig
rice	Reis	80	achtzig

90	neunzig
100	hundert
200	zweihundert
1,000	tausend
2,000	zweitausend
1, 000, 000	eine Million
1st	erste(r)
2nd	zweite(r)
3rd	dritte(r)
4th	vierte(r)
5th	fünfte(r)
6th	sechste(r)
7th	siebte(r)
8th	achte(r)
9th	neunte(r)
10th	zehnte(r)
11th	elfte(r)
12th	zwölfte(r)
13th	dreizehnte(r)
20th	zwanzigste(r)
21st	einundzwanzigste(r)
100th	hundertste(r)
1000th	tausendste(r)

FURTHER READING

HISTORY & SOCIETY

Bailey, George. *Germans.* (1972)
Bradley, John. *The Illustrated History of the Third Reich.* (1978)
Calleo, David. *The German Problem Reconsidered: 1860–1978.* (1980)
Craig, Gordon. *The Germans.* (1982)
Dawson, William H. *German Life in Town and Country.* (1977)
Holborn, Hajo. *A History of Modern Germany: 1840-1945.* (1969)
Jones, Brangwyn G. *Germany: An Introduction to the German Nation.* (1970)
Kirsch, Henry. *German Democratic Republic: A Profile.* (1985)
Lowie, Robert H. *Toward Understanding Germany.* (1979)
MacDonald, Ian. *Get to Know Germany.* (1975)
Marsh, David. *New Germany at the Crossroads.* (1990)
For good background read any of the classical works by Goethe and Schiller, Heinrich Heine and Friedrich Hölderlin, to name a few. A selection of German and English/American authors follows:

Grass, Günter. *Headbirths*; *The Germans Are Dying Out*; and *The Flounder.*
Mann, Thomas. *Buddenbrooks.*
Mansfield, Catherine. *In A German Pension.*
Stael, Madame de. *Germany.*
Twain, Mark. *A Tramp Abroad.*

USEFUL ADDRESSES

TOURIST INFORMATION

Tourismus-Zentrale Hamburg, Burchardstrasse 14. Tel: 300510.
Tourist-Information im Bieberhaus, Hachmannplatz. Tel: 30051244/245.
Tourist-Information im Hauptbahnhof (Main Station), Haupteingang Kirchenallee. Tel: 30051230.
Tourist-Information am Hafen (Port), Landungsbrücken. Tel: 30051200.
Tourist-Information am Flughafen (Airport), Ankunftshalle D. Tel: 30051240. Daily 8am–11pm.
Tourist-Information im Hanseviertel, Poststrasse. Tel: 30051220.

CONSULATES

Denmark - Heimhuder Strasse 77. Tel: 414005-0.
France - Pöseldorfer Weg 32. Tel: 414106-0.
Greece - Abtei 33. Tel: 440772.
Japan - Rathausmarkt 5. Tel: 333017-0.
Portugal - Gänsemarkt 21. Tel: 343478.
Russia - Feenteich 20. Tel: 2295301. Visas: 2295201.
Spain - Mittelweg 37. Tel: 443620.
Turkey - Tesdorpfstrasse 18. Tel: 443041.
United Kingdom - Harvestehuder Weg 8a. Tel: 446071.
United States - Alsterufer 27. Tel: 411 71-214; Visas: 411 71-213.

ART/PHOTO CREDITS

INDEX

Z